Sociolinguistics

C000092930

Glyn Williams offers a trenchant critique of mainstream socio-linguistics and the sociology of language. He takes as his starting point the philosophical roots of the theory of language in society, arguing that they lie in a specific perspective on society which derives from eighteenth- and nineteenth-century social philosophy. This perspective is consensual in nature, and has been lost in the 'taken-for-granted' nature of sociolinguistic theory. It involves a view of society as consisting of rational subjects manipulating language and leads to the mistaken belief that language reflects society. Williams goes on to present a critical overview of the various sub-fields of the study of language in society, and shows how they share a particular view of the nature of society – a view which is not far removed from the 'common sense' social philosophy of American society.

Sociolinguistics has been in great need of a book which emphasises the sociological rather than the linguistic side of the subject, and Glyn Williams' book goes a considerable way towards redressing the balance. Williams is provocative and controversial, taking on as he does all the leading figures of the discipline, including Labov, Fishman, Hymes, Gumperz and Milroy among others. But the clarity and strength of his argument, firmly grounded in the history of western thought, will make the book essential reading for anyone researching language in society and for advanced students of sociolinguistics.

Glyn Williams is a Reader in Sociology at the University College of North Wales, Bangor. He has written many books, including *The Sociology of Welsh*.

Sociolinguistics
A Sociological Critique

Glyn Williams
Foreword by Joshua Fishman

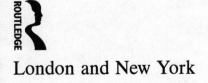

London and New York

First published in 1992
by Routledge
11 New Fetter Lane, London EC4P 4EE

Simultaneously published in the USA and Canada
by Routledge
a division of Routledge, Chapman and Hall, Inc.
29 West 35th Street, New York, NY 10001

© 1992 Glyn Williams

Typeset in Times Roman by
Falcon Typographic Art Ltd, Edinburgh
Printed in Great Britain by
T J Press, Padstow, Cornwall

British Library Cataloguing in Publication Data
Williams, Glyn
  Sociolinguistics: a sociological critique.
  I. Title
  306.44

Library of Congress Cataloging in Publication Data
Williams, Glyn
  Sociolinguistics: a sociological critique / Glyn Williams.
  p. cm.
  Includes bibliographical references and index.
  1. Sociolinguistics. I. Title.
  P40.W49 1992
  306.4′4 – dc20 91–31695
ISBN 0–415–06513–5
      0–415–06514–3 (pbk)

Contents

Foreword
What can sociology contribute to the sociolinguistic enterprise?

At the 1964 Summer Linguistic Institute at which American socio-linguistics was 'born', ten scholars who claimed to be crucially interested in that field-to-be convened, studied and argued in order to give it shape. Roughly half of these were linguists and roughly half were sociologists but, in the formation of the field and in its rapid worldwide ramifications via publications, conferences and courses, the linguistic half clearly and constantly outweighed the sociological half. Why was sociology such a junior (or even silent) partner in the formation of sociolinguistics? There are probably many reasons why that was (and still is) so. To my way of thinking, this was primarily the result of two hundred years of modern sociology in which the notions of 'language', 'language groups' and language-focused group-processes received very little attention. Accordingly, modern sociolinguistics was 'born', focusing on the problems, theories and methods that sympathetic linguists, particularly anthropological linguists, were familiar with – and these definitely did not include disciplinary sociology.

Every new beginning has to take off from what came before and anthropological linguistics – from Sapir to Ferguson, Gumperz and Hymes – was simply what had come before. It was both the conscious and the unconscious point of departure for sociolinguistics, and the 'socio' side has been paying the inevitable price ever since, particularly in English and in German sociolinguistic circles, which have long been intellectually and methodologically aligned or attuned to each other.

It seems totally unsurprising to me that whereas almost all linguistics departments include courses in sociolinguistics today (not a mean accomplishment for an area of specialisation which began barely three decades ago), almost no sociology departments do so. Indeed, the two fields are as remote from each other now as they were in the early 1960s. After three decades, sociolinguistics has remained just as it was: a province of linguistics and anthropology, and a rather provincial province at that.

This book is a welcome beginning to the process of ameliorating and rectifying this negative state of affairs. It is written by a well-trained and stimulating sociologist who has taken sociolinguistics seriously. It follows a theoretical sociological perspective which is not well known or frequently followed in the Anglo-American-German sociological establishment. These are the main reasons why I am delighted to greet this book, its author and the sociolinguists who will invest the time and effort needed in order to digest the plentiful and stimulating material presented in the pages that follow. These sociolinguists will embark on a voyage which will inevitably take them to other shores as well.

Other books on sociology and sociolinguistics will ultimately follow this one, I am sure. Sociology currently lacks a dominant, theoretically integrated mainstream, and various sociological perspectives on sociolinguistics need to be examined carefully. A plea for more sociological expertise is not the same as a plea for this or that theory or data-analytic approach. However, sociology is also much more than a sophisticated theoretical–ideological critique. Like all sciences, it progresses (or should progress) from that point of departure to the formulation of specific hypotheses, to the collection of new empirical field-data, to the analysis of this data by publicly replicable methods and to the testing (confirmation or disconfirmation) of the original theories and hypotheses that initially set the entire process in motion. This book does not do all of that and perhaps no single book could. It is a beginning, virtually a first along a long neglected and difficult road. That is the reason why I so encouraged the author while he was working on it and why I so congratulate him now. Not only is it a worthy accomplishment in its own right but it should also stimulate, perhaps I should even say aggravate, others to try their hand at the same task: to bring specialised sociological knowledge, based on specialised sociological theories, hypotheses and methodologies, into the sociolinguistic heartland from which these have all been excessively absent for so long.

There must not be a third or yet a fourth sociologically innocent and ignorant generation of sociolinguists! This book is a welcome beginning in what I hope will be a multi-pronged, multi-theoretical and multi-methodological effort to keep that from happening, an effort which will inevitably broaden the sociological contributions to sociolinguistics which this book has attempted to provide. I have no doubt, particularly not after this first beginning along that path, that the sociolinguistic enterprise of the future will be as informed of sociology and society as it is of linguistics and language, that its theoreticians, researchers and practitioners, will be well and explicitly trained in both disciplines and that all will then look back upon our own time with puzzlement, wondering why it took so long for such an obviously desired state of affairs to come about.

Joshua Fishman
Yeshiva University, New York

Preface

My interest in the study of language in society derives largely from having been raised with a minority language as my mother tongue. This experience throws one into a variety of situations in which the respective languages in a bilingual community have to be justified, this justification sometimes being achieved through the denigration of the other language, and with it the denigration of a language group. Invariably this process involves the legitimation of the dominant, state language and, with it, the fostering of a negative identity among many members of the minority language group. The associated discourses are, in themselves, interesting, even if one's early experiences involve taking them for granted, without much reflection. However, if one is exposed to the intellectual discipline of the social sciences they must be placed in quite a different perspective. To a certain extent my own experience involved a realisation that there was a persistence in the tendency to speak from the place of the dominant, and that the theoretical orientation of much that passed as objective social science did little justice to my experience as a member of a minority language group. This suspicion was reinforced in my discussions with social scientists from other language minorities who were studying their own language and society.

It follows that my interest in the academic study of language should encompass a critical perspective. This interest, over the years, I have shared with numerous colleagues who share my concern about the predominant theoretical perspective in the study of language in society, albeit that their critical awareness derives from sources different from my own. Among those whose insights I have benefited from are five colleagues who have gone to the trouble of reading an earlier draft – Pierre Achard, Louis Jean Calvet, Bernard Conein, Françoise Gadet and Bob Hodge. I need hardly add with reference to such gifted colleagues that the limitations of the book are no fault of theirs. I also owe a debt to Joshua Fishman who has not only been open in his acceptance of criticisms of his own contributions to the sociology of language but has encouraged the entire venture.

Introduction

This book attempts an overview of sociolinguistics and the sociology of language. Most subdisciplines of sociology have responded to the on-going changes in sociological theory. This tends to involve a reflexive orientation on the part of those sociologists associated with the various subdisciplines who continuously address theoretical issues within the context of the substantive issues associated with that subdiscipline. Sociolinguistics and the sociology of language, to a very great extent, appear to be exceptions to the case. There are those who would insist that these areas are not subdisciplines of sociology but, rather, are either subdisciplines of linguistics or constitute a coherent discipline in their own right, albeit one that is in its infancy. Be that as it may, the sociological input is central to both areas and, as such, changes in sociological theory and developments in theoretical critiques cannot be ignored. There is a strange lacuna in the role played by theoretical critique in sociolinguistics and the sociology of language, perhaps on account of the emphasis that is placed upon empirical positivism and theory building.

Any such critique must take account of the historical and it is necessary to look at the past from the point of view of the debates that emerge in a scrutiny of theoretical issues in the study of language in society. I will argue that these problems are often grounded in particular discourses on language and society that emerged in the early developments of sociology and linguistics during the nineteenth century. Thus the first chapter seeks to consider the main themes that emerged in these developments, particular emphasis being placed upon some of the central sociological concepts that have subsequently been employed in the study of language in society.

The inheritor of this historical tradition who undoubtedly had the greatest influence upon the recent growth in sociology was Talcott Parsons. His influence was particularly prominent at the time when sociolinguistics and the sociology of language were emerging as areas of some intellectual and institutional significance during the 1960s and 1970s. It is essential therefore to outline his understanding of the nature of society and culture and this is done in the chapter 2.

It is probably correct to say that within mainstream sociology the study of language is dominated by the ethnomethodologists who devote much of their energy to conversation analysis. It is they, as much as anyone, who have sought to redress some of the problems which derive from the Parsonian influence. However, I argue in chapter 6 that they have also retained the fundamental social philosophy of that which they seek to redress.

Before reaching a discussion of conversation analysis three chapters are devoted to issues and orientations which have been more faithful to the Parsonian view of society. Thus chapter 3 discusses speech variation and in particular the work of Labov; chapter 4 focuses upon language contact by looking at the important early work of Fishman and Ferguson as well as considering later developments of this orientation; and chapter 5 considers the implications of the applied aspects of these orientations in a discussion of language planning. Taken together these three chapters constitute the main thrust of sociolinguistics and the sociology of language during the 1960s and 1970s.

Chapters 7 and 8 discuss topics which many would relate to anthropological linguistics and psycholinguistics. In chapter 7 I consider the ethnography of communication and the heavy reliance on the concept of culture therein. This has considerable influence upon many sociolinguists and this is nowhere more evident than in the methodological emphasis of network analysis. Even though those at the forefront of the study of ethnolinguistic vitality which is discussed in chapter 8 are psychologists by training, their emphasis is very much upon social psychology. This allows us to consider the issue of social identity and the particular problem of language as reflection which derives from a very specific philosophy of language.

The concluding chapter seeks to draw the critique together by a consideration of the main thrust of the theoretical orientation which I maintain dominates sociolinguistics and the sociology of language, and by focusing upon the possibilities and limitations of alternative perspectives, albeit perspectives which are very much at the margins of the study of language in society. I argue that the criticism must go beyond the simple polarisation of conflict and consensus perspectives in that it must also consider the problems which these perspectives share. Furthermore, the two alternatives which I consider, Marxism and French Discourse Analysis, useful though they may be in redressing some of the problems which I identify, should not be seen as a panacea, but rather should be addressed as part of an ongoing debate on the nature of language in society, a debate which hitherto, I would argue, has been confined to the margins of this field of intellectual study. My goal here is synoptic, being no more than a sketch in the hope of provoking an enlarging of what is, in my view, a much needed debate.

1 Historical antecedents

The end of the eighteenth century and the beginning of the nineteenth century marked a period of considerable turmoil, not only in the world of politics but also in the world of ideas. The discourse on language and society which emerged during this period laid the ground for what is contemporary sociolinguistics. In this opening chapter I intend to survey these antecedents in order to ground the subsequent critical discussion of contemporary work on language and society. In so doing it is necessary to treat ideas as a philosophical discourse so that the inherent logic which holds statements about language and society together in a 'taken for granted' manner is made explicit. By so doing it becomes possible to evaluate critically the limitations of any thesis premised upon the background assumptions of such a discourse.

THE IDEA OF PROGRESS

By the end of the seventeenth century the scientific endeavour based upon rational assumptions had been firmly established. Furthermore, humankind was seen as firmly in control of its own destiny, thereby allowing the emergence of debates about the social nature of human endeavour. These developments coincided with the emergence of a distinctive political order in Europe and much of the ensuing discussion focused upon the nature of humankind and its relationship to authority.

Clearly, many of the ideas circulating in Europe during this period derived from Greek philosophy and an awareness of this continuity was responsible for the heavy emphasis upon the idea of progress as a phenomenon that is never ending. This involved two assumptions. First, that knowledge was cumulative, a central proposition of science, and second, that knowledge was equivalent to ability. Thus, by linking these two beliefs, progress was inevitable in that time alone led to a more able society. As we shall see, the second assumption also had profound implications for the legitimation of European superiority in that it served as the basis for comparison within the evolutionary framework.

From the time of Bacon in the seventeenth century the progressive development of knowledge was viewed as natural and normal. It was in the following century that the idea of progress was set in the context of civilisation, with the concept of civilisation involving culture as well as ideas and institutions. This was the inception of linking progress with the idea of social complexity. However, this emphasis did not come to the forefront until the nineteenth century; prior to which the tendency was to relate progress to civilisation. Perhaps it was Leibniz, writing as early as 1697, who was the forerunner of Spencer and Darwin in emphasising that change did not occur in stages but rather was a gradual and cumulative affair. It was Leibniz also who claimed that the future was predictable from a knowledge of the present, much as did Marx, Comte and others in the nineteenth century. This view evidently encompassed the idea that progress is the natural and normal trend of humankind. Yet it was also felt that it relied upon the periodic obliteration of institutions and beliefs which stood in the way. As in any period, these views were in general circulation within the intellectual community, and at about the same time Vico sought to view history as progress in terms of his thesis on the Three Ages of Man.

These views also appear in Kant's *Idea for a Universal History* where he presents mankind as proceeding through a steady and progressive evolution towards a state of perfection. As in the futurology of Leibniz, Kant's work constituted a form of conjectural history that was the forerunner of social evolutionism involving a search for a law of progress, a preoccupation that persisted from the Enlightenment to the nineteenth century. Such a conjectural history allowed Kant to demonstrate the reality of progress while simultaneously seeing evolution as culminating in an inevitable social perfection. This optimistic discourse on mankind was the converse of the prior, pessimistic view of mankind as inherently sinful.

Perhaps the work which tended to foresee the preoccupations of the nineteenth century was Condorcet's *Progress of the Human Mind*, published in 1797, in that it was, simultaneously, a statement of belief in never-ending human progress, psychological principles and a preoccupation with an extensive social and cultural history of civilisation. In this he anticipated the work of the nineteenth-century philosophers who took a global perspective on human society and sought to demonstrate that the progress of civilisation rested in the human mind by tracing human evolution from one type of society to another. Thus, he traced the evolution of social organisation from clans, through tribes to 'modern' polities. It is here that we witness the equation of progress over time with the idea of an evolving social complexity. This is a theme we shall return to in due course. Condorcet's conception of human society as a 'developing' feature was not restricted to social organisation but also encompassed theories of the origin and evolution of language, writing and the arts which were the diacritica of civilisation, thereby relegating those societies without one or other of these traits to a condition outside civilisation. The ethnocentrism of a view where the highest form is equated with the features of Condorcet's own society was not considered. It is an idea that culminates in Spencer's focus on progress as development from a homogeneous to a heterogeneous social form.

Herder placed this theme of progress and social development within the analogy of the life cycle by referring to human progress in terms of stages of child, youth, mankind and old age. By inference, the course of civilisation was seen as childlike thus linking with the belief that progress was hindered by ignorance. Hegel adopted a somewhat similar position later in comparing human progress with a biological analogy involving plant life.

Although many such philosophers conceived of future society in terms of egalitarianism, democracy and a rationality fostered by universal education, they also insisted that conflict served as a motor for progress, claiming that conflict had to be overcome if society was not to stagnate. In a sense this was a statement about an ideal future in terms of the present, since it was claimed that progress was hindered by ignorance, inequality, economic exploitation and religious super-stition – the bases of conflict. Yet the French Enlightenment claimed that the state, through legislation, could eliminate any interference to progress thereby making progress a feature inseparable from the polity. The state was to be the custodian and guarantor of cohesion and harmony.

On the other hand, the Scottish moral philosophers doubted that progress based on the accumulation of knowledge could enable one to predict the future. Thus Ferguson stated that he could see no evidence for consistent progress in the history of nations and that the converse of progress was as predictable as progress itself. He was also highly critical of the ethnocentrism of the arguments which saw progress as tied to the superiority of European nations.

It was from these antecedents that the main thrust of evolution as a process emerged during the nineteenth century. The emphasis was on the successive stages through which human society had passed and how the past helped explain the present. It involved a transition between the extremes of primitive and civilised, with the latter seen as superior, thereby allowing the moral philosophers to see part of their goal as ascertaining how to promote development towards a more perfect society. A central feature of this work was the concept of nature in the sense of an uncorrupted condition. It was felt that by looking at the origin of things the true essence or the nature of things could be encountered.

It should be evident that the seeds of nineteenth-century evolutionism had already been sown in the previous century and, indeed, even earlier. No one acknowledged this inheritance more than Comte who stressed his debt to Condorcet, Hume and the Scottish moral philosophers and recognised that his work derived ultimately from Aristotelian philosophy. However, before proceeding to a discussion of the work of Comte and other nineteenth-century social evolutionists including Hegel, Spencer, Morgan and Tyler, it is necessary to consider the important distinction made by Nisbet (1969:161–4), whereby social evolution is distinguished from biological evolutionism, for, even though the social evolutionists did play heavily on the biological analogy, their evolutionism was, in one sense at least, quite different from biological evolutionism. Nisbet (1969:162) emphasises the distinction between biological theory's standing as a population and statistical theory with organisms and organic phenomena capable of being described collectively only in statistical terms, and the theory of social evolution's dependence upon typological construction. The typologies tend to be constructed out of social constructs such as social class, kinship, units of culture etc., which are held to be institutional and normative bases of human behaviour. This emphasis upon typological construction is one we will return to time after time in subsequent chapters.

Comte's work leaned heavily on that of Condorcet, particularly with reference to history as science, which foresaw the 'progression of the human species' and the associated belief in the social analyst's ability to plan the future. The historical perspective allowed an understanding of the central developmental tendencies of social evolution which could be projected to the future:

> The aim of every science is foresight. For the laws established by observation of phenomena are generally employed to foresee

their succession . . . it is quite in accordance with the nature of the human mind that observation of the past should unveil the future in politics, as it does in astronomy, physics, chemistry and physiology . . . it is clear that knowledge of what social system the elite of mankind is called to by the progress of mankind is called to by the progress of civilisation – knowledge forming the true practical object of positive science – involves a general determination of the next social future as it results from the past.

(Comte 1896:94–5)

This confidence in science was merely a reiteration of Condorcet's belief that science was to guide and shape social development. A new science, social science, by assimilating the methods of the natural sciences, was to become equally objective, as precise and as predictive.

The observation that there was order with continuity was central to Comte's views on social evolution. This does not mean that he saw evolution as unilinearly inevitable, for, while he held that change in time was natural or normal, there was also what he referred to as statics. He emphasised that a great mistake among his predecessors was to think in terms of a false dichotomy involving order and change, for if change was natural within a dynamic context, then order existed in change. The driving force of that change was human knowledge. While the principle of order in change was accepted by his successors their understanding of the motor of change differed.

It should be clear that by Comte's time the idea that evolution was not haphazard, but directional, was well established. Thus Comte envisaged three stages, each characterised by different types of human knowledge which co-varied with the intellectual disciplines. Hegel held similar ideas concerning his spirit of freedom, and Marx's conception of change involved the same directional inevitability. By and large an air of Eurocentrism prevailed in that the direction of change was inevitably towards the qualities of nineteenth-century Europe. It has been suggested (Peel 1971:198) that conservatives such as Spencer favoured their own societies over all past ages, whereas nineteenth-century social critics such as Comte or Marx saw their own society as merely a stage on the way to a superior form.

Since the main objective of social evolutionists was to discover the provisions for change within the nature or structure of the entity being observed, immanence was inevitable (Nisbet 1969:170). Thus the directional nature of change derived from the inherent forces which engendered growth. Not that change proceeded at a single pace; it could be arrested. In this discussion of an inherent force, once again we witness the analogy with the growth of an organism. Of course, this was no more than an elaboration of what Liebniz had stated at the beginning of the eighteenth century. It was the inner composition of the social system that was the driving force of change, whether it be Marx's economic laws of motion, or Comte's laws of social dynamics.

Whereas the eighteenth-century philosophers postulated numerous stages prior to the present, each one seemingly with his own magic number, the nineteenth century witnessed the emergence of a view which merely contrasted the past with the present. Thus this opposition was collapsed into two logically and sociologically contrasting states or types of society. Saint-Simon was an important contributor to such developments, arguing that modern society was the society of production, contrasting with previous society which was preoccupied with power and domination. At the time he was writing the emerging production was industrial production, a period of profound change which affected the way in which the new batch of sociologists interpreted human society. Industrialisation, as a productive process, was accompanied by urbanisation, secularisation and institutional change, as well as by numerous changes in family life, politics and culture, all of which were to be lumped together and referred to as 'modernisation'. The eighteenth-century philosophers, in pursuing 'natural history', rejected any conception of accidental causes of change and adopted an outline of 'ideal' states through which society progressed. This led to a focus on the generalised, idealised elements of the society at any one moment in time. Even though a society might only have displayed some elements of the typology, clarity insisted that this was sufficient to fit into the general framework. The emphasis was on the integrating principles of the type, the ordered interrelated patterns that lent meaning to the whole and served to sustain it. This much was also true of the nineteenth-century proto-sociologists with reference to a uniform industrial society as a type. If society was progressive then the converse of industrial society was pre-industrial society.

The tendency to a polarisation involving past and present was presented as a succession of two logically and sociologically contrasting types of society. There are numerous examples: Spencer's militant and industrial society, Toennies' *Gemeinschaft* and *Gesellschaft*, Maine's contrasting social orders involving status and contract, Durkheim's mechanical and organic solidarity, and Weber's two forms of rationality. It was a common theme during the nineteenth century. When the polarisation was linked with progress in terms of social complexity, we encounter another of the main concerns of nineteenth-century sociologists - the concern with social breakdown. Of course this did nothing to dent faith in inevitable progress, for it was linked with the idea of adaptation. Progress was seen as an integral part of the change from a state of primitiveness to civilisation.

> . . . whether man has won or lost in this change (from the primitive to the civilisation state) is no longer an open question if one considers the destiny of his species. This consists in nothing less than the progress towards perfection.
>
> (Kant, 1963:60)

The inevitability of progress is clear. One form of civilisation replaces a previous form which was unimproved, as a consequence of which its demise was inevitable. It was a clear expression of the survival of the fittest, a theme to be echoed by later followers such as Hegel and Spencer.

The voices raised against the inevitability of progress were lost in the biological analogies which permeated what has become known as Social Darwinism, and which is most characteristic of the work of Herbert Spencer. Spencer conceived of social changes in terms of evolution, a process which involved the increasing differentiation of society. This differentiation was premised upon the increasing specialisation of functions. Society involved integration, that is, the mutual interdependence of the structurally differentiated parts and the coordination of their functions, an idea which derived from Montesquieu. It is here, together with the work of Comte that we witness the emergence of what later became known as structural functionalism. Social change involved the displacement of mechanical solidarity, and progress involved the integration of the organic solidarity within a new form of the quest for order. It was held that the new, more complex, social organisation required a new form of control. According to Spencer this was evident when a historical dimension was introduced in that there was a temporal coincidence between the emergence of the state as a source of control and the emergence of the idea of the individual and progress.

The biological analogy, characteristic of medieval philosophy and well developed in the ideas of Hobbes, was strong in the work of Spencer. He maintained that societies and institutions competed for living space and that the only ones which survived were those which were able to adapt themselves to the changing environment. If the structural parts of a culture do not adapt to the demands of the environment, the culture will be destroyed by its competitors. The idea of progress as involving the change to a more complex, more differentiated and more integrated society ordained a greater sense of power in the struggle for survival. Thus the more complex society will displace the less complex.

Within this argument Spencer combines the Montesquiean idea of a closely knit interdependence of institutions with the ideas of Comte and Condorcet on progress by postulating a global and permanent trend towards increasing interdependence or integration. As we have seen, Condorcet and other Enlightenment writers emphasised that the progress of civilisation depended upon the accumulation of knowledge. Although Comte did discuss the problem of coherence of social institutions, his main emphasis was similar to that of Condorcet. Their interest was in the development of a social system conducive to moral improvement whereas Spencer was concerned mainly with deducing ethical norms from social evolution. The displacement of the least powerful, be it a social or a cultural group, was the consequence of that very lack of power. The issue of survival of the fittest justified their demise as the price of progress.

This evolutionary perspective which sees progress, not only as inevitable, but also as involving a very specific social form, presents numerous problems. Among them is that the inevitability of the process means that the existing social form will, in time, disappear, because it is inferior in the sense that it is unable to make the adaptive adjustments which constitute progress. It would appear to impose the blame for the disappearance upon the very form which disappears rather than upon that which survives. It becomes a self-justifying prophecy. It is also an inherently conservative perspective in that the function of adaptation is to generate a condition of equilibrium and harmony. Within Spencer's work there is a tendency to superimpose a typological construction of society, which derived from existing ethnographic work, upon a philosophical conception of society in change. It was essentially an inductive process which created 'types'. These 'types' were labelled in accordance with the theoretical position while being 'discovered' on the basis of what had been said about them.

STATE AND COMMUNITY

Social breakdown was seen as a general crisis which affected all of European society. It was evident that the French Revolution and the industrial revolution were having profound effects upon all aspects of society, and it was this which lay behind the preoccupation with a search for social order. A series of assumptions was established which claimed that order was best represented through homogeneity while conflict derived from difference. The production of a discourse which set a premium on the freedom and dignity of the individual raised the Hobbesian problem of how a social order could derive from a situation in which individuals enter into free competition in a 'war of all against all'. Some form of organic solidarity involving specific moral order was necessary in order to offset the anomic tendency. Nisbet (1969) maintains that the counter-revolution of those such as Chateaubriand, Maistre, Haller and Bonald, reacting to the rationalist philosophers whose ideas inspired the French Revolution, produced a series of concepts which contributed to a conservative discourse on society. These ideas influenced the work of later French social philosophers such as Comte and Saint-Simon. Similarly, Kant's work on the moral imperative fired a German tradition that was equally conservative. It is from this tradition that the Durkheimian idea of a mechanical solidarity, or Toennies' *Gemeinschaft* as the source of the individual's moral shelter derives. The Romanticism of this train of thought is clarified when this form of community is opposed to its converse – the organic solidarity of the *Gesellschaft*. Urbanisation and industrialisation were held to generate a change in the social order from one which depended upon the moral imperative to one dependent upon association. Durkheim claimed that the solidarity based upon association, his organic solidarity, had corresponding social norms: 'the division of labour gives rise to legal rules which determine the nature and the relations between divided fractions, but whose violation only entails restitutive measures without any expiatory character'(1933:206). The cooperative law which Durkheim referred to derived from 'that part of social life' formed by 'the bonds engendered by the division of labour' (1933:119). It also reflected, in part, the dependence of Durkheim's ideas on his conception of society as consisting of mutually dependent parts. This *conscience collective* was not a static quality but was subject to change as society changed.

While Comte argued that specialisation was a threat to the orderly progress of society, Durkheim claimed that the increasing division of labour led to a new form of social cohesion in the form of organic solidarity. This new solidarity grew alongside, but eventually overshadowed, the mechanical solidarity based upon the similarity of the 'conscience' of individuals (Durkheim 1933:226). Thus Comte's emphasis upon order and progress was replaced by Durkheim's social solidarity, a concept which derived from Saint-Simon. In this respect we find an unbroken line of political consensus which focuses upon what holds society together rather on than why it falls apart.

It has become commonplace to relate social distinction to the concept of social role. This concept appears to derive from the work of Maine and Durkheim on the division of labour, and that of Weber on bureaucracy. However, the manner in which Montesquieu drew upon Roman jurisprudence and, in turn, his influence upon the Scottish moral philosophers are also relevant. Role is conceived of as involving the rights and duties which constitute a status, that is, it involves the behaviour that is the consequence of occupying a determinant position in the social structure. The reference to rights and obligations derives from the legal tradition of Rome and was related to social relations in the eighteenth century. These ideas were later related to Durkheim's remarks on the division of labour with roles being seen as the consequence of that division. Mechanical solidarity was associated with the fixing of the individual in a rigid structure and associated also with the primitive end of the evolutionary schema. It was the detachment of the individual from any particular position that provided the basis for the full emergence of social roles, and this only became reality in highly complex societies. The social complexity associated with evolution was linked to specific role systems. The rights and obligations associated with social roles were legitimised through normativisation. Two points require emphasis. First, that this conception of role fits neatly with the conception of social order, with social actors neatly slotted into positions in such a way that a harmonious coexistence is emphasised, providing there is some feature which ensures conformity with the principles of rights and obligations. Second, there is a legitimation of the evolutionary schema, and of the Durkheimian view that progress is linked to the evolving division of labour.

This social dichotomy when associated with evolution leads to a discourse which focuses upon state/community relationships. It is evident in the work of Rousseau and Locke, but their work shows affinity with that of other philosophers including Machiavelli, Hobbes and Montesquieu. The basic theme of Rousseau's work is that, in a state of nature, society was based upon the moral principles which generated integration; but as society became more complex, the state became necessary in order to conserve the moral imperative. As we have seen, the superimposition of time upon society in such a way that social change proceeds in a unilinear direction with a degree of inevitability means that *Gemeinschaft* must give way to *Gesellschaft*, thereby implementing and justifying the state in society. Economic and other developments undermined the simplicity of society and stimulated a high degree of relative inequality. As a consequence there emerged a need to eliminate the dependence of a person upon his/her fellows and to make each individual dependent upon the state. It was the state which was to produce the moral character in man/woman. The state was no longer conceived of as the creation of rational individuals striving for certain goals, but, rather, it was held to be associated with human beings seen as the product of their groups or associations. Justice in the state was held to be the equivalent of the state's moral rationale which involved equity, if not the equality of rewards. The state of nature from which man/woman was held to derive was not, as Hobbes would have it, morally defective, but his argument earned him infamy with reference to the concept of the 'noble savage'. This form of original society was based upon equality which was held to be a perfect state. 'Development' generated inequality and a departure from the pure state of nature. It led to the placing of power in certain hands, thereby destroying natural liberty. In this sense it is not the state and the community which are in opposition but the state and the individual. None the less, Hobbes' argument did lead him to present an alternative in which this contradiction is eliminated and the integration of the state and the community made complete, for the objective of the state is to teach its citizens to 'respect the sacred bond' of community. It is a collectivist rather than an individualist conception. The creation of the 'moral and collective body' of the state is meant to transform 'natural' individuals into 'moral' beings, into citizens with appropriate moral notions and sentiments. While the state is the creation of individualism the individual is also the creation of the state, since the state compels the individual to act as a member of the community. Thus it is the conscious identification with the good of the state that makes the citizen morally good. In order to achieve this goal Rousseau emphasised the need to strive for political unity: 'if the general will is to be able to express itself, that there should be no partial society within the state' (Rousseau 1950:142). He advocated the elimination of all intermediate groups which in any way militated against the individual assimilating into the rational state. This theme was ruthlessly adopted by the Jacobins in their castigation and elimination of languages and cultures in their search for a single, united France (Calvet 1974). It was a theme which echoed Hobbes' advocation of the monopoly of force on the part of the state, despite the quite different conception of the natural order that each held. Hobbes had no sympathy for any customs, traditions or moralities that existed outside of the framework

of sovereign law. This led him to advocate the supremacy of territorial/
national values over those of localism and internationalism. For
Hobbes the political community was the only possible haven from
the ills and torments of society since he held a view of individuals
as locked in a state of nature involving political, cultural and
psychological separation from one another. It was this Aristotelian
concept of the state as the source of fulfilment of the individual which
Hobbes shared with Rousseau, Machiavelli, Spinoza and others.

Fichte, a student of Kant, also pursued the ideals of Jacobinism.
Kant shared with Hobbes the belief that individualism had to be
curbed:

> in man those natural capacities which are directed to the use of
> his reason are to be fully developed only in the race, not in the
> individual. . . . The means employed by Nature to bring about the
> development of all of the capacities of men in their antagonism
> in society, so far as this is, in the end, the cause of lawful order
> among men.
>
> (Kant 1963:12–13)

The state was seen as the means by which the latent force that was
inherent in nature's provision for progress could be actualised:

> The history of mankind can be seen in the large as the realisation
> of Nature's secret plan to bring forth a perfectly constituted state
> as the only condition in which the capacities of mankind can be
> fully developed, and also bring forth that external relation among
> states which is perfectly to this end.
>
> (Kant 1963:11)

This is the essence of progress, a condition impossible without the
state. Government was seen as the actualisation in society of what was
latent, desirable and inevitable in nature's provision for progress.

This linking of progress with the state in order to generate what was
latent in nature, and which constitutes the essence of community, is
also evident in the ideas of Mill. He emphasised that people must be
ready for government and that this involves passing through the early
stages of development. Order is a condition of progress rather than an
end in itself. Thus the state forms order in the sense that it organises
the 'moral, intellectual and active worth already existing' while also
promoting the 'general mental advance of the community'. These two
objectives were related. In contrast to civic thinkers such as Hobbes,
Locke and Montesquieu, Mill saw the state as playing an active rather
than a passive role.

Both Marx and Spencer looked forward to the victory of the individual over the state, thereby following Rousseau's perception. Both felt that the diminished power of the state involved the withering of the entire supra-individual, sociocultural nexus of restraint. In contrast, Durkheim claimed that the growth in the division of labour, while contributing to an organic solidarity, led to an intensification of the mutual dependence of individual and social group. The importance of his conception of social group as something other than an amalgam of individuals is a fundamental development for later sociology. Despite accusations of idealism, the super-organic anticipated much that was to follow in sociology. In claiming that the determining cause of social facts should not be sought in the states of individual consciousness he stated:

> Collective representation, emotion, and tendencies are caused not by certain states of the consciousness of individuals but by the conditions in which the social group in its totality is placed.
>
> (Durkheim 1938:106)

In this respect Durkheim shared with Marx the belief that the individual states of consciousness were moulded by social conditions of which the individual was not aware. Durkheim felt that there existed a 'coercive effect' which social things exerted over individual behaviour. This meant that such things must have an 'existence of their own'. Individual behaviour is a 'reincarnation' or a mirror of social entities with an existence independent both of the concrete expression in a given individual and of the observer's logico-empirical procedures. This leads him to conclude that 'sociological phenomena cannot be defined by their universality', and that 'a movement repeated by all individuals is not thereby a social fact'. In contrast, the generality and social constraints of a genuine social fact derives from the exterior and collective 'consciousness'. Social facts are held to be 'collective' representations or ideas expressed by the group mind and expressed or 'reincarnated' in the minds and behaviours of the individual members of the social group.

These ideas were consecrated as the *raison d'être* of the state during the first half of the nineteenth century. Given the discursive power of such ideas it was essential that any source of opposition to the established states in the form of stateless nations had to incorporate these ideas into their own discourse. Thus the nineteenth-century nationalists such as Kossuth, Korais, Palacký, Mazzini and Davis did not refute these ideas but argued that their particular nations were worthy of achieving the condition of statehood on a par with all of the already existing states. This was usually done by an appeal to the relationship between community, language, culture and territory, reminiscent of the early German writers such as Herder. This involved the ideals of a united, progressive humanity, devoted to rational and beneficial ends. The rationalism of the Enlightenment was retained.

What is evident in the discussion about the community and the state is that it is impossible, within the terms in which they are discussed, to envisage the two as existing in a condition of mutual antagonism or opposition. The manner in which nature and reason are resolved among the Enlightenment writers presents this problem. The community is held to derive from the existence of a moral order and is the repository of that moral order. On the other hand, social change leads to a displacement of the very ingredients of community in the name of progress. But the state is invoked as the saving grace which exists to uphold or even to create anew the moral order. Thus, if the community exists together with the state, then it is inconceivable that the two can be in opposition. Furthermore, this position is strengthened if the community is held to change as a consequence of progress, and if the state is the source and guardian of that progress. There is a contradiction here between the community as the basis of the moral order and a state which is the guardian of the moral order because of the eventual demise of the community. It can only be resolved by placing the state as the ultimate source of a morality which looks to tradition and history for its existence outside of the confines of the state. Of course this position, as one would expect, given the historical conjuncture in which it appears, was the converse of the previous historical epoch when the proto-state was in a position of obvious conflict with the medieval political unit. It was also the converse of anarchists such as Kropotkin and Stirner who advocated the abolition of the state in favour of the community.

THE COMPARATIVE METHOD

During the second half of the nineteenth century social theorists sought to fill gaps in their knowledge of universal history by what was known as the 'comparative method'. This was based upon the belief that the existing sociocultural system is, in differing degrees, comparable with extinct cultures. Thus if Victorian sociologists or anthropologists wished to know what society was like in Stone Age England they could obtain an insight through the study of a Stone Age sociocultural system then in existence in some part of the world. Thus Pitt-Rivers claimed: 'the existing races, in their respective stages of progression, may be taken as the bona fide representatives of the races of antiquity' (Pitt-Rivers 1906:53). The application of the comparative method, as it is known, involved arranging the varieties of contemporary institutions in a sequence of increasing antiquity by assuming that the older forms were the simpler ones.

Evidently this is merely another expression of the Enlightenment belief, that, within the conception of progress, European civilisation represented an advance on an earlier, more primitive condition. Any such idea of progress involved the existence of some base line of origin as a basis for comparison. Alongside the idea of a 'state of nature' was the 'savage' who existed in such a state and who served as an example of whence the contemporary European derived. Thus Tyler and Morgan believed that contemporary institutions could not be understood without recreating evolutionary antecedents. This dedication to diachronic study involved a belief that present society derived from the past and that 'traces' or survivals from the past could be recognised and identified. This cultural survival was a feature which 'did not fit in with its cultural medium. It persists rather than functions, or its function somehow does not harmonise with the surrounding culture' (Malinowski 1944:28). This view persists in those perspectives which look to the past for the core of a culture, with the present being merely a contamination of that perfect past. Such perspectives fail to see culture as a dynamic entity, constantly created and recreated but, on the contrary, lead to culture being equated with 'tradition' as a survival from the past.

The concept and theory of culture was a major theme prior to the French Revolution. It was Locke who claimed that knowledge derived from enculturation rather than from an innate condition. Drawing upon comparative ethnographic examples he argued that this was equally true of moral rules of conduct. Since behaviour derived from knowledge, differences of experience would generate both individual and national differences in behaviour. Yet Locke also insisted upon the existence of universally valid moral beliefs and rules of right and wrong and modes of conduct. This substantiated the claim that the 'primitive' was to be led to 'civilisation' through the moral force of Christianity. Locke's conception of culture as social heritage was echoed by Turgot who added the importance of the symbolic with reference to culture. If culture was heritage it tended to be seen in terms of a group's 'customs' or 'way of life'. Furthermore Turgot emphasised that there was no direct relationship between evolution and ability, stating that genius was distributed across cultures, a view which clashed with what was to become commonplace among the

nineteenth-century evolutionists who equated progress with knowledge as ability.

The concept of culture was linked with the idea of progress. This
much is evident in the Social Darwinism of Spencer. The idea of
progress as involving change to a more complex, more differentiated
and more integrated society was related both to the historical and
the comparative perspective. In combining Montesquieu's idea of a
closely knit interdependence of institutions with the ideas of Comte
and Condorcet on progress, by postulating a global and permanent
trend towards increasing interdependence or integration, Spencer
was concerned mainly to deduce ethical norms from social evolution.
Progress involved competition between societies in the struggle for
survival. Success in this struggle depended upon the ability of a society
to adapt, with culture playing an important role in such adaptation.
With characteristic ethnocentrism, English society was presented as
the most complex and evolved social form, and the features of this
society were assumed to be the most successful in the struggle for
survival. All other cultures were judged in relation to this standard.

A view of history which saw a specific line of development which
culminated in the Europe of their time was shared by most of
the nineteenth-century social philosophers. Furthermore, what now
existed in Europe was to be the fate of the rest of the world in the
future. This was the early statement about the diffusion of a modernity
which was counterposed with traditionalism as a feature which was
displaced in time. These concepts were equivalents of civilisation
and primitiveness, and once the traits of each were established on
the basis of comparison, it was possible to assert the superiority of
specific societies, and to denigrate others. It was also possible to
label societies along a continuum according to the traits which they
displayed. Comparison became located within a presumed order of
growth and development. Yet this sense of development was weak
and the various forms of societies and cultures were ranked in relation
to a series of stages devoid of process.

On the other hand, it is not surprising that these ideas flourished
when they did for they were very effective means of justifying
the colonial activities of European states in various parts of the
world. Salvation was offered to the 'primitive' or 'barbarous', who
could be brought into civilisation and thereby paternalistically saved
from the hardships of the evolutionary journey through the various
intermediary stages. With religion as the moralising force which
would salvage the 'primitive' from the state of nature, the Christian
missionaries were given free rein to preach their own brand of

salvation. This denigration of culture and society was extended to encompass Britain in the work of Tyler as he emphasised the modern/traditional distinction which played such a central role in the denigration of the Celtic languages.

The presentation of an argument which, simultaneously, invokes the idea of an inevitable progress, social change over time, and distinctive social and cultural forms, raises certain problems. The inevitability of the evolutionary process means that the existing social and cultural forms will, in time, change. Furthermore this change assumes a specific form since the emphasis on competition leads to the disappearance of inferior societies and cultures, leading to a homogeneous, integrated, whole. Not that the individual carriers of culture disappear. Presumably they melt into the successful society as part of the process of homogenisation. This process imposes blame for cultural demise upon the very form that disappears, rather than upon the surviving form. The entire process becomes a self-fulfilling prophecy premised upon the superior/inferior dichotomy. Many of these problems derive from the confusion of knowledge and ability. If progress derives from knowledge, and if knowledge is equated with ability, then what is termed 'modern' must be more able than its converse, and the entire system is justified.

FUNCTIONALISM

Giddens (1984:228), echoing Gouldner (1970:117), has suggested that functionalism was responsible for the decline of evolutionary thinking. Yet it should be clear that functionalism and evolutionary thought coexisted quite happily in the nineteenth century and continue to do so in contemporary sociology. What was important in the difference between the views of Comte at the beginning of the century and those of Durkheim towards its end was the shift from an emphasis on order and progress to the synchronic study of order, with a methodological emphasis upon comparison. It was Durkheim who incorporated the idea of utility from the Positivists into functionalism. As a consequence, the emerging functionalist theory tried to show how the persistence or change of any social institution was not to be discussed in terms of 'survival', but rather in terms of its ongoing impact upon other institutions and behaviour. There is here the Montesquiean idea of the interrelationship of parts within an integrated whole. A social institution had to be explained in terms of its place in, and its contribution to, the wider society of which it was part.

It should be evident that this functional integration was the basis of social order for Durkheim. He saw the usefulness of the division of labour not merely in terms of increasing productivity, but also in terms of the production of an 'organic solidarity' so essential in his conception of order. He envisaged men as being bound together within the new division of labour and thereby being restrained. In this respect it was emphasised that things which were not functionally useful in economic terms could still be socially useful. Such a stand was essential in order to demonstrate that the new economic division of labour was not merely related to individual gain. A new morality would regulate and interconnect occupational specialisation while also contributing to social solidarity. This morality was functional, necessary and useful for the maintenance of social order. Yet the precise nature of the social function was not spelled out; while it was claimed that survival involved functional usefulness, the empirical nature of this function was to be determined through practice. This emphasis on the importance of moral values Durkheim shared with Weber and in this respect both of them looked to the non-rational in man.

In many respects the legacy of Durkheim's functionalism was most evident in anthropology. While in the USA Boas' rejection of evolutionism and his emphasis upon synchronic study had some relationship to Durkheim, he was writing before the publication of Durkheim's highly influential *The Elementary Forms of Religious Life* in 1912. It also seems that Durkheim's work reached the USA through the English anthropologist Radcliffe-Brown during his period at the University of Chicago. The functionalism of Radcliffe-Brown's work is described in the following terms by Gardner (1973:36–7):

> Radcliffe-Brown did not hesitate to view society as a biological organism and to deal with such abstract notions as social structure and social relations. He construed society as a system of inter-dependent parts, searched for analogous structures among diverse groups, and attempted to make those general comparisons which would illuminate the nature of social institutions.

Yet his conception of social structure was, in one important respect, different from that of Durkheim. I have already underlined the fact that for Durkheim society was an abstraction. Although Radcliffe-Brown substituted the term social structure for society, he tended to see society as no more than the sum of the individuals within that society. This difference between structure and aggregate is important in that, as Piaget (1935:6–7) emphasises, the elements of a structure are subject to laws in terms of which the whole is defined.

Furthermore, the laws are not reducible to the constituent parts, since they confer on the whole, features different from the properties of the elements.

The two also differed in another respect. Durkheim argued for a study of 'primitive' society in order to shed light on the understanding of 'complex' civilisation. In contrast, Radcliffe-Brown studied 'primitive' society without reference to any other form of society. There is evidence here of a separation of British social anthropology from the evolutionist tendency of the previous generation, a tendency which persisted in France.

The functionalism in Durkheim's work referred to a correspondence between the activity of a phenomenon and what he called 'the general needs of the social organism'. These needs varied according to the complexity and size of the society in question. Radcliffe-Brown substituted 'necessary conditions of existence' for Durkheim's term 'needs':

> I would like to substitute for the term 'needs' the term 'necessary conditions of existence' or if the term 'need' is used, it is to be understood in this sense. It may be noted, as a point to be returned to, that any attempt to apply this concept of function in social science involves the assumption that there *are* necessary conditions of existence for human societies just as there are for animal organisms, and that they can be discovered.
>
> (Radcliffe-Brown 1935:178)

Ekeh (1974:70) has indicated how this suggests that Radcliffe-Brown was generalising to human society as a generic type and thereby made 'the necessary conditions' appear to refer to 'the least common function of all human societies' (Ekeh 1974:70). This is in direct contrast to Durkheim's tendency to relate 'need' differentially to human societies. Furthermore it was Radcliffe-Brown's rejection of any definition of function which did not relate to this conception of social structure which gave rise to the term 'structural functional'.

As we have seen, Durkheim placed significant emphasis upon the concept of social solidarity, a social feature which Radcliffe-Brown discussed in terms of 'harmony' or 'unity'. They shared the view that social systems maintain themselves for significant periods of time in a steady state during which social cohesion among the members is characteristic. In contrast to Malinowski who discussed function in terms of the biopsychological needs of individuals, Radcliffe-Brown emphasised that, for him, function referred only to the contribution an institution makes to the maintenance of social structure. Social conflict as such was not accepted as a normal, or fundamental aspect of the human condition.

THEORIES OF LANGUAGE

As we have seen, the eighteenth-century philosophers used reason to discover a social solution to social problems, believing that they could discover the rational structure of the social realm. In this respect they opposed the divine right absolutism of the previous age which claimed that language was the gift of God. Language, for them, became an object of human creativity. My objective in the second part of this opening chapter is to discuss theories of language in the eighteenth and nineteenth centuries in the context of this intellectual climate. In this respect the approach departs from much of what linguists have written about the history of their subject in that they have tended to discuss the history of linguistics as if it were separate from the philosophical observations on society. Consequently, one reads such work with the feeling that it is more about what the early linguists, if indeed they should be defined as such, did rather than what they thought.

Pecheux (1982:6) has suggested a three-fold tendency in linguistic theory:

(i)   the formalist–logistic tendency which involved a relationship between determination and explication and which was evident in seventeenth-century philosophical thought;
(ii) the historical tendency which predominated in the nineteenth century but which has its roots in a much earlier historical period. It involves tracing linguistic variation and change and has tended to focus upon historical linguistics;
(iii) the linguistics of speech in which the emphasis is upon communication, including poetics and rhetoric.

The fascinating theme which runs through these three tendencies is the contradiction between unification and differentiation. As a Marxist, Pecheux would tend to see this contradiction as involving the difference between the need for unification of the political totality in the form of the state, and the trend towards differentiation that characterises capitalist society. The system must simultaneously unite and divide; make uniform while also differentiating. Be that as it may, the three tendencies are not uniformly divided among the philosophers of the eighteenth and nineteenth centuries, but, rather, they often overlap. Thus it might be preferable to discuss the historical developments of orientations to language in chronological order while bearing in mind the relevance of Pecheux's three-fold categorisation.

EARLY ANTECEDENTS

The ideas of early empirical and rationalist philosophers including Bacon, Locke, Leibniz and especially the Port-Royal School had a significant influence upon what was to follow. It is among them that we witness the rejection of the idea that language was a divine gift and its replacement by the belief that language was invented and developed by man. This break is the backbone of the idea of progress. Since the transmission of thought depended upon language and since reason, the very essence of progress, was a feature of thought, then evidently progress involved language. It was this reasoning that lay behind the Utopian quest for a universal community with a single universal language, an idea that can still be encountered in a different form in discussions of *langues véhiculaires* or in the work of Habermas (1979) when he discusses universal pragmatics. Not that linguistic nationalism was missing. Indeed it was central to much of the eighteenth-century discussion on language.

The empiricism of the British social philosophers involved the thesis that all human knowledge is derived externally from sense impressions and the operations of the mind upon them, in abstraction and generalisation. It contrasted with the rationalism of Descartes who made claims for the irrefutable truths of human reason. This division features prominently in the emergence of contemporary linguistics.

Bacon, as one of the foremost empiricists, argued that while language was the means of conveying thought between men, nevertheless the existing form of language was inadequate for this purpose. He claimed that language had stagnated in the sense that the existing structure was inadequate to express new ideas. He rejected the assumption that languages are conditioned by reason, claiming that language limits reason and that the limitations of language made reason fallible. This theme is also common to Locke who argued that the individual ways in which peoples expressed certain complex ideas created a barrier between human communities. That is, complex ideas are untranslatable. Leibniz is often heralded as the forerunner of the symbolic logicians; even though he disagreed with Locke on several points, he was another philosopher who pursued this theme and who had a profound influence on eighteenth-century thought on language.

He argued that language allowed man to reason with himself but that existing language was inadequate and there was a need to develop a world-wide language involving a universal symbolisation of thought, free from the vagueness and uncertainties of natural language. This would be the basis for an absolute precision in reason which, in turn, would lead to the discovery of absolute truth.

The nationalist ingredient derives from the ideas of those such as Mandeville (1962) who claimed that men (sic) needed government, and government needed law as the basis of social order. Such a law must be written and therefore relied heavily on language. This relationship between law, the language and the state became the basis for the claim on behalf of a single language of reason by which a state was consolidated. Thus even though several languages may be spoken within the geographical territory of the state all other languages had to be subordinated to the interests of the language of reason, *qua* language of the state. Thus there emerged a dichotomous relationship between the language of reason and *patois* or all other languages which, implicitly, lay outside of reason.

Given this argument we find some speakers of non-state languages seeking to legitimise these languages by resorting to the Babel thesis which claimed that all existing languages derived from a single original language (Calvet 1987). This theme persisted in the work of de Brosse and Court de Gebelin. The original language was associated with the perfect state of nature and its associated reason. Thus if a language could be shown to display features of the original language it could also be assumed that this preferred reason also survived making the speakers of that language superior. Poisinet de Sivrey, entering into the debate concerning which came first, language or society, claimed that the Celts had been the first to form a society and that thereby were closest to the original language. Evidently both arguments, the one focusing upon the language of the state and the other upon proximity to an original language, were premised upon the belief in language complexity within which languages were not equal. When linked with the emerging evolutionism there emerged a conception of language evolution. Of course this theme was interlinked with the pre-dominant theme of the time, involving the quest for progress through reason. On the other hand, if ideas could not be communicated until the existence of language, the emergence of language meant that ideas could now be transformed into new ones. The interdependence of language and ideas is firm. Rousseau linked this idea with social complexity associated with the complexity and variety of ideas, thereby underlining the uneven evolutionism of language. Language was used to measure the progress of a people and to demonstrate that progress was at work in the development of language through time. This evolutionary theme involved a blind search through correlation for some contact between languages and the progress of those who used them. The analysis of language revealed the level of civilisation achieved by its speakers:

> elle [the analysis of language] nous donne l'histoire même de l'esprit humain et des développements chez chaque nation. . . . D'après la langue d'un peuple, en un mot, on peut peindre d'une manière plus exacte que d'après ses monuments historiques: on y suit sans peine les progrès des sciences et des arts, et la route qu'ils ont tenue.
>
> (Court de Gebelin 1776:82–3)

Diderot (1877: vol xviii:232) claimed that a nation could not emerge from the state of barbarism until its language had attained a certain level. Morellet and Chevalier de Jaucourt elaborated upon this, the latter claiming that the knowledge of various languages, especially those of the *peuples savants* would promote the advancement of the sciences. Science was regarded as the major factor in progress, and if science was heavily reliant on language then scientific accuracy was linguistically determined. The empiricists were interested in language in order to discover the origin of the ideas of man, taking a view of language having as its sole purpose to communicate and analyse ideas. This led to the argument among the French philosophers that French was the best language for expressing thought and ideas, thereby reinforcing its existence as the language of reason. In discussing language contact it was claimed that the new language which emerged reflected the traits of the most advanced people (Turgot 1913), and Condorcet (1955) agreed that the new form was superior. It was argued that the further development of language involved geniuses, but for geniuses to emerge a nation had to have a certain level of development of its language thereby legitimising the denigration of cultures through language.

These early thoughts on language planning were also found in attempts at standardisation. In England the early phoneticians derived their inspiration from the empirical attitude of Bacon and Hume and focused considerable attention on spelling and pronounciation. It was the 'English school of phonetics' which sought to cultivate a standard form or 'the King's language'. Inevitably a focus on a standard draws attention to the non-standard and Cobbett was clearly aware of the class nature of language varieties (Robins 1967:123), and also of the link between speech variety and social mobility. Voltaire (1953:166) stated, 'C'est le peuple ignorant qui a forme les langues', while adding that educated men (sic) had finally learned the best way to employ the haphazard language created by the masses. Similarly, de Brosse (1801:77) recognised a distinction between the proper language of a nation and the vulgar one of the masses. The Italian Garvina claimed that a language was corrupted when the vulgar speech became dominant enough to be adopted by the nobility. Even so, de Brosse claimed that even this form would, once more, be subdivided into class varieties. Yet there was also a criticism of the role of the Academy in standardisation, on the grounds that it involved a form of absolutism inappropriate for the new era of democracy. This concern with democracy in turn was problematic in a country where less than half the citizens spoke French and led to a call, not for democracy to accommodate the other languages spoken within the state boundaries, but rather to a demand that all citizens should learn French (Achard, 1980). Since language was held to reflect the character of the people who spoke it (anticipating the ideas of Herder and even Whorf), it was best that a single language be available as an expression of that character.

This standardisation of state languages involved the legitimisation of what were previously seen as vernaculars which became items worthy of study. It was this elevation of what became termed 'Modern European languages' which led to a focus upon the question of language universals. The empiricists stressed the individual variations of particular languages while the rationalists emphasised what was common to all languages. The Port-Royal School was an important influence with reference to the second emphasis.

Important though these early philosophers were to subsequent philosophical discussions of language, it is perhaps the rationalists of the Port-Royal School who left the greatest imprint. They emphasised the interdependence of thought and language as well as the importance of linguistic and cultural relativity. A feature of the logico-philosophical school of the seventeenth century was the emphasis placed on the relationship between meaning and reference. Logic was held to be the art of thinking and it would appear that grammar, seen as the art of speaking, was homogeneous with logic since the same principles applied to both. Pecheux (1982) argues that within this conception there was a difference between seventeenth- and eighteenth-century reasoning with reference to ontology. The determinative relationship of the seventeenth century, through the relationship between comprehension and extension, is concerned exclusively with the order of being, without any addition from thought. We are on the level at which being designates itself. In contrast, eighteenth-century thought introduces the essence of thought. This difference has led to Foucault, in his work on the Port-Royal Grammar, to state:

> Grammar is not to be taken as the prescriptions of a legislator, at last giving the chaos of utterances their constitution and laws . . . it is a discipline which states the rules to which any language must conform for it to be able to exist.
>
> (Foucault 1969:xiii)

That is, logic is the foundation and the 'art of speaking' merely conforms to the rules that constitute that logic. Thus the 'correct' use of speech involves bringing the subject back to the truths of the world of essences. Explication thus becomes the means by which to reduce the discrepancy between my thought and the entities to which my discourse refers, that is, between what is learnt in childhood and what is subsequently learnt. Thus correct usage becomes a pedagogical exercise.

Pecheux goes on to state that the subordination of the fields of grammar and rhetoric to that of knowledge is marked in the seventeenth-century conception of the relationship which the speaking subject maintains with his/her discourse. Thus when we find a discussion of pronouns as substitutes for nouns, the position of the subject becomes simply the effect of a rule, one of both etiquette and economy, it is completely dependent of the enounced and is logically reduced to it: 'they perceived that it was often needless and indecent to name themselves: Hence they introduced the pronoun of the first person.' Commenting on this importance of knowledge Foucault (1972) saw discourse as the invention of the seventeenth century in the same way as 'man' was the invention of the nineteenth century. He advocates a return to a preoccupation with discourse. Foucault emphasised that he referred not only to the Port-Royal School but also to Hobbes who referred to language as being imposed upon the collectivity (Foucault 1972:82).

The distinction between essential properties and contingent properties continues into the eighteenth century and is evident in the distinction made between truths of reasoning and truths of facts where the truths of reasoning are necessary and those of fact are contingent. By resolving a necessary truth into simpler ideas and

truths we bring out the determinations of an idea. Thus, for example, it was claimed that the idea which God has of the triangle is
expressed in the individual and this must contain all of the properties
of the triangle. Eighteenth-century philosophy made the transition
with respect to the concepts of seventeenth-century rationalism, a
shift that involved reducing, from God's point of view, all expli-
cative relations to determinate relations. At this time most theories of language started from the principle that there was once an
'Adamic language' which plainly revealed the natural order common to angels, to men and to all intelligences in general, but of
which contemporary language only retained a distorted trace in the
practical correspondence between logic and grammar. An immense
effort of decoding was therefore necessary in order to ascend to
the lost origin. This was in line with the empiricist philosophies of
the eighteenth century and contrasted with the seventeenth-century
world of eternal truth. In this respect we find the principle of
variation according to which there are no a priori truths. The following passage from Maupertuis, published in 1752, is characteristic:

> Since languages have departed from this original simplicity, and
> there are perhaps no longer people in the World savage enough to
> instruct us in the search for the pure truth which each generation
> has obscured, and on the other hand, the first moments of my
> existence cannot help me in this search . . . since, then, I am
> deprived of these means for my instruction and am obliged to
> accept a multitude of established expressions, or at least to use
> them, let us try to make out their meaning, their force and their
> scope; let us ascend to the origin of languages and see by what
> stages they have been formed.

(Maupertuis 1752:31)

This question of the origin of languages preoccupied all science
and philosophy in the eighteenth century. It argues that in order
to understand the origin of language, which is associated with the
faculty of thought, it is necessary to ascend to the 'state of nature', a
new and empiricist fiction which mirrored the rationalist fiction. The
beginning of language involved the production of sounds emitted in
relation to immediate objects and at the command of needs, but it
is also the natural extension of the language of action: 'that which
nature imposes on us by virtue of the configuration she has given
our organs' (Condillac 1947:197). It is here that we encounter the
basis for a theory of enunciation involving a combination of the

gestures of the 'language of action' and the sounds of articulated language.

These preoccupations of the eighteenth century crystallise during the next two centuries. They develop into a philosophy of language and the linguistics that correspond to it. The new conceptual form is dominated by subjectivity and involves a reworking of the Aristotelian opposition between the contingent and the necessary through the inference of the predicate in the subject (concept) to which it applies. The analytic judgement consists of the awareness of a necessary relation, whereas the synthetic judgement, which is a new concept, is an act of the subject who posits a connection between the concept and something outside it. This new conception of the relationship between the necessary and the contingent, and the notion of an act of the subject that became attached to it, linking subjectivity and contingency, constitute the common foundations of modern thought, in which the links between logico-philosophical reflection and preoccupation with language become ever closer. It would seem that the seventeenth-century opposition between necessary and contingent has been superimposed by the objective/subjective which characterises the modern philosophical idealism. It is here that we witness the descent of Husserl's phenomenology from the Port-Royal themes.

Thus the Port-Royal School was concerned to suppress the discrepancy between thought and truth by multiplying the forms and levels of the representation of an object, so as to be able to analyse it, setting out to decompose, combine and arrange it. A logic of ideas, signs and judgements replaced the logic of concepts, categories and proofs (Foucault 1969:xviii). This developed into a theory of representation that would allow the conception of the secret necessity of what appears to us to be contingent. In turn this developed into the element of modern idealism in which the subjective is subordinated to the objective. As a consequence it is possible to treat ethics, religion, politics etc. as analogous to logical-mathematical entities and to apply to them the same operation. A return to this approach has been central in the work of many French sociolinguists, an approach which challenges the implicit assumption of mainstream sociolinguistics.

LINGUISTICS AS SCIENCE

There is a tendency among historians of linguistics to play down the eighteenth-century contribution to science and to emphasise that linguistic science was a product of the following century. This involves a disregard for the serious scientific study of language undertaken in the eighteenth century. It was of course a period when a faith in science was emerging and most fields of knowledge were drawn into the realm of scientific inquiry. Despite the naïvety in his work, de Brosse did establish the principles of systematically studying language as a mechanism. Both he and Court de Gebelin employed the comparative method in their attempt to establish laws of language change. Turgot's work on rules of etymology are also important in this respect. Perhaps of major importance for subsequent scientific studies of language was the emphasis placed on the filiation of languages which derived from the philosophical emphasis placed upon evolutionism and progress. As we have seen, the debate concerning the derivation of all languages from a single language was an old one, and the nature of the original language was discussed in terms of the emerging nationalism of the state. True to the evolutionary perspective, attempts were made to recreate the original language. However, there were dissenting voices, and both Turgot and Condillac argued that there had been more than one original language, with new languages developing wherever new societies were formed. Subsequent language contact and the associated borrowings made the reconstruction of the mother tongue impossible. While these philosophers employed language to support their philosophical systems, this also involved an attempt to establish a science of linguistics.

When William Jones in 1786 first proposed that Greek, Latin, the Celtic languages and Sanskrit had a common origin, he was in effect asserting that the comparison of contemporary languages could yield reliable information concerning the nature of languages spoken by chronologically remote peoples. Jones' ideas were systematically pursued and in 1837 Grimm's formulations of the regularities of vowel changes in the Indo-European languages provided a fresh confirmation of the validity of the comparative method applied to linguistic phenomena. By the 1860s the triumphs of 'philology' in outlining the steps in the evolution of Indo-European phonology, grammar and semantics served, along with palaeontology and archaeology, to demonstrate the validity of the comparative approach.

The gathering of comparative linguistic data during the eighteenth century was not entirely a haphazard exercise since it was guided by the general theory of social evolution and progress, and by the early principles of the comparative method. The direction which this field took prior to the seminal work of Jones on Sanskrit was elaborated towards the end of the century. The early work involved such exercises as the compilation of comparative word lists involving several languages and this was later expanded to accommodate phonetics, semantics, grammatical structures and the spatial analysis of language. The tendency to look to comparison between features of language and to accommodate links between different languages in the form of universal features fitted neatly into the philosophical conception of society and history. Thus, establishing links between languages served to demonstrate an elaboration of the Babel thesis either in its original Biblical form or in terms of legitimising state languages. Similarly, demonstrating the common attributes of all languages was useful in arguing that humanity was subject to a single evolutionary pattern which was relevant to different degrees among different peoples. Such an approach to language was, in effect, an inevitable consequence of the social philosophy of the time. The work of Harris on universal grammar similarly served to extend the argument concerning universal thought processes and the quest for a universal basis of ideas, thereby following Locke and Condillac. Perhaps what we have stated above (pp. 14–15) about the comparative method is most evident in the work of Burnett who, in common with many of his contemporaries including Herder, held that the origin of language could be brought to light partly through the study of existing languages by seeking evidence of primitivity and 'traces' among the languages of what were held to be 'primitive' people. He claimed that such languages were devoid of differentiation of word classes and syntactic rules, and cited the language of the Chinese as 'exceedingly defective'.

By the time Rask, Grimm and Bopp were producing their observations on historic linguistics the questionable assumptions of earlier writers had receded and it is claimed that theirs was a 'scientific' work. None the less their work derives from that of their predecessors and many of the background assumptions are retained. Thus, following Herder, Grimm related his discovery of sound correspondences within Indo-European languages and other language families to the emergence of nationhood among the ancestors of Germanic peoples. Similarly, Bopp's work involved attempts to recreate the ancient Scandinavian language. In both cases there was reference to a fall from grace of a condition of primitive integrity reminiscent of Rousseau's ideas. Even at the end of the century this preoccupation with evolutionism and language was still evident. William McGee, the first president of the American Anthropological Association, had the following to say:

Possibly the Anglo-Saxon blood is more potent than that of other races; but it is to be remembered that the Anglo-Saxon language is the simplest, the most perfectly and simply symbolic that the world has ever seen; and that by means of it the Anglo-Saxon saves his vitality for conquest instead of wasting it under the Juggernaut of a cumbrous mechanism for conveyance of thought.

(Quoted in Harris 1968:255)

This confusion of race, culture and language was not uncharacteristic of the ideas associated with evolutionism and the comparative method in the nineteenth century.

NATION, LANGUAGE AND THOUGHT

Evidently during the eighteenth and nineteenth centuries language was part of the search for the cultural origins of human populations. This was particularly true of the German preoccupation with what is referred to as the 'sunken folk cultures' of past eras. It involved a search for lost manuscripts which could serve to indicate the earlier form(s) of a particular language as well as legitimising that language through its literacy. Folk customs and folk speech were also part of this endeavour. It often assumed a link with the soil in the sense of being an autochthonous form. This quest was associated with the emergence of linguistic tools or the conceptualisation of language and its relationship with the discovery of grammatical structure as the underlying dynamic of all verbal communication. A metaphysical unity of the language of a people and of the representation of the world that it serves to present is the essence of this perspective. Characteristic of this approach is the work of Herder. However, as Manicas (1988:80) emphasises it is a mistake to associate Herder with a racist orientation.

Marcellesi and Gardin (1987:20) have suggested that de Michaelis equated national culture with 'opinions of the people' and national language with 'language' in his interpretation of a question posed by the Berlin Academy of Sciences in 1757 which asked: 'What is the influence of people's opinions on the language, and of language on the opinions of the people?' In this respect he was merely elaborating on what has been discussed above about the legitimisation of the language of the state. This prize-winning essay by de Michaelis led Herder to develop his thesis on language as the manifestation of the people that speak it. True to his time he claimed that a language was a depository of the experience and knowledge of past generations. Language, according to Herder, is also the centre of our knowledge of the world, the entity which conditions and sets limits on thought. People think as they speak and speak as they think. Language is the tool, the content and the form of human thinking. The Kantian theory of perception involving sensations produced by the external world being ordered by categories imposed by the mind, was related to language, and language became the mirror of the nation. This approach was again typical of its particular historical conjuncture when the creation of a sense of nationhood in the name of the state was in operation. A nation's speech was an individual phenomenon possessing intimate bonds with national thought, national literature and national solidarity. Again we find that Herder is merely continuing an earlier line of thought in that he answers the question concerning the priority of language or thought by stating that their interdependence pointed to a common origin and a common evolution. Much of his thesis involved a hypothetical reconstruction of speech within evolution.

The ideas of Herder were pursued by von Humboldt. For him, culture derives from the people, language expresses the spirit of the people, the love of the nation. The diversity of languages corresponds with the diversity of mentalities. Language was an interior form independent of the world but which organises the world. Thus what is often referred to as a language community is replaced by the concept of nation, while the notion of the mode of thought of a collectivity is replaced by the idea of the spirit of the nation. Language creates or helps to create representation of the world, something that is impossible without language. Thus language transforms an objective world into a different world, a world of the spirit. Similarly, language constitutes the people and is thereby the basis of collective identity, but the language also creates the nation and the nation is identified with the language. In a sense the language represents a collective memory of its speakers, this collective memory representing the basis of a conception of common identity that is the nation. Even though Herder never intended his ideas to encompass race, the idea that those born to speak a certain language within a certain national territory have a particular perspective of the world has led commentators to infer a racist conception of language (Marcellesi and Gardin 1987:23). Similarly, it can be argued that the equation of language with nation serves to prevent a social conception of language since in each case, when the social is invoked, it involves either the people or the nation. The language is reduced to its official form within which the people are viewed as homogeneous, as uniform.

Von Humboldt also claimed that some languages displayed a greater advance than others as instruments and models of thinking and in this respect he was reiterating the ethnocentricity of the Eurocentric evolutionist model.

The most evident later development of this line of thinking involves the work of Sapir and Whorf, the North American anthropologists. Their work was characteristic of the tendency among this school to derive structural categories from observation, as opposed to structural analysis which saw empirical study as merely a means to an end. The main objects of their study were the various native American languages. They were highly influenced by empiricism and by the influence of Boas in his insistence on detailed synchronic, empirical, rather than abstract, theoretical study, and also by Kroeber's emphasis on culture areas. In accordance with the evolutionary perspective there had emerged a tendency to see the grammatical system of native American languages as primitive and lacking in the semantic power and the so-called grammatical refinement of those languages used in the western world. Hawkes (1977:29) has suggested that it was the desire to record the dying languages of the native Americans rather than the empiricist foundation that was responsible for the development of what is referred to as descriptive linguistics.

While this school is well known for its methodological developments it was, of course, not devoid of theory. Gumpertz (1982:13) suggests that the structural analysis of these studies furnished empirical evidence for the contention that human cognition is significantly affected by historical forces. It was claimed that perception and mental retention is a function of culturally determined predispositions to perceive and assimilate. History-bound conventions determined forms of human action and thought processes. Cultural differences replaced primitiveness and the associated standards of rationality and efficiency as an explaining principle.

As prominent members of this school, Sapir and Whorf envisaged a relationship between the grammatical system of Amerindian languages and the world view of the speakers, with the former influencing the latter. This opposed the prevalent philosophy that human linguistic reasoning is describable in terms of universal logical processes which are independent of the way in which propositions are expressed in particular languages and cultures. For Sapir, meaning was both culturally and subconsciously patterned. In stating that languages operate by means of some kind of inherent structuring principle which simply overrides the 'objective' observations and expectations of the non-native speaker who listens from 'outside', Sapir was close to a phenomenological position in stating:

> it becomes almost impossible for the normal individual to observe or conceive of functionally similar types of behaviour in other societies than his own or in other cultural contexts than those he has experienced without projecting into them the forms that he is always consciously finding that one is in unconscious subjection to.
>
> (Sapir 1949:10)

Yet Sapir refers to cultural distinctions in terms of an undifferentiated, functionally integrated, internally homogeneous system.

One of the successes of this perspective was its ability to show that the grammatical patterns that they had isolated were remarkably stable over time. While pronunciation, vocabulary and other aspects of language were subject to change, core grammatical systems tended to survive intact often for many centuries.

Although there is a tendency to associate Sapir and Whorf, the ideas of the two scholars were by no means identical. Sapir saw language as formed in the social world and suggests that it is not until after it is formed that it operates to shape a world view. That is, if man sees only an objective world the existence of the world is not in doubt. Language to a great extent organises our thoughts and thereby contributes to condition our way of conceiving of the objective world. Thus Sapir conceived a relationship of interest in which language contributed to culture and culture shaped reality. In contrast, Whorf, as did von Humboldt, saw the external world as merely chaotic without the intervention of the linguistic system; the external world exists but it is not possible to know it scientifically until the knowledge which one has of it is related to language.

There is also a difference with reference to their respective positions on language and thought. For Sapir only the lexis of a language is the organiser of the experience of the people that speak it. In contrast, there is no direct relationship between society, the representation that it has of the world and correctly used grammar (phonetics, morphology and syntax). Also Sapir appears to admit that with reference to vocabulary there is nothing in language that depends upon culture: the evolution of the latter and the evolution of the former are not parallel, isomorphic, and consequently it does not seem possible to establish a cause/effect relationship between them. The rapport between language and society, according to Sapir, lies in a conception of language as the instrument of socialisation. In effect, social relations cannot exist without it. Sharing a language is a particular symbol of the solidarity that unites individual speakers of that language. External to the communicative function, language puts into operation the bond of a physical group. As such, language plays a considerable role in cultural accumulation and in the transmission of history both in 'primitive' societies through oral history, and in advanced societies. Culture is present in a linguistic form. Furthermore, the relationship between language and culture is not mechanical but rather it is a detailed knowledge which permits a deepened comprehension of the culture. In this respect there is not the simple correspondence between the form of a language and the form of the culture of its speakers. Rather, language and culture, for Sapir, constitute two different realities, with language evolving more slowly than culture. The collective psychology of a group and the physical environment are the forces which determine change and reflect the language.

For Whorf, on the other hand, the role of grammar is not to reproduce certain ideas giving them an oral form. Rather it models ideas. He states:

> The linguistic system fashions the ideas, it is the programme and the guide of individual mental activity, the cause of their analyses of impressions, the cause of the syntheses which operates his mental stock.
>
> (Whorf 1956:12)

In this respect he reverses the ideas of Sapir in stating that language is not a consequence but rather a cause.

J. A. Fishman (1980:31–3) has summarised several criticisms of Whorf's ideas, criticisms which, it should be emphasised, derive from the inability of positivistic research to confirm hypotheses which derive from these ideas. Perhaps the most relevant of these criticisms for the present purpose is that Whorf was overly preoccupied with the idea that his subjects existed within a monocultural/monolingual situation, while at the same time ignoring the existence of varieties within the single language. Also, there is the criticism that language is dynamic in nature and that, according to the perspective of those making the criticism, grammars are consciously changed by their speakers. Of course the assumptions of these criticisms can themselves be criticised, but the main surge of the criticism is that Whorf's view of language structures as deriving from some ancient past, and as being unmodifiable, thereby involving an origin beyond the memory of mankind, is exaggerated. Again the criticism focuses upon the ability and willingness of speakers to consciously change language, thereby implying that people are not trapped by their various grammars to the extent that Whorf implied. Third, there is criticism of language as cause which derives from those who see the relationship between language and society as a circular one. They argue that language use and language structure may identify a social reality, and also reflect a social reality, but they are not the prime causes of that reality. This view would seem to depart from the phenomenological position while also assuming the existence of a reality independent of conception. In addition there is disagreement as to whether mind fashions language or vice versa. Most such criticisms are not really criticisms in the sense that they criticise the argument in terms of its own internality, but rather rely upon alternative arguments to sustain the criticism.

Ultimately, of course, an argument which presents language as the cause of culture, and culture as the determining factor of behaviour is inherently conservative. It raises numerous problems associated with multilingualism and language contact. On the other hand, it does raise some interesting questions about the relationship between language and society, especially with reference to the tendency to treat language as a reflection of the social. This it shares with the Saussurean perspective which has been so influential in recent years.

THE SAUSSUREAN REVOLUTION

The shift to the study of spoken language was associated with the development of methods of transcription in order to enable the recording of 'unknown' languages. The objective was to produce bodies of phonetically accurate texts from which to derive general principles of sound change. This line of enquiry led to an awareness that to undertake such research on isolated words was insufficient to account for what was regular or stable about the language behaviour of particular populations. The nature of linguistic features and associated method made it difficult to formulate general principles of change. This led to a new emphasis on contrastive relationships among acoustically similar sets of sounds. It involved combining empirical observations and abstractions based on contrasts at the level of sound and meaning. The difference between the two is evident in Saussure's contrast between *langue* and *parole*.

The tradition deriving from the seventeenth-century writings of Locke and Descartes involved a doctrine of language within which primacy was accorded to the subject as the self-defining point from which the orders of thought and of the world are constructed.

Language, in this perspective, becomes a simple receptacle for the contents of consciousness – as a conveyor of information and a means of communication but subordinate to and dependent upon the intuitive relation between the subject and his/her ideal and impressions. Saussure's work argued against this position.

Writing at the turn of the century, Saussure paralleled Durkheim's quest to establish the specifically social territory of sociology through a reconceived linguistics which came to be established as part of a new science of signs or semiology. Through his characterisation of signs as arbitrary the rules of combination of the linguistic system, arbitrarily and socially organised, at last came into view. He proposed that language should be studied not only in terms of its individual parts but also in terms of the relationship between those parts, and synchronically, that is in terms of its current adequacy. This emphasis on the synchronic was momentous because of its recognition of language's current structural properties as well as its historical dimensions.

Saussure criticised those who 'regard language, when reduced to its elements, as a naming process only – a list of words, each corresponding to the thing it names'. Rather, he insisted, that 'the linguistic sign unites, not a thing and a name, but a concept and its sound-image'. The sign comprises two elements: the *signifie* or signified (the concept) and the *significant* or signifier (the sound-image). This is the case with reference to speech: in the case of the written language it would be a concept and a written word; in the case of any other branch of semiology it would be a concept and some other entity. In every semiology the link is between, on the one hand, the subjective and the objective, the ideal and the material, the private and the social. While the concept is a feature of the internal state of mind of the speaker or listener the sound image is a feature of the public world shared in common with others. The process of signification involved in language consists in the movement from sound image to concept and back, the movement backwards and forwards from signifier to signified. Jakobson (1963:162) emphasises how the conception of the sign is the same as its medieval definition as something which stands for something else. Where he breaks new ground is in his insistence that signification depends upon the relation holding between the units making up a language. A word can be exchanged for something dissimilar, an idea, or with something of the same nature, another word. Thus it is not merely that it can be 'exchanged' for a given concept, that is that it has this or that signification, but one must also compare it with the similar, that is with other words that stand in opposition to it. Thus differences carry signification. Saussure states: 'In language there are only differences' (1915:115).

For Saussure, therefore, language consists in two parallel and interdependent series, the signifier and the signified. Each series is constituted by the relations between its elements, sounds and concepts respectively. These relations and the elements themselves are produced by differences. Here we witness the basis of Saussure's distinction between *langue* – the whole set of linguistic habits which allow an individual to understand and to be understood – and *parole*, its usage in speech. Priority is given to *langue* within a synchronic framework – the relations constituting *langue* at any one time rather than a diachronic form involving the evolution of language.

La langue is:

a social product of the faculty of speech and a collection of necessary conventions that have been adopted by a social body to permit individuals to exercise that faculty.

(1915:61)

Since it is a social product it invites investigation as 'an associative and co-ordinating faculty', a world of social facts of which the individual speech-act is only the embryo. *Parole* on the other hand refers to the actual speech-act. This involves the way in which any speaker selects and combines elements of the given linguistic system. Thus 'I' in speaking becomes 'me' in most contexts. The system of pronouns exemplifies language and the utterance 'I' exemplifies speaking.

This system is social and exhibits regularities subject to investigation:

Among all the individuals that are linked together by speech some sort of average will be set up: all will reproduce – not exactly, of course, but approximately – the same signs united with the same concepts . . . . For language is not complete in any speaker, it exists perfectly only within a collectivity.

(1915:64–5)

Thus the distinction between language and speech distinguishes the social fact from the individual choice. Furthermore language is:

The social side of speech, outside the individual who can never create nor modify it by himself, it exists only by virtue of a sort of contract signed by the members of a community.

(1915:66)

Saussure here shares with his contemporary Durkheim, the ideological opposition of society and the individual, an opposition which is mediated and resolved by the fiction of a 'contract'. We also witness signs of a historical structural functionalism in his claim that for every society language is inherited from predecessors: there is no question of any one individual being able to change a single word of the language. Yet signs are unstable, that is, their meanings do change over time as, therefore, does the relationship between signifier and signified. He makes only a weak attempt to account for this change and this is not surprising when we recognise that, in a manner reminiscent of the functional integration of society among his sociological contemporaries, he holds that there is an internal coherence and comprehensibility; an autonomy of the system of signs itself. Language becomes autonomous, a self-contained system, it is self-defining, whole and complete. It is capable of a process of transformation, that is, of generating new aspects of itself in response to new exegermus. It has this capacity because it allows no single, unitary appeal to the 'reality' beyond itself. In the end, it constitutes its own reality.

Reference has already been made to how Saussure's conception of language has dislodged the subject from the position it occupied in philosophy since Descartes. The subject is no longer the source of meaning, the guarantor of the relation between word and object. Thus the subject was decentred from being the secure foundation of thought and the world the subject became a result of certain relationships which were both prior to and exceeded it.

For the historical linguist the work of Saussure indicates that structural analysis, in addition to revealing the regularities of sound change, also leads to a level of grammatical description which transcends geographical, social and individual variability and thereby captures what is common to particular populations of speakers. Saussure and his dialectologist contemporaries were keenly aware of the complexity of relationships between structural grammatical distinctions and human population boundaries. However, the ideology of the nineteenth and twentieth centuries and its emphasis on history and group identity, led to people being seen in terms of discrete national or ethnic units with their own independent traditions and cultures and with a language or dialect characterised by a distinct grammatical structure. These structures were held to reflect the basic underlying characteristics of the group.

Hawkes (1977) partly accounts for the separate and independent growth of the study of language in North America discussed above in terms of the failure to translate Saussure's work into English prior to 1959! The linguacentrism of academics rather than historical philosophic tradition or the impact of ideology is held responsible. There is a faith in the quality of Saussure's work commensurate with his current respect in academic circles.

LANGUAGE AS A REFLECTION OF SOCIETY

It should be evident that Saussurean linguistics introduces a philosophy of language quite distinct from what was considered in the earlier pages of this chapter. From the time of Bacon a philosophy of language emerged which involved the separation of language and thought, with the latter preceding the former. With all human knowledge deriving from sense impressions, the individual subject was the source of its own thought, language becoming the reflection of that thought. Thus language was linked to reason via the rationality of the human subject which was capable of employing language as a means of self-expression. One consequence of such a position that we will encounter in subsequent chapters is that the individual employs language to express an identity.

Extending this argument to a discussion of the relationship between the individual and society, we find a retention of the idea that the social somehow precedes language. Thus language can also be a conveyor of the social. Discourse becomes an intermediary between thought and reality. In some respects this argument is reminiscent of the Marxist theory of knowledge which is, of course, a variety of philosophical materialism. It is based on the metaphysical view that there is a material world which exists independently of our consciousness of it, whereas consciousness, on the other hand, cannot exist independently of matter. Thus the reflection theory of knowledge holds that the material world is knowable by consciousness, because consciousness reflects material reality. The test of truth is practice.

The consequence of this position which separates language from the social is that the relationship between them becomes unproblematic; language merely reflects society. It leads to the tendency to analyse language in terms of the social through empirical correlations in which the social is the independent variable, and language the dependent variable. For most sociolinguists this is sufficient, and there is no awareness of the relationship between correlations and theory.

The Saussurean position refutes this cosy relationship between language and society. The autonomy of the subject is undermined. Since the sense of a word or sentence is no longer its reference to an entity outside language, that language becomes autonomous, a self-contained system. Furthermore, meaning no longer resides in individual words or sentences, but depends upon the relationship constituting language. This means that the subject is no longer the source of meaning, the basis of securing the relationship between word and object. The subject is decentred from being the secure foundation of thought and the world. Language no longer reflects society, but rather, language is society.

CONCLUSION

In this chapter I have tried to do several things. First, I have tried to emphasise that linguistic theory has not emerged separately from the social philosophy of its time. Rather, it must be seen as a manifestation of the ongoing debate on the nature of society and the social world. Second, I have claimed that the assumptions which underlie many of the conceptions of society, as they enter into contemporary sociolinguistics, derive from highly questionable claims for the nature of society made by social philosophers. These assumptions cannot be separated from the concepts as they are now employed. Thus, there is good reason to query much, if not most, of what has become axiomatic in both sociology and sociolinguistics. This, in turn, means that the claim for objectivity in the social sciences must be rejected. Third, and developing from the previous arguments, I suggest that if indeed sociolinguistics rests on such a flimsy epistemological base, then it should give rise to a sustained critique of the field, a critique which has, thus far, been muted. Such a critique is the objective of the following chapters. However, before proceeding to a consideration of the sociolinguistic material, it is necessary to lead the discussion of the sociological tradition considered above towards the sociological perspective which has dominated sociolinguistics in recent years, and which has been most responsible for its present condition.

2 Parsonian structural functionalism

The intellectual tradition of society discussed in chapter 1 was inherited by the American sociologist Talcott Parsons who integrated several strands of thought into what has become known as structural functionalism. This brand of sociology dominated the discipline for many years and in many respects it remains centre stage among sociologists. Alvin Gouldner had the following to say about Parsons' importance and influence:

> Intellectually viable or not and socially 'relevant' or not, it is Parsons who, more than any other contemporary social theorist, has influenced and captured the attention of academic sociologists, and not only in the United States but throughout the world. It is Parsons who has provided the focus of theoretical discussion for three decades now, for those opposing him no less than for his adherents.
>
> (Gouldner 1970:168)

Structural functionalism is the perspective which has been adopted uncritically by most sociolinguists to the extent that sociolinguistics can, to a very great extent, be regarded as the structural functional discussion of language in society. This may be as a consequence of the direct intellectual influence of Parsons and his sociological followers, or it may be, as J. A. Fishman (1990) has recently suggested, merely the consequence of intuition among sociolinguists who were working in the same cultural environment as these sociologists, at the same historical conjuncture. That is, in order for common perspectives to emerge, it is not necessary that a single author or school has to be slavishly followed if we recognise that the sociological discourse in question is, to an extent, the intellectual equivalent of a society's common sense. This chapter will be devoted to an elaboration of structural functionalism. As such I do not intend the discussion to be exhaustive but rather I will focus upon those features of the perspective which are central to the subsequent critical discussion of sociolinguistics.

THE ACTION FRAME OF REFERENCE

Perhaps the most appropriate starting point for a discussion of Parsons' work is the action frame of reference, with action being discussed in the following terms:

> Action consists of the structures and processes by which human beings form meaningful intentions and, more or less successfully, implement them in concrete situations. The word 'meaningful' implies the symbolic or cultural level of representation and reference. Intentions and implementation taken together imply a disposition of the action system – individual or collective – to modify its relation to its situation or environment in an intended direction.
>
> (Parsons 1966:5)

Following Weber, the objective of Parsons' work was to begin from the elements of action, seen as viewing the world through the eyes of the studied, to the most complex forms of organisation. However, he was also very much aware that the actions could only be understood within the context of the system of organisations. This, of course, was the central assumption of his belief that actions, and the motives, thought patterns etc. which organise them, are generated in and organised by the social system.

A central assumption of social action is the Kantian principle of free will which Parsons subsumes within the idea of voluntaristic action. However, the autonomy of the human subject is qualified by the relationship between the normative and the conditional. Within the action frame of reference values play a determining role and the human actor, within social action, is the expression of such values. Weber considered 'action' as 'including all human behaviour when and in so far as the acting individual attaches a subjective meaning to it' (Weber 1964:88). Savage (1981:99) clarifies an important point when he emphasises that while Weber's social action refers to the action of individuals it does not reflect an individualistic system of values. There is also the supra-individual realm of culture, of 'complexes of meanings' to which the individual must comply. Thus some individual forms of action are the effects of this realm which means that subjectivity is not entirely a freely constituting human subjectivity. Parsons similarly underlines the importance of the interrelationships between the actor, goal of action, situations of action and the normative orientation to action.

The situation of action involves the condition of action involving objects outside of the control of the actor, being physical, social and symbolic objects with which the agents of action must come to terms; and the means which are available in the action complexes. Thus limits are set upon the actor's subjectivity. Similarly, the goals of action set limits. While they relate to a future condition desired by the actor, they always exist within forms of systems of action – the situational.

Perhaps the greatest constraint on individual voluntarism in Parsons' framework involves the normative orientation of action. It is here that we recognise his claim that:

> Social systems are those constituted by states and processes of social interaction among acting units. If the properties of inter-action were derivable from properties of the acting units, social systems would be epiphenomenal, as much 'individualistic' social theory has contended. Our position is sharply in disagreement: it derives particularly from Durkheim's statement that society – and other social systems – is a 'reality sui generis'.
>
> (Parsons 1971:7)

The normative orientation of action is articulated to the cultural system in value-patterns or organisations of a cultural or ideal character. Action on an organised basis is facilitated through certain values which constrain and direct an actor's motivation and orientation. The primary element of values involves the religious realm of orientation through which fundamental conceptions of right and wrong, good and evil etc., are constituted. It is through the ultimate reference of values that normative orientation is claimed to structure or organise action. It is the manner in which culture specifies values that determines the action which the actor 'should' take. This claim is elaborated to encompass social action by the claim that certain values contain orientations towards other actors which then become shared. This, in turn, leads to the collectivity as:

> a unity, a unity in the sense that society can be thought of as pursuing a single common end (or system of ends) and not merely discrete individual ends.
>
> (Parsons 1937:247)

For Parsons, action denies individualistic explanations of social relations and relates it, instead, to culture.

Culture, as conceived here, involves values, meanings, ideas, rules etc. – the ideational. It contrasts with the other level, that of 'nature', each level being subject to different forms of determination but with action as the articulation of the two levels:

> Action must always be thought of as involving a state of tension between two different orders of elements, the normative and the conditional. As process, action is, in fact, the process of alteration of the conditional elements in the direction of conformity with norms.
>
> (Parsons 1937:732)

It seems therefore that the normative is of central importance. It is particularly important where objective determination of action is absent, that is, in situations of choice. Savage (1981:96) argues that Parsons' theory of action does not involve the Kantian idea of an indeterminate and freely constituting individual since action constitutes a relation between the ideational and the natural. It is here that Parsons' work is to be distinguished from phenomenology and ethnomethodology since the actor is not a free actor, but is subject to conditioning forces. Thus voluntarism refers to the link between the normative and the conditional with the human actor being the means by which the normative is represented. Voluntaristic action is never really 'voluntary', while subjective action is never a self-constituting subjectivity. Evidently what is central to this distinction is the Durkheimian distinction between the individual and society, a distinction repeated by Weber (1964) in his discussion of the supra-individual nature of culture, complexes of meaning and systems of values. The individual becomes the means by which the supra-individual realm of meanings is represented. Similarly, for Parsons, the individual conceives rather than constructs his situation.

All action occurs in situations involving, on the one hand, physical, social and symbolic objects with which the agent of action must come to terms and, on the other hand, the means available in the action complexes. Given that the ends or goals of action are also an important feature of action it would appear that the subjective element is evident, but Parsons links ends closely with the normative orientation of action and especially its articulation to the cultural system. Thus systems of action are defined in terms of the systemic character of value-patterns, organisations of a cultural or ideal character. Values constrain the actor's orientation while also directing him/her. Thus 'social action' depends upon the existence of certain social values

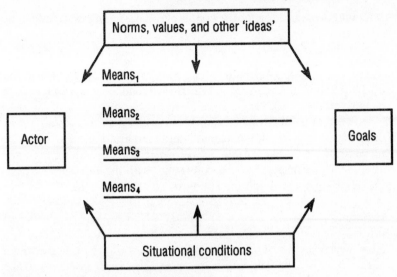

Figure 2.1 Voluntaristic sources of action.
Source: Turner (1986) p. 61, fig. 3.1.

which are the precursors of social order. It is through values that normative orientation may be said to govern or organise action, that is, the culturally determined values indicate the direction which the actor should take. Social action only becomes possible because of the existence of values which manifest orientations to others which become shared. It is from this sharing that the social collectivity emerges:

> the collectivity . . . [is] a unity, a unity in the sense that society can be thought of as pursuing a single common end (or system of ends) and not merely discrete individual ends.
>
> (Parsons 1937:247)

Collectivity derives from value consensus, a value consensus whose central feature is moral obligation.

Parsons went on to emphasise the importance of functionalism in his schema:

> The structure of social systems cannot be derived directly from the actor–situation frame of reference. It requires functional analysis of the complications introduced by the interaction of a plurality of actors. . . . The functional needs of social integration and the conditions necessary for the functioning of a plurality of actors as

a 'unit' system sufficiently well integrated to exist as such impose others.

(Parsons 1949:229)

These assumptions are, obviously, very close to the functionalism of Durkheim, Spencer, Radcliffe-Brown and others discussed in chapter 1.

However, pursuing the ideas of voluntaristic action, Parsons developed Pareto's distinction between logical and non-logical action. The former refers to a relationship between goals and ends where the actor adopts a scientifically valid interpretation, with the end deriving from the actor's proposed action. The latter, on the other hand, involves action which cannot be judged in terms of the logical nature of its reasoning since it is based on criteria which are not reducible to rational or scientific judgement. Such action is guided by 'ultimate ends' which involve man's conception or view of the universe which is the basis of a meaningful relation to the world. A consequence of this seemingly theological conception is that ultimate values are unknowable which, in turn, means that logical action cannot apply. Social action involves action which is orientated towards others as opposed to action geared to individual ends and, as such, it depends upon the integration of ends in systems, an integration that is only possible if there is some higher form of existence of ends – the ultimate ends of action that lie beyond the criteria of science and rational action.

Evidently ultimate values are unknowable, being

a rationalised expression of something else, something vague, less defined. This 'something' of which an end is a logically formulated specification, I call a value-attitude. This conception, it is evident, is arrived at negatively – it is the name for an unknown.

(Parsons 1935:306–7)

This is underlined in Parsons' critical reference to Durkheim's empirical analysis of ethical and religious behaviour:

If the reality underlying religion is an empirical reality, why should religious ideas take the symbolic form in a way which scientific ideas do not? Why could that reality not be represented directly by the theories of sociological science?

(Parsons 1937:429)

This apparent defence of religion against the reason of science is, of course, much more than that. It is an argument that the social component cannot be subject to scientific investigation and explanation in the same way as the object world. Thus the rules of religious ideas are normative whereas those of science are factual. Consequently normative orders must be defined in terms of aspects of norms – ends, rules, etc. Religious ideas may be subjectively comprehended, but they cannot be conceptualised and scientifically analysed.

Here Parsons turned to Weber who claimed that the investigator/analyst as an actor is an integral and necessary part of action. Thus an analysis in terms of meaning must involve a comprehension of meaning of the actor to the actor, the values which govern the action. This inter-subjectivity is, of course, a central feature of ethnomethodology, thereby representing an overlap with the work of Parsons. For Weber it depended upon the overlap between the values of the investigator and those of the object of his/her investigation, that is, an overlap between cultures. This was accepted by Parsons:

> Not only are the non-scientific values of the investigator himself and his culture involved, but also those of the persons and collectivities which are the object of his investigation. At the level of *verstehen*, scientific investigation is basically a process of meaningful communication.
>
> (Parsons 1967:138)

Clearly, values can only be known by means of values, that is, an element of cultural relativism must always be involved despite Parsons' attempt to overcome the problem by drawing upon scientific objectivity. Furthermore, as Savage (1981:114) emphasises, it is not possible to relate the unknowable with the knowable without the involvement of speculation. Thus concrete action cannot be derived from the symbolic that is seen to govern it since there is a permanent discrepancy between the two: 'the discrepancy between norm and actual course of action is one main aspect of the non-logicality of action' (Parsons 1937:213). This problem Parsons accepted and his analyses of values were limited. Thus a discussion of the normative and its role in social action is difficult, to say the least.

It should now be clear that action is the relation between given values and the conditional elements of action. In his later work Parsons extends the link between the normative and the conditional to involve the link between the cultural system and the personality and social systems, the latter two being empirical systems. The level of culture involves the cognitive, expressive and evaluative ideas which are seen as symbols for the empirical systems of action. These ideas

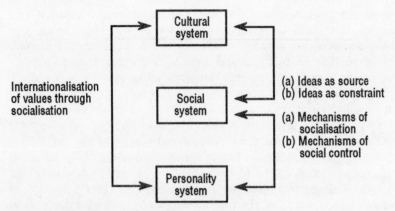

Figure 2.2 Integration among systems of action.
Source: Turner (1986) p. 67, fig. 3.3.

provide the pattern configurations for the action complex. However, the cultural realm is not conceived of as constituted by an aggregate of individuals, nor by individuals themselves, but rather by an atemporal and symbolic organisation of ideas, values and norms in such a way that the empirical system of action is made possible.

On the other hand, these empirical systems of action – the personality and social systems – are seen as motivated action deriving from the relationships of individuals, and of modes of action organised around the living organism. The operationalisation of this link between the ideational and empirical systems involves the institutionalisation of culture in social systems and its internalisation in personality systems. This then guides choice through goal orientation and the normative regulation of means and expressive activities. Thus, in a sense, the personality and social systems reflect culture. However, this is not the same as claiming that motivation is an expression of values or the realisation of culture. Parsons rejects this idealist emanationism, as he calls it, claiming that motivational and value influence on action are distinct even though action is a product of both. Even so, there is no escaping the fact that the cultural–ideational realm is the primary form of deterministic action. The personality system internalises values and the social system institutionalises them in the context of social processes. Much of his argument in this respect relies on an argument which involves: 'realisation of that which is already immanent in the human individual' (Savage 1981:125). Thus his account of socialisation emphasises that it is a process whereby a human subject capable of acting on the basis of value orientations is created. Personality derives from socialisation and the human subject is only really human in the sense of being integrated into the social system and fulfilling the requirements of the personality as a system when capable of responding to values. As Savage (1981:126) shows, Parsons fails to theorise the mechanisms of personality formation and enculturation is merely the realisation of an immanent capacity.

In his discussion of culture and the individual Parsons was particularly concerned about the tendency for psychologists to resort to individual reductionism by ignoring: 'the organisation of action about the exigencies of social systems as systems' (Parsons 1951a:539). He was similarly concerned about the tendency for North American cultural anthropologists to view social systems merely as the embodiment of culture. On the other hand, his critique of Durkheim clearly indicates his dissatisfaction with those who saw culture as a simple reflection of the social world and the tendency to sociologise personality. Rather, he sought to emphasise that while action can be reduced to the elements – actor, end, situation and norm – it was essential to recognise that action is organised in the sense that it exists in the form of systems (fig. 2.1). The three most important of such systems are the personality, social and cultural systems which involve organisation in terms of need dispositions, role expectations and value orientations respectively (fig. 2.2). These systems are all involved in most individual action and are therefore integrated. Let us consider the social system and in particular its relationship to social roles.

The social system involves, above all else, the relationship of actors to one another – interaction, the fundamental basis of which is the social role. While roles involve individual personalities the concept of differentiation distinguishes social action from individual action in the sense that the action elements are differentiated. Thus the social system is differentiated from the other systems of action. While the cultural system may be functionally significant to the social system in the sense that the cultural system involves symbols which provide guides for action, it is not equivalent to it. Similarly, within the social system the role may be the basic unit but collectivities or collective actors involve more than merely role relationships. Thus the social system must involve consistent relationships with the other two systems of action.

It should already be evident that an important function of the personality system is that, through socialisation, it produces socialised individuals and is thereby of fundamental importance to the social system. Similarly, action is not possible without motivation *vis-à-vis* the conditions and norms of action. Thus, for example, the individuals' need-dispositions must be consistent with social features of roles and role expectations. However, the personality system and social system link is consolidated by the third system – the cultural. This much is evident in Parsons' use of the role concept.

Role appears as an interactional concept involving two or more actors, with what these actors do in their social roles being related to the functional significance for the system. Roles involve role expectations, patterns of evaluation which organise reciprocity, expectations and responses to these relations, all of which involve patterns of meaning which make interaction possible – they involve elements of culture.

What we have here is a reference to the problem of social order. One aspect of Parsons' work on culture relates to the Hobbesian problem of how social order is sustained, a problem we referred to in the preceding chapter. Organised value orientations ensure that action is orientated to the action of others, thereby ensuring consensus in terms of social interaction. It is shared values, related to social norms learnt through socialisation, which constitute the basis of social order. However, Parsons goes further in claiming that the fulfilment of social roles is essential for the survival of the social system since they are indispensable to its functioning. Additionally, the cultural system, through the normative system, is the means whereby the functional problems are realised. It is here, within the process of normativisation, that the social and cultural systems are in contact.

The link between value orientation and function is evident in several aspects of Parsons' argument. Thus in relation to institutions it is held that institutions reflect value standards in complexes of status–role relationships with the effect of integrating role relationships under a standard value pattern. Functional subsystems are conceived of somewhat differently in that they involve a number of institutions held together by their functional primacy *vis-à-vis* the social system as a system of action.

In order for social systems to operate it is necessary to resolve problems associated with environmental adaptation in order to meet basic physical requirements, the achievement of collective goals associated with a common agreement among societal members, the generation of a universal motivation and tension management, and the integration of the parts of the social system. This, in turn, depends upon the existence of four major structural features – the major subsystems of the Parsonian schema. These four are, respectively, the economy, the polity, kinship, and community and cultural organisations. The form of these structural subsystems depends upon the value system of the particular society under scrutiny.

Pattern variables or patterns of cultural value orientation are important for the relationship between institutions and functional subsystems. It is the pattern variables which determine the nature and extent of choices confronted by the actor and this is, therefore, one of the constraints on the free action of the individuals. This choice is further limited by the need for such choice to coincide with that which is objectively required by the social system. It is evident that the cultural specifications of the pattern variables must meet the social requirements of the action system, thus giving the link between society and culture. This is not to imply that the social system is to be reduced to sets of cultural values since the social system is organisational. Neither is culture a natural product of social relations. The social and cultural systems are distinct with reference to determination and constitution, despite the fact that there is some form of determinate relationship between them in that it is the cultural system that is decisive as a condition of existence of social relations and social development.

EVOLUTIONISM

We have already seen in chapter 1 that when social change is associated with a sense of inevitable progress there emerges an evolutionary discourse. Furthermore most functionalist theories are evolutionary. Parsons is no exception and he conceives of social evolution as change in a definite direction leading to a higher level of sociocultural existence: 'Our perspective clearly involves evolutionary judgments – for example, that intermediate societies are more advanced than primitive societies' (Parsons 1966:110). In adopting such a stance, at a time when cultural anthropology in the USA was deeply involved in the evolutionary debate, Parsons renounced ideas of cultural relativism – a view which discusses cultures in their own terms rather than as a feature of universal social development – since it, 'regards the Arunta of Australia and such modern societies as the Soviet Union as equally authentic "cultures" to be judged as equals in all basic respects' (Parsons 1966:110). Evidently the two perspectives are incompatible, the adoption of one implying the rejection of the other.

Clearly any perspective which assumes the inevitability of progress must refer to the driving mechanism of that progress. For Parsons this is what he refers to as an enhanced adaptive capacity which can either derive from within the society by forming new structures, or, as a consequence of cultural diffusion, from without. It involves four categories – differentiation, adaptive up-grading, inclusion and value generalisation. Differentiation is the division of a unit or structure into two or more units or structures and relates to progress when each new unit has a greater adaptive capacity than the preceding unit. Adaptive up-grading involves an increase in the range of resources available to a social system. Thus an increase in social resources will lead to an increase in adaptive capacity. Taken together, differentiation and adaptive up-grading constitute another functional problem since the action elements then produced must be integrated. Inclusion involves the integration of the complex elements and structures within the normative system. However, social systems are not always able to cope with the changes which accompany differentiation and adaptive up-grading and it is those normative systems which are best equipped which will improve the capacity for advance. Finally, value generalisation refers to the ability of a system to alter its value system. This process, as a consequence of the other processes, must involve the value patterns having a greater level of generality so that the wider range of goals and functions of its units can be legitimised.

However, these four processes do not occur randomly but, rather, they are incorporated within a conception of a determinate order. Within Parsons' cybernetic hierarchy, systems high in information but low in energy 'control' systems which are low in information but high in energy. This means that 'ultimate reality' – the major environment to the action complex – is the main element of control with the systems of action being secondary to it:

> The cultural system structures commitments *vis-à-vis* ultimate reality into meaningful orientations towards the rest of the environment and the system of action, the physical world, organisations, personalities, and social systems.
>
> (Parsons 1966:9–10)

The cybernetic hierarchy determines the system of action. The system of action – the differentiation between personality, social and cultural systems – is part of the evolutionary process. Time is invoked to highlight the increasing differentiation between the four major systems of action. Thus a primitive society is defined as one where there is a low level of differentiation between the social and cultural systems, and between the biological organism and the personality system. From this Parsons presents a series of evolutionary 'stages':

primitive, intermediate and modern. The distinguishing feature of these 'stages' is the extent to which the cultural and social systems are differentiated. Thus in primitive societies there is little differentiation between the two systems, primarily because there is an undeveloped language system. In order to move to the intermediate stage there has to be a development of an elaborate, formal, system of codes. The appearance of a written language is crucial in this respect since, together with the symbolic content of a culture, it can be embodied in forms separate from particular action contexts. These, in turn, act to stabilise and standardise social relations, thus permitting the separate development of the social and cultural systems. Similarly, the distinction between intermediate and modern societies rests upon the formation of a legal system which facilitates the independence of norms from particular political and economic interests in the same way as writing promotes the independence of the cultural system from the condition exigencies of society. Law formalises the normative system.

Evidently time is invoked to demonstrate that non-human factors are suppressed by human ones, that is, cultural factors. Human action involves the intervention of values in behaviour. Indeed values become a measure of humanity and history is the process of the development of humanity. The human capacity to create and transmit culture means that adaptation in social evolution involves a more generalised capacity to cope with the environment. Here religion plays a central role, being seen as the primary evolutionary universal. However, for it to operate effectively it must be implemented in action systems and must therefore involve communication via the secondary primary evolutionary universal – language. The other two primary evolutionary universals are kinship, which is responsible for reproducing the species, and technology, which facilitates the control and manipulation of the physical environment.

The existence of these four universals – religion, language, kinship and technology – is characteristic of all human societies, but additional universals are necessary in order for the social system to develop beyond the primitive 'type'. Thus social stratification and systems of cultural legitimation permit the emergence from primitiveness, and the addition of bureaucracy and money markets permit further 'progress', while the appearance of generalised norms and the 'democratic association' are held to be essential features of 'modernism'. Perhaps the most interesting of these universals is 'democratic association' since it highlights Parsons' ethnocentrism and political bias.

Parsons claims that the more complex and expanded the society the greater the necessity for political organisation, an elaboration of the eighteenth-century claim for the importance of the state as the basis of social order. Political organisation is important, Parsons argues, partly in order to accommodate the expanding 'consensus'; furthermore, only a democratic association is capable of mediating consensus. Conversely, communism cannot achieve this level of consensus otherwise communist states would not oppress the citizenry through 'education'. Communism can only legitimise itself and cannot mediate consensus. As a consequence communist societies are limited in their evolutionary potential.

POWER

Power was weakly conceptualised in the structural functionalist perspective and it is not until Parsons' late work that it is clearly outlined. In his later work he modified his earlier views which he referred to as the 'traditional' view of power. In his criticism of the work of C. Wright Mills, Parsons refers to a 'misleading and one-sided' view of the nature of power in which power is seen as held by a single person or group to the degree that it is not possessed by the person or group over whom it is wielded (Parsons 1960:220). That is, power is defined in terms of mutually exclusive objects, with power being used to attain objectives at the expense of others. Power serves sectional interests. Consistent with his liberal view of society this was unacceptable to Parsons.

As with the concept of creative conflict Parsons argued for an alternative conception of power in which a relationship exists from which both sides can gain. In so doing, in contrast to the zero–sum perspective which began with the question of the distribution of power, Parsons emphasised that the production of power is also important. Indeed, the question of the distribution of power in theoretical terms is secondary to the manner in which power is produced and reproduced. Thus power is generated by a social system much as wealth is generated in the productive organisation of an economy. As with money, power has a function in the polity or goal-attainment system seen as the mobilisation of effective collective action in the attainment of the goals of the collectivity. While money is seen as a symbolic form of differentiating value, power is seen as the

> generalised capacity to serve the performance of building obligations by units in a system of collective organisation when the obligations are legitimised with reference to their bearing on

collective goals and where in the case of recalcitrance there is a presumption of enforcement by negative situational sanctions.

(Parsons 1969:361)

Being defined in terms of the polity power is no longer some arbitrary relation between individuals but, rather, is a mechanism of significance for the system. Furthermore it involves legitimation. All power involves a certain mandate which not only confirms rights on power holders but also obligations towards those over whom power is held. Thus power cannot exist or function without its social conditions of existence. The collective goals rest on the common value system which sets out the major objectives which govern the actions of the majority in a society. It must also be grounded in the relational system involving the normative guidelines provided by the institutionalisation of power.

Power facilitates the achievement of collective goals through the 'agreement' of the members of a society to legitimate leadership positions and confirm leaders with the mandate to seek to achieve the goals of the system. Everybody gains from this process but it implies trust on the part of the majority. Power also derives from authority, with authority being seen as the institutionalised legitimation which underlies power. A consequence of the associated binding obligations is that there is no such thing as 'illegitimate power'. Power is the activation of the 'binding obligations'.

Within his perspective Parsons saw two channels through which one party may seek to command the actions of another, and two models of control, giving a four-fold typology. Ego controls the situation in which alter is placed or will try to control his/her intentions; the models depend upon whether sanctions are positive (rewards) or negative (punishment).

EQUILIBRIUM AND SOCIAL INTEGRATION

We have already seen how order is maintained by the normative system but this issue reappears in Parsons' discussion of equilibrium. This is yet another idea which has a long history, being evident in the work of Comte, Spencer and Durkheim. For Parsons a society in a condition of equilibrium is one in which conflict is absent, since everyone knows what is expected of him/her in any role context, and where such expectations are the basis of action. Evidently this is another ideal type. Yet Parsons regards it as the objective which every society seeks to attain. As such it involves maintaining viable interrelationships between system units and in this sense it reflects the biological analogy of Comte who saw society as an organism which must continuously retain equilibrium.

It is in the discussion of integration within and between action systems that Parsons draws together the problems of adaptation, goal attainment, socialisation and social control or latency. The associated structures are viewed in terms of their functional consequences for each of the four requisites and the interrelationships among structures are discussed in terms of how their interchanges alter the requisites that any single structure must meet.

We have already seen how, in a simple way, equilibrium can be attained by subjects being socialised into specific roles involving the associated expectations which are sanctioned by positive and negative aspects of role performance. Thus within a perfectly integrated system Parsons claims that motivation is harnessed to fulfilling role expectations. However, Parsons' theoretical model is far more complicated. Each of the four action systems – culture, social structure, personality and organism is confronted by functional problems involving adaptation, goal attainment, integration and latency. Together the four action systems constitute an overall action system. Within this system the organism is central to resolving adaptive problems, while the personality, in its involvement with goal-seeking and decision-making, is most involved in goal-attainment problems. Similarly the social system is viewed as an organised network of status norms integrating the cultural system and the needs of personality systems are crucial for the general action system. Finally, the cultural system, being the repository of symbolic contents of interaction, is crucial for the maintenance of institutional patterns (latency). In addressing the issue of the interrelationships among the four subsystems he concludes that culture circumscribes the social system, social structure regulates the personality system, while personality, in turn, regulates the organismic system. Furthermore, each system provides what he calls the 'energy conditions' necessary for action in the respective systems, with the organism providing the energy necessary for the personality system which, in turn, provides the energy conditions for the social system. Finally the organisation of personality systems into a social system provides the conditions necessary for a cultural system. Thus there is a two-way reciprocal flow of input and output with systems exchanging information and energy. This is Parsons' cybernetic hierarchy of control.

Built into this cybernetic hierarchy of control is a schema for the discussion of social change. It is not correct, as some have

INSTRUMENTAL FUNCTIONAL IMPERATIVES   EXPRESSIVE FUNCTIONAL IMPERATIVES

INSTITUTIONAL ORDERS

ADAPTATION	GOAL ATTAINMENT	PATTERN MAINTENANCE/ TENSION MANAGEMENT	INTEGRATION
ECONOMY	POLITY	KINSHIP	CULTURAL AND COMMUNITY ORGANISATIONS
(major sub-system) made up of	(major sub-system) made up of	(major sub-system) made up of	(major sub-system) made up of
INSTITUTIONS (e.g. factory system, banking system)	INSTITUTIONS (e.g. political parties, state bureaucracies)	INSTITUTIONS (e.g. nuclear family, marriage)	INSTITUTIONS (e.g. schools, churches, media organisations)
Each institution is made up of	Each institution is made up of	Each institution is made up of	Each institution is made up of
SETS OF ROLES Specific *norms* giving concrete behavioural prescriptions define roles. These concrete norms are underpinned by:	SETS OF ROLES Specific *norms* . . . . underpinned by:	SETS OF ROLES Specific *norms* . . . . underpinned by:	SETS OF ROLES Specific *norms* . . . . underpinned by:

FUNDAMENTAL VALUES

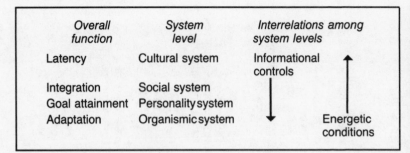

Figure 2.4 Parson's cybernetic hierarchy of control.
Source: Turner (1986) p. 73, fig. 3.7.

asserted, to state that Parsons' work tends to ignore strain while also ruling out inherent sources of conflict and deviance. As we shall see, Parsons' discussion of the relationships between the systems contradicts this claim:

> No one system of value-orientation with perfect consistency in its pattern can be fully institutionalised in a concrete society. There will be uneven distributions among the different parts of the society. There will be value conflicts and role conflicts. The consequence of such imperfect integration is, in the nature of the case, a certain instability, and hence a susceptibility to change.
>
> (Parsons 1951b:231)

The claims for the lack of relevance of Parsons' theory for social change derives mainly from what are termed conflict theorists who might be better advised to focus more on the consensus nature of the discussion of change and conflict rather than implying their absence.

The information–energy exchanges among the action systems constitute the potential for change within or between the respective action systems. Thus an excess in either information or energy in the exchange can constitute one source of change. For example, an excess of motivation will affect the enactment of roles, and even the reorganisation of roles, of the normative structure and even of cultural value orientations. On the other hand, a deficiency of energy or information supply can lead to internal or external readjustments in the structure of action systems. Such readjustments or adaptations are a consequence of strains or tensions in the system which interfere with the tendency towards stability and integration, and social change is, in effect, the tendency of the system to reassert equilibrium.

Parsons maintained that his theoretical schema was undeveloped and incomplete in that it lacked 'a complete knowledge of the laws which determine processes within the system' (Parsons 1951b:483). In order to overcome this deficiency he stressed two points. First, the structural categories of action, associated with the logical require-ments of the action frame of reference, allow him to identify patterns which can be designated as relatively stable and constant. Structural analysis involves classifying these patterns into categories. Second, the functional dimension involves formulating the relation between this and the environmental conditions articulated with it. It is this that points to the mechanisms of the functioning of the system, both internally and externally, and which explains the orderly response to environmental conditions. Thus he indicates what is required in order for systems of action to remain in equilibrium and, as such, they complement the dynamic of the structural categories.

Regarding structural functional theory as incomplete Parsons stated that 'a general theory of the processes of change in social systems is not possible in the present state of knowledge' (Parsons 1951a:486). Since a complete knowledge of the laws of social systems is not avail-able it is necessary to restrict discussion to a theory of subprocesses of change within social systems as opposed to a change of systems. The resultant emphasis upon structure and function leads to many of the problems associated with the Parsonian discussion of social change.

One area which Parsons claimed was inadequately theorised and which thereby was treated as a given, was culture. As we have seen, he argued that the integration of need dispositions of actors with a set of cultural patterns through institutionalisation was essential for social equilibrium. However, if there is some disturbance at the system level a lag may result before the other systems return to a position of equilibrium. For example, a disturbance at the level of role expectations will result in disequilibrium involving need dispositions. The integration of need dispositions generates a resistance to change at the social level. Consequently, if social change is to occur it must not only alter role expectations but also it must do this by overcoming the resistance to change.

The position of culture in his framework is ambiguous. He does not claim that culture is the most important factor of change, but does state that the associated value patterns are the main organisational factors in determining the impact of the factors of change. He argues that stable systems can absorb internal strains and that the value system is an important feature of this neutralisation of strain. It seems that culture determines the direction of social change and, to this extent, his theory of social change is inherently culturist. This directionality relates to the Weberian concept of rationalisation:

> there seems to be no doubt that there is an inherent factor of the directionality of change in social systems, a directionality which was classically formulated by Max Weber in what he called the 'process of rationalisation'.
>
> (Parsons 1951b:499)

Yet it is important to recognise that Parsons also emphasised that there is no primary source of change but rather referred to the order of importance or a hierarchy of the variables. However, culture was capable of 'transmission without loss', that is, culture in terms of knowledge, moral standards and expressive symbols, persists beyond its particular relationship to the social and personality systems. For this reason it is capable of controlling the direction of change.

SOCIAL STRATIFICATION

The functionalist theory of social stratification again points firmly in the direction of the Durkheimian tradition. Social stratification is seen as 'normal' in the sense that it is a common feature of all societies. Consequently it must serve a positive function *vis-à-vis* society:

> social stratification is a generalised aspect of the structure of all social systems . . . it is a condition of the stability of social systems that there should be an integration of the value-standards of the component units to constitute a 'common value-system' . . . stratification in its valuational aspect . . . is the ranking of units in a social system in accordance with the standards of the common value system.
>
> (Parsons 1953:93)

Equally important is the Durkheimian concept of the division of labour, a concept which obliges us to consider Parsons' ideas about the economy.

In his criticism of economists Parsons focused upon the reification of the economy and the tendency to relegate sociology to a residual role involving the explanation of what was held to be non-rational or non-optimising behaviour. Again he draws upon Weber, viewing economy not as a mode of organisation or structure, but in terms of an orientation, thereby distinguishing the economic from the non-economic in terms of types of action. Furthermore, the determination of the society–economy relation lies in the realm of values and their effectivity. He departed from Weber in his contention that economic rationality should not be seen as individual orientation but as an integrated system of action.

Returning to Parsons' subsystem schema (fig. 2.3), the economy is seen as the subsystem primarily concerned with the problem of adaptation, its goal being to produce facilities for society. Thus the economy produces wealth whereas the polity produces political power, integration produces solidarity and the maintenance of the value system produces prestige. This last point involving the existence of a common value system leads to stratification being seen as: 'stratification in its valuational aspect . . . is the ranking of units in a social system in accordance with the standards of the common value system' (Parsons 1953:93). The link between economy and society becomes clearer when, in discussing American society, he states that society gives prominence in its value emphases to the contribution that units make 'to the production of valued facilities . . . whatever these may be. . . . This puts the primary emphasis on productive activity in the economy' (112). Despite the absence of a single goal to which the system is committed, the primary system goal involves: 'the maximisation of the production of valued possessions and cultural accomplishments' (112). However, American society places great stress upon 'equality of opportunity', but side by side with this is the claim that talents are differentially distributed and therefore inequality is inevitable. Indeed, this is also seen as a good thing in the sense that it is one basis of motivation that the individual should seek social mobility and self-improvement. Structural arrangements are necessary in order to motivate individuals to play the required roles. Associated is the concept of social status which, Parsons argues, 'is a function of the individual's productive "contribution" to the functions of the organisations concerned' (116). That is, status depends upon capacities and achievements on behalf of the organisation.

Status was, however, important in Parsons' schema: 'Our system of stratification revolves mainly about the integration between kinship and the occupational system' (120), with family income and status deriving from occupational earning and position. The strength of the American system lay in its openness, there being, for Parsons, no fixed, unambiguous class system, no hereditary upper class, no clear-cut hierarchy of prestige, considerable opportunity for social mobility and a toleration of diverse avenues to success. Furthermore, automation was rapidly eroding the lower class while the large increase in productivity was opportunity-producing on a large scale. Evidently productivity was related to values in the sense that the most important value involved the extent of contribution to productivity. Given the opportunity for social mobility, some means by which this could be made accessible to all had to be found. This involved education as opposed to access to possessions, hence the stress upon equal educational opportunity.

Failure to achieve mobility is of course inevitable, but Parsons explains this through emphasising the importance of motivation. Society has to motivate members to fill certain positions in society and to motivate them to perform the duties attached to these positions. If all the tasks were equally easy to fill and perform, and were all equally important to the survival of society, and if everyone was equal in their abilities and talents in relation to the required tasks there would be no problem. However, as stated, talents are differentially distributed which means that a society must have some form of inducements or rewards available in order to encourage those with the most suitable abilities to fill the most important positions. These involve rewards both in material and prestige terms. Any discrepancy between the reality of the situation and the morality which the argument is based upon is dismissed, either by blaming the victim or by arguing that discrepancies will, in time, disappear through the inexorable working of universalistic values and the stress upon equality of opportunity.

CRITICISMS

It is not the intention of this chapter to produce a critique of Parsons' ideas, but rather to present those ideas in order that their importance in sociolinguistics and the sociology of language will be evident. The main criticisms will appear when the various enterprises of the two subdisciplines are discussed. None the less it is important to discuss some of the criticisms that have been made of Parsons' ideas. By now these criticisms are numerous, despite the fact that attempts have been made to defend the Parsonian tradition. However, it seems evident that they have been either disregarded or ignored by sociolinguists and those involved in the sociology of language.

The first criticism that requires attention involves the extent to which Parsons' schema corresponds to reality. This argument involves two separate implications; first, that his perspective is little more than a portrayal of American society informed by the dominant American value system and that, as such, it cannot stand replication elsewhere in the world. The second aspect of the criticism is more profound.

It derives from, as much as anyone, Ralph Dahrendorf (1958), who compared functionalism with utopia. He claimed that Parsonian concepts portrayed a world devoid of developmental history, that experiences only consensus over values and norms, displays a high degree of integration among its components and displays only mechanisms which reproduce the status quo. The utopianism derives from the lack of possibility of deviance, conflict and change.

Some have replied to Dahrendorf by saying that he has over-responded and that his criticism does not stand up to careful scrutiny. Yet there is no doubt that the problematic is a continuation of that developed by Comte and Durkheim among others and that it is essentially consensual in nature. It is an argument which always portrays a system striving towards equilibrium and integration. In this respect it conforms with the emphasis in the work of Durkheim and Radcliffe-Brown with reference to a search for social processes which serve the goal of social order through integration and equilibrium. Thus there is an overemphasis upon the role of socialisation and social control in the process of institutionalisation. Deviance and change are reduced to residual processes or to a kind of Durkheimian pathology. Indeed, it is argued that change can only be discussed in terms of stages rather than process since it is a phenomenon which always strives to retain or regain equilibrium. This equilibrium being the end product, the kind of change that can be discussed is evolutionary change, and change is akin to the search for progress in the work of Durkheim and Spencer.

The accusation that functional analysis is inevitably teleological and tautological has been applied not merely to Parsons' work but also to that of Durkheim, Radcliffe-Brown, Malinowski and Marx. Perhaps its main influence involves the inappropriateness of theories which are teleological and tautological for generating testable propositions *vis-à-vis* the real world and, subsequently, for building sociological theory.

Savage (1981:222–6) argues that the teleological problem is most evident in Parsons' work when he discusses evolution. He states that Parsons' attempt to demonstrate a general trend in evolution involves the means of conceptualising the mechanisms and processes which constitute evolution. Thus evolution becomes the process of realisation of a pre-given objective. One of the associated problems is the difficulty of knowing that the implied capacity for adaptation cannot be known to exist. Parsons resolves this by beginning from an already realised level of development and working backwards. The past is explained in terms of the present; not merely any present, but a present couched in terms of the features of evolution. Furthermore, the mechanisms of the past are seen in terms of the future in terms of effectivity, that is, they have a purpose.

For Parsons, action always involved goal attainment, this being a basic system requisite. Teleological propositions become inevitable since social action can only be conceived in terms of the ends sought. Turner (1986:81) argues that this is not true of goal striving since Parsons does show the progress of events that are involved in this progress. On the other hand, he suggests that this is not true of the other three requisites of adaptation, integration and latency. However, Nagel (1953:537–58) has argued that if such work is phrased in terms of 'under conditions $C(1-n)$ concept x causes concept y' it is acceptable in that it involves explanation of the covariation of x and y. Others have argued against this stance on the ground that statements are often not capable of being transposed in this way because the essential existence statements are absent. This issue is summarised in Nadel's statement to the effect that:

> To pronounce at once upon the ultimate functions subserved by social fact is to short-circuit explanation and to reduce it to generalities which, so prematurely stated, have little significance.
> (Nadel 1951:375)

Another defence of the teleology in Parsons' work involves the claim that teleological propositions can involve reverse causal chains. This is expressed as follows by Turner (1986:83):

> By emphasising that the function served by a structure in maintaining the needs of the whole could cause the emergence of that structure, Parsons' functional imperativism forces analysis to be attuned to those causal processes involved in the initial selection.

He denies the teleological argument by stating that it is possible for the systemic whole to exist prior in time to the structures that emerge while adding that no essential purpose for the systemic whole is suggested.

Finally, there is the issue of tautology. Parsons implies that if the four requisite systems of adaptation, goal attainment, integration and latency are not met then the whole system is under threat. Without specification about the relationship between the system requisites and survival requirements the argument becomes tautologous, that is, it is an argument in which the items meet the survival needs of the system simply because it exists and therefore must be surviving.

CONCLUSION

The consensual and politically conservative nature of Parsonian structural functionalism should now be evident. Perhaps it is most clearly expressed in his discussion of social stratification and power. Not only is inequality regarded as inevitable as a consequence of the uneven distribution of ability, but it is also advantageous in that it serves as an incentive for the industrious. The only compensation for the poor is that society at large holds a responsibility to support the needy. Not surprisingly, power is similarly claimed to be of benefit to society in that it is tied to serving the needs of society. A critical sociology which addresses the political implications of power and inequality is irrelevant.

Having established the background to the kind of consensus functionalism which dominates most of sociolinguistics and the sociology of language, it remains, in the subsequent chapters, to outline specific critiques associated with this particular perspective.

3 Speech variation

INTRODUCTION

Much of what passes as sociolinguistics seeks to show a systematic relationship between language use and social structure. Unfortunately there is a tendency to treat social structure merely as background information and, as Breitborde (1983) has suggested, the main concern seems to be to investigate the personal calculations of individuals in language-use decisions. None the less some of the work undertaken by sociolinguists, despite the deficiencies in matters of sociological theory, have become accepted as axiomatic working assumptions. The objective of this chapter is to consider some of this work, to show how it relies heavily upon structural functionalism, and to suggest some of the limitations that derive from adopting such a perspective.

Given the reflection view of language, in which language is claimed to be a manifestation of society such that social variation is mirrored in language, it is not surprising that the main focus of sociolinguistics is on the manner in which linguistic change, as exemplified in speech patterns, relates to social change. In most of the work this involves treating the speaker as a rational actor employing speech in order to convey an identity. Speech is seen as the product of social convention or norms and the objective of much of the research in this field is descriptive in the sense that its aim is to discover the relevant speech norms. It should already be evident from the preceding chapters that the assumptions in this mix of linguistics, sociology and psychology are highly questionable and it should not be taken for granted that behaviour is conscious, let alone rational; that the objective of this rationality is the expression of identity to relevant others; that norms exist as some simple expression of society; nor that language is a reflection of society. Such assumptions are the feature of a particular discourse on society, one that draws upon and claims to contribute to some objective truth or reality. It is not surprising therefore that this epistemology adopts many of the approaches of science, albeit in the guise of a social science.

The scientific nature of this discourse is evident in what is referred to as variable rules. This approach involves the claim that speech is subject to constant variation without which inter-personal communication would not be possible. It is further claimed that this variation is only subconsciously perceived by the listener and that speakers are unable to make any direct pronouncements about these rules. The function of the variation is to provide information to the listener about the speaker.

The nature of the 'rules' relates to the scientific and empirical nature of the work which seeks to establish rules which can be applied to the relationship between linguistic and non-linguistic factors. While the analogy with scientific rules is retained it is recognised that social science differs from pure science in the sense that the best that can be achieved is a series of generalisations. The sociolinguist who has contributed most to the development of variable rules is William Labov who states his objective in the following terms: 'to connect theoretical questions with a large body of intersubjective evidence which can provide decisive answers' (1969:757). His work is a response to the tendency for generative grammarians to focus exclusively upon the individual, making no reference to social groups and the relationship of such groups to social norms (Dittmar 1976:135). On the other hand, the work of Labov and his followers does pay allegiance to the generative transformational grammar of Chomsky. In this respect the source of origin of the work in linguistics is explicit whereas we find little reference to the theoretical input from sociology. The most evident link is that whereas most linguists seek to establish categorical rules those who seek to establish variable rules, as we have seen, do so in line with the sociological tendency to establish regularities in terms of generalisations. An awareness of this difference between the 'scientific' endeavours of linguistics and sociology is essential for an understanding of variable rules. The objective is to identify general trends from surveys of language use which, it is claimed, demonstrate 'trends or norms in populations' (Wardaugh 1986:181). Evidently it is, first and foremost, a statistical exercise and the claim for theoretical relevance is a matter for subsequent interpretation of the statistical regularities.

Clearly the objective of Labov's early formulation was to specify various effects of linguistic and social variables in determining the frequency, for the population being studied, of some linguistic variants as opposed to other variants. Since the emphasis is upon frequencies it is possible, not merely to demonstrate that two forms are in alternation, but also to specify which form is used by whom, with which degree of frequency, in which situation. However, some (Kay 1978) claim that this approach fails to allow for interaction between the social and linguistic constraints operating within a rule, despite the claim that such interaction is inevitable as a feature of linguistic change. This criticism leads to advocating implicational scales as an alternative to the study of the correlations between social and linguistic factors (Gal 1979:19).

The emphasis upon empirical correlationism raises other methodological issues. The most common form of correlation is that the form '*a*' or the variety '*a*' tends to appear in, or to correlate with, situation '*x*'. What is overlooked time after time is that correlation simply shows an empirical relationship between variables; it does not explain that relationship. The failure to recognise the fundamental difference between causation and association is all too evident in work on speech variation where the absence of a concept of levels of analysis means that causal effectivity is absent. We can legitimately speak of causation only when discussing phenomena of the same order. The mismatch of levels between the process of linguistic data gathering which focuses upon the individual and the social emphasis on groups is particularly important in this respect (Dittmar 1976:137). There is also the problem of conceptualising 'language' and 'society' separately rather than seeing language as an integral part of social process – there is much more to such an integration than merely correlating data from two areas of study. A distinction must be made between causality and relationships of probability, and even where causality is demonstrated the resulting explanation lies in epistemology. It is, perhaps, the lack of awareness of the epistemological which is the fundamental weakness of most studies of speech variation.

It is interesting that the criticisms of variable rules have tended to focus upon such issues as the implication of the statistical information for mental processes and for language acquisition rather than questioning the assumption that the statistical correlations are indeed manifestations of cognitive processes and practices. Such criticisms involve methodological and empirical issues and bear little relevance to theoretical issues which often tend to be taken for granted. In the remainder of this chapter the theoretical aspects of speech variation will be in focus and it is appropriate to begin with a consideration of the concept of speech community which is the frame within which all such studies are located.

SPEECH COMMUNITY

While recognising that the meaning of a concept relates to its theoretical problematic (Althusser 1971) it would seem to be unnecessarily complicated to allocate the same concept to different phenomena within the same discipline. The concept of community is a case in point. It is a concept which has a long history in sociology and yet, in many respects, it appears to have developed within sociolinguistics with a somewhat different meaning. For this reason alone it is useful to consider the manner in which the concept is employed among sociolinguistics before considering the implications of such a use.

This is not to claim that there is not an overlap between the concepts of community as employed in sociology and sociolinguistics respectively. Indeed, both appear to retain an interactional and a spatial ingredient. That is, there is a sense in which an enclosed area is occupied by interacting individuals and these features somehow contribute to the essence of community. What is distinctive is the manner in which sociolinguistics creates the boundary of the enclosed space on the basis of linguistic, rather than social features. This is not surprising given the claim that language reflects society. Thus Gumperz (1972b:219) refers to speech community as 'any human aggregate characterised by regular and frequent interaction by means of a shared body of verbal signs and set off from similar aggregates by significant differences of language usage'. Speech communities are classified according to their linguistic similarities and differences. However, Labov (1966:7) suggests that this 'community' has some further quality being an aggregate of speakers:

> That New York City is a speech community, and not a collection of speakers living side by side, borrowing from each other's dialects, may be demonstrated by many kinds of evidence. Native New Yorkers differ in their usage in terms of absolute values of the variables, but the shifts between contrasting styles follow the same pattern in almost every case.

The qualifier 'absolute' contrasts with 'relative' to make it clear that, what Gumperz refers to as norms and rules, Labov interprets as subjective values. Again we are brought back to the twin issues of norms and values, the cornerstone of structural functionalism. Furthermore, the shared values constitute a norm which allocates to the group its essence, an essence reminiscent of culture either as rule-bound behaviour, or as the values governing behaviour. Thus each community is different because of the manner in which its membership evaluates stylistic variation. Culture is added to interaction and space as the diacritica of community.

Despite the negative reference to a collection of individuals the group is not defined as a social group unless, of course, we take a very large step and assume that the normative consensus is akin to Durkheim's 'conscience collective'. Rather the group is defined in terms of shared linguistic features. Thus two features of the speech community are highlighted – the shared linguistic features and the subjective values of the speakers. As Romaine states in referring to Labov's Martha's Vineyard study they are drawn together in the claim that speech is an entirely conscious act involving the tendency to assert 'local solidarity in a strong way through positive identification with life on the island' (Romaine 1982:13). Thus, solidarity, an essential feature of community, is conveyed through language and represents a subjective identification with the life style characteristic of the community. Community itself becomes a subjective entity. The objective element at first appears to be language – the methodological starting point of establishing the boundaries of the community – and yet language is held to be a subjective quality. This is repeated in Milroy and Margrain (1980:25–6):

> These results show that even in a single speech community . . . there are many differences in the manner in which speakers take hold of 'pieces' of the language and use them as symbols of community loyalty.

What we are not told is what this 'solidarity' and 'loyalty' is pitted against. If, as seems to be implied, the 'solidarity' is a product of the normative consensus then it is a feature of social order and, in this respect, is reminiscent of Durkheim's mechanical solidarity. Thus it is not a community loyalty against the state. Furthermore, since there is a parallel tendency to conceive of the state as the product of all communities, loyalty to the community is akin to loyalty to the state.

The community is presented as a homogeneous, self-contained entity, but since the community is defined by actors who share a common value orientation, rather than by social groupings, it is unlikely that the community is socially homogeneous. Indeed Labov, and Milroy and Mangarin indicate that the community consists of a variety of social groups. Labov specifically refers to a variety of social classes. It would appear therefore that the community is akin to a Weberian status group – a group whose members share a similar life style, to the extent that they are drawn together across class lines.

Yet despite this apparent Weberian point of reference, social class, as we shall see below, tends to be discussed partly in Durkheimian terms, the emphasis being upon individual differentiation. This is not surprising since, as Romaine (1982:14) emphasises, the approach 'takes the individual as the starting point of analysis, largely to avoid this problem of defining group boundaries'. I would go further and state that the individual as the starting point of analysis is a consequence of beginning from a preoccupation with linguistic data and being confronted with the necessity of undertaking exhaustive analyses of finite data within a linguistic methodological framework. It is therefore not surprising that 'group' in terms of the linguistic data frequently assumes the character of the aggregate of the idiolects, and in social terms as the aggregate of the individual speakers.

It is not surprising therefore that a speech community can be conceived of as 'the national unity of a people or . . . communicative networks of interaction' (Dittmar 1976:106). Indeed the range of possibilities makes it difficult to envisage how the concept can be effectively and meaningfully operationalised. It is even possible to envisage a situation where speech communities overlap in terms of both space and membership. Indeed Labov, at one time, in discussing what he claims is a single speech community, states that different age groups within the general population of the speech community 'belong to slightly different speech communities' (Labov 1972:158). It is clear why speech communities should be so variable and, as a consequence, so elusive; if community is built out of boundaries of language use conditioned by social norms, and if social norms are the product of socialisation patterns, then any social unit can be responsible for variations in socialisation depending upon the level of generalisation concerning the importance of socialisation practices.

In her discussion of speech communities, Romaine (1982:17) refers to Gauchat's concern with the problem of explaining the origins of language if the individual could not change the language, and to his conclusion that, consequently, it is the group that is responsible for changing the language. However, to imply that the activity of the group is the product of an authorless norm is to fall into the same structural functionalist trap as Labov who claims that the locus of grammar lies in the community, and that the speech of any social group will be less variable than the speech of any individual.

It seems at times that the norm referred to by sociolinguists is the standard variety associated with the dominant class or, in the conceptual terms of almost all sociolinguists, the high class. Yet this claim is not that clear cut in that the usual claim is that this class is 'closer to the norm' than any other social class. Thus the norm tends to be some form of ambiguous ideal, unrelated to any specific class. As a consequence it becomes even further divorced from social construction and the argument becomes one of relative proximity to this elusive norm.

Some clarification of the nature of the norm is available in Labov's discussion of linguistic change. He suggests that such change is embedded in social class, the 'proof' being based upon the correlation between social class and linguistic features. The relationship between the two variables that is inherent in this correlation is then related to 'social pressures and attitudes [which] come to bear on linguistic structure'. The elusive norm has been reduced to a set of social pressures and attitudes. The only further explication involves a rather confusing argument involving the relationship between status, prestige and esteem. This argument claims that the lower classes seek to accrue status through imitating the upper class and that it is this that serves to establish the norm. It is an argument premised upon the idea of the rational individual striving for upward social mobility characteristic of the philosophy of individual liberalism.

One feature which the concept of speech community shares with the sociological concept of community is interaction. This much is evident in the quotation from Gumperz's work cited above. It encompasses a view of things reminiscent of the social dialectology of the nineteenth century with the emphasis on boundaries determined by language which in turn is determined by social factors. The important features of Gumperz's definition are interaction and language use although we should not disregard his reference to verbal signs. The concept once again appears to be the product of linguistic rather than social factors since the boundaries are defined by linguistic features. However, it would be a sterile concept if it was discussed simply in terms of linguistic uniformity. Thus we have the possibility of 'differences' in language use which relate to interactional factors. The attributes of difference which serve to define the speech community are linguistic rather than social and they have the result of producing 'aggregates' rather than social groups in the sociological sense. Thus, it would appear that the speech community is an aggregate of individuals in interaction.

The empirical construction of the speech community is evident in Labov's (1966) New York study. Accountability to the data is sought by (i) isolating a 'variable' – usually phonological; (ii) quantifying a large number of tokens of the variable; (iii) presenting a mathematical result either in terms of a binary percentage score or as a 'weighted index' score; and (iv) demonstrating co-variance between group scores and such social parameters as socioeconomic class (Milroy 1980:35). This methodological procedure tells us a great deal. It underlines the primacy of linguistic features as the definitional imperative and emphasises the reliance on co-variation for the appearance of any social input. Without a theoretical basis for the explanation of co-variance we are left with description and the concept, as a consequence, appears to be disassociated from theory.

Returning to the interactional feature of the conceptualisation of speech community we find Agar (1973:130) and Gal (1979:12) emphasising that frequent and significant interaction between members of the speech community results in a form of communication which is not readily understandable to outsiders. Interaction becomes a form of code not unlike the conception of culture as behaviour. Gal (1979:12) states: 'Members have the background knowledge necessary to interpret each others' variable behaviour.' It is not clear what this background knowledge refers to, and at times it would appear to resemble the norm referred to above. We do find reference to individual speech variation conveying 'information about the social context and the speaker's attitudes or intentions' (Gal 1979:12) which are held to reflect the social identity of the speaker. Thus the correlational method referred to above is employed to reveal differences of social identity. We are still left with the problem of what conditions the 'attitudes and intentions' which, in the long run, are reduced to a form of psychologism.

Dorian (1982) has some reflections on this particular point. Following Hymes (1972) she emphasises that knowing how to say something appropriately is as important as knowing how to say something. It is this, she claims, which distinguishes the speech community participant from the speech community member. Thus it would seem that there are some members of the speech community who do not participate in its activities. We find a kind of code of linguistic behaviour which closes the community. There is a shift from defining the speech community in terms of distinctive linguistic features to a definition based upon behaviour in context. Furthermore, internal variation is not based upon proximity to a preferred norm as in Labov's work but, rather, upon the behaviour skill with reference to communicative competence. Community is now primarily spatially defined, the population within that space being divisible into participants and members.

I would now like to return to the work of Gumpertz and a more recent definition of speech community as

> a system of organised diversity held together by common norms and aspirations. Members of such a community typically vary with respect to certain beliefs and other aspects of behaviour. Such variation, which seems irregular when observed at the level of the individual, nonetheless shows systematic regularities at the statistical level of social facts.
>
> (Gumperz 1982:24)

This summarises what has been stated above – that the speech community is a functionalist concept involving rational actors operating under the influence of an uncontrolled and unspecified social norm. These norms relate to shared values which serve as the basis for an empirically, rather than socially defined group. This view calls for assumptions about cognitive processes if any form of explanation is sought.

Gumperz (1982:26) proceeds by stating that the dynamic nature of the speech community means that a bounded community sharing an assumed norm is no longer evident. That is, the homogeneous speech community is a rarity. This is yet another manifestation of the Durkheimian evolutionary schema with the transition from mechanical to organic solidarity, from *Gemeinschaft* to *Gesellschaft*, being reflected in the nature of the speech community as homogeneous or heterogeneous. As evolution proceeds so the conditioning force of the normative order also changes. If this normative structure is the basis of social order then the speech community is the unit of social order as reflected in speech. This is the sense in Dittmar's (1976:106) claim that the heterogeneity of speech communities relates to 'literary standards and grammatically different local dialects'. As we shall see in chapter 5 the standardisation of language involves the state and its agencies of legitimisation. Thus the transition from homogeneous to heterogeneous speech communities posited by Gumperz increasingly appears to be a restatement of the evolutionary schema and of the role of different agencies in the creation of social order within such a condition of change.

It should be clear that for the sociologist looking for the primacy of the social structure in any explanation of speech behaviour, as is implicit in the reflection thesis, speech community is a very frustrating concept. This is largely because it involves several assumptions. Among them is that speech is a reflection of social structure and that therefore it is possible to establish the boundaries of the speech community on linguistic grounds alone and that this will, simultaneously, involve the creation of a socially relevant community. Second, that social structure and social order are the product of the normative process. We are left with social norm as the only social basis for the creation of the speech community. However, norm is the very basis for human subjectivity and, as a consequence, speech community becomes a subjective or emic concept.

REGISTER

In a recent paper Ure (1982) has summarised the conventional work on register which she defines thus:

> The register range of a language comprises the range of social situations recognised and controlled by its speakers – situations for which appropriate patterns are available. The inventory of contrasting textual patterns provides a classification of situations; speakers select from this range when they negotiate registers; they are thereby able to exercise control over the relationship and type of activity in which they are engaging according to the current social norms.
>
> (Ure 1982:5)

It is clear that the Hobbesian problem of the tension between social order and social freedom is evident here. An image of rational actors making voluntary decisions from among alternatives is presented side by side with the idea of a higher level social order conditioned by a free floating norm. The individuals are claimed to 'control' the social situations but within these situations a 'norm' specifies what is 'appropriate'. Furthermore, the objective of the exercise is 'control', not over other individuals, but over the associated relationship.

Given this explanation for registers there is a need to confront the issue of social change *vis-à-vis* registers and the reference to 'current social norms' makes this evident. Ure claims that change derives from technology, and/or both social and individual 'transition'. This transition conveys an image of change from one stage to another, that is, it is devoid of process. Furthermore, the agency of change is unclear. What is clear is the application to language of the structural functional approach to social change in which adaptation derives from the disruption of a consensual equilibrium and obliges the other integral parts of the system to adapt in order to regain or re-establish the lost equilibrium, albeit in a modified form. Thus a living language . . . extends its range and adapts to new patterns of interaction and new technologies. Language adapts as its speakers adapt, and in periods of social or personal transition unsettled language patterns reflect the fact that the situations in which they are used are unfamiliar.

(Ure 1982:6)

Apart from the reification of language in this statement it is evident that language is seen as a manifestation of society, albeit within a particular model of social explanation. We are told more about the controlling factors of change when Ure refers to socialisation in stating that actors are socialised into the language norms of a particular speech community and that this is the driving force of change in the register range.

We are also told more about the nature of social change:

The register range of a language is one of the most immediate ways in which it responds to social change. The difference between developed and underdeveloped languages (Ferguson, 1968) is fundamentally one of register range, and language context, which contributes to language development (Becker, 1948) is mediated by particular registers (Rubin, 1958).

(Ure 1982:6)

The additive nature of the scientific orientation of sociolinguistics and the associated uncritical, slavish adherence to previous work means that this model of social change should, by now, be familiar. Languages, and presumably the societies which we are told they reflect, are dichotomised into 'developed' and 'underdeveloped', the polar ends of the familiar evolutionary continuum. The route to development is through diffusion in which contact with the 'developed' somehow provides the magic effect – communication is the source of ultimate benefit in the form of development. Furthermore, since 'language users are aware of the choices that they make', it follows that there can be no element of coercion or power in the process since adaptation is a matter of conscious, rational choice. Conversely, of course, a failure to modernise is either the fault of the 'underdeveloped' or is the consequence of irrationality. The arrogance of this modernisation theme with reference to language is evident in the following passage:

However, like Greek, Pidgin has a political status in the modern world, being with English one of the state languages of Papua

New Guinea, a function unique for a pidgin; in this function Pidgin suddenly requires an extended register range such as Greek or Welsh have, to meet the needs that arise out of independence and modernisation.

(Ure 1982:7)

Even a bastard can gain access to the throne and thereby achieve comparability with the classical greats, providing he is accompanied by an appropriate queen. The opportunity is open even to the most humble, they must merely seize that opportunity. On the other hand, the diffusionist model insists that such status can only come about through contact with the modern source of ultimate and inevitable advantage: 'it is principally due to the geographical boundaries of mountain and sea that the gaelic-speaking community has been able to remain separate' (Ure 1982:8). A minority language can only survive through separation from the source of modernisation and, consequently, a minority language can only survive as underdeveloped.

The theme discussed so far in Ure's work is summarised in the following quotation:

> The range of activities for which a language is used is an aspect of the cultural, economic and social organisation of the society; the register range changes as the society changes, and one of the most important aspects of this change is the development of new registers, part of the process of modernisation.

(Ure 1982:10)

As a consequence it is possible to rank languages on a continuum from underdeveloped to developed or, in the more customary parlance, from primitive to modern, by a consideration of the respective register ranges of such languages.

Ure distinguishes between register and domain in the following terms: 'Domains are not the same as registers. A register is a register of a language, whereas domains of language use may draw upon more than one language' (Ure 1982:7). None the less, by referring to domain in terms of language use and register in linguistic terms, she claims that it is possible to draw the two concepts together and ask the question: 'which register relates to which domain?' The link to evolution which she has already claimed for registers thereby also becomes applicable to domains:

> Modernisation can be described in terms of institutional domains. . . . An institutional domain, as the term is used here, should be described in sociological and economic terms; it comprises a set of

occasions of language use that arise because society is organised the way it is.

(Ure 1982:8)

Modernisation is reduced to the inevitability of social organisation – progress must profit.

It is easy to see how the evolutionary argument relates to multilingual settings since it is a statement concerning the relative standing of the respective language groups. However, it should be clear that register must also be applicable to monolingual settings and that it must be discussed within the same evolutionary context. Evidently within monolingual settings the register range covers the whole range of customary activities. However, Ure claims that there can be variation to this trend: 'Within the North American English-speaking community we may expect differences in the scales of formality adopted by subgroups who do not qualify as "educated"' (Ure 1982:9). This rather unfortunate linking of formality with degree of education suggests that within the monolingual, modern, community, education replaces communication and diffusion as the basis of integration with development. Yet she fails to relate register variation in such communities to social class, with the consequence that educational 'failure' is explained in linguistic rather than social class terms:

> It is noticeable that children whose register range is restricted, being educated through a second language or dialect and forbidden the use of another tongue in such contact situations in school, frequently end their school careers as underachievers, as is often the case with immigrant children in schools in the United Kingdom.

(Ure 1982:15)

Language rather than position in the socio-economic order is responsible for under achievement and the link between the two is not pursued.

LABOV AND CLASS VARIETIES

William Labov is undoubtedly one of those whose work has set sociolinguistics upon its present course. His work during the 1960s into the relationship between speech variation and social class established a pattern for a great deal of subsequent research. On reflection it is quite remarkable that the treatment of social variables in a systematic way within sociolinguistics derives from the early work of Labov and no earlier. At first glance the objective of his work does not appear to be too ambitious, merely seeking to demonstrate that linguistic change co-varies with social change and thereby establishing the social nature of language:

> If we have, as a result of Labov's work, a better (though still very imperfect) understanding of the role of sociolinguistic variation and how it operates, this is primarily because he has success-fully brought to bear upon the question rather more sophisti-cated sociological concepts and techniques than have been applied hitherto . . . .
>
> (Lyons 1972:xvi)

This may well be the view of a linguist; for the sociologist, on the other hand, the amount of sociological input and discussion in Labov's work is limited and, as we shall see, his use of sociological concepts raises a number of interesting questions. To return to the objective of Labov's work, the apparent narrowness of his objective is displaced by a closer scrutiny which makes it clear that he views his work as part of a broad view of language and society, a view which encompasses a desire to produce universal statements about the nature of linguistic change in relation to the nature of human evolution.

The emphasis upon the linguistic in his work is explicit, indeed he claims that his objective is to create 'a socially realistic linguis-tics' (Lyons 1972:xix), claiming that 'the basis of inter-subjective knowledge in linguistics must be found in speech' (xix). He aims to achieve his objective by the positivistic process of isolating linguistic variations and seeking to establish correlations and co-variations with corresponding social factors. Yet, despite the claim that language reflects society and that, consequently, the independent variable in any explanation of the relationship between language and soc-iety must be social in nature, the emphasis in his work is most emphatically on the linguistic. Indeed the amount of sociological analysis and interpretation is very limited and this makes the entire exercise appear to be descriptive rather than analytical. That is, the impression is given that he merely seeks to describe the relationships between social and linguistic variables rather than employing one set of variables to explain the other. Of course establishing a relationship between language and society and claiming that the latter determines the former may be sufficient to establish a claim that language reflects society but surely such a claim should go further; it should involve a consideration of the conceptualisation of the social and the relationship of this conceptualisation to the mode of explanation of that relationship between language and society.

As we have already seen, the speech community, defined as a structured set of speech norms which are subject to variation, or as a set of shared attitudes towards language, is the operational frame for Labov's work. Since the objective of his work is to establish the nature of speech variation he is obliged to encompass a discussion of the dynamic nature of such a norm and of the formation of the normative order writ large. While the unity of the speech community depends upon the sharing of a common norm the speech community is not treated as socially homogeneous and, even though Labov does not claim as much, it would appear that it is a shared norm which holds the heterogeneous social structure together as a coherent unit. Thus language becomes a feature of social order.

Within the speech community the dimensions of differentiation which receive attention are those of age, sex, ethnicity and social class, with the last receiving by far the greatest attention. It is appropriate therefore to focus attention upon the concept of social class employed by Labov. Given the emphasis on the speech community it is not surprising that the conception of class relates, both in the work of Labov and his followers (cf. Shuy, Wolfram and Riley 1968) to the community studies of American sociologists such as Holingshead and Warner. It should be emphasised that for such sociologists one of the main objectives was to explore the local basis of differentiation as opposed to the state-wide system which most sociologists deal with.

Labov insists upon both a subjective and objective conception of class stating: 'social stratification is the product of social differentiation and social evaluation – the product of the normal workings of society' (Labov 1972:44). It is easy to see why he must include the subjective evaluation for, as we shall see, if his explanation of language change relies upon the listener's perception of the relationship between speech and social class then a subjective view of class must be built into the explanation. This means, of course, that regardless of what claim is made to the contrary, any explanation is inherently a social psychological explanation. However, the assumption involved in discussions of subjective class is that an objective class structure exists in reality but, for one reason or another, the lay person is unaware of its form. The reasons given for this lack of awareness vary from a claim that the subjective evaluation consists of a false consciousness to a claim that it has something to do with the absence of class varieties of language, with language being a prominent feature in making the objective class structure explicit. Consequently subjective and objective class systems are not alternatives and any explanation that is rooted in an analysis of subjective class must refer to the objective dimension and the inherent logic associated with it. None the less, it is possible to assert the significance of the subjective structure as in the phenomenological claim that behaviour is structured by the actor's consciousness rather than by some objective reality. It is worth emphasising, once again, that this is a social psychological stance, not unlike the concepts of prestige and status which Labov also draws upon. Status and prestige cannot be enjoyed unless others recognise the prestige claim and defer to it. Thus the existence of status rankings depend upon an awareness of prestige rankings. Class and status are analytically distinct even though they may interpenetrate. However, there is no necessary correlation between them. But we should also recognise that the existence of prestige rankings, and the awareness of the existence of status groups who share a similar amount of prestige, differs from one community to another. It is here that Labov's dependence upon the field of community studies is evident as also is his reference to class as being defined by participation in a set of shared norms (1972:120). The shared norms in this respect are speech norms allowing him to discuss his very specific conception of social class by reference to his concept of speech community. The consequence of this is that any findings that derive from his study are limited to the speech community from which those findings derive, thus making any generalisation to the wider society difficult to say the least. It should also be added that the perception and awareness of prestige arrangements also vary *within* the community with location in the status structure being important in this respect. Thus we find that much of Labov's discussion of differentiation is coloured by specific limitations on the scope of his findings. This is not the same as the main theme of this work – that limitations are placed upon the analysis by the nature of the theoretical framework and associated conceptualisations. None the less it is something which should be kept in mind in the following discussion.

In his discussion of objective class on the other hand, Labov focuses upon social differentiation, a very specific conceptualisation of class in which the key element is the manner in which differences exist between objective groups rather than on the nature of the power relations that exist between them. He draws upon numerous dimensions of differentiation including occupation, education, income and location of residence. Of course these dimensions do appear to relate to one another but only within a specific context – that of consumption relating to a meritocratic order in which success derives largely from educational achievement. The 'fairness' of such a system relies heavily upon the creation of what is referred to as 'equal educational opportunity', quite a different concept from that of equality. The essence of this particular discourse on inequality involves the idea of opportunity such that failure within the system does not derive from any inherent lack of fairness in that system, but rather from the failure of the individual to take advantage of the opportunity offered him/her. The reward of success within the system is measured in terms of income and the associated consumption patterns. It is very much a system which involves individuals in competition with one another rather than one which sees society as a system of social groups in conflict.

The assumption behind the use of employment as a dimension of differentiation is that occupations are differentiated on the basis of the contrasting skills that are required for the various occupations, and that these skills can be ranked in terms of social preference or desirability. This allows occupations to be grouped into the different categories which serve as the basis for the different social classes. Thus occupations are first of all divided into manual and non-manual and thereafter into skilled, semi-skilled and unskilled. What is questionable about this process is the basis for ranking the various skills. Most systems of occupational class are not independent of the phenomenon to be explained since they involve some kind of ranking by prestige. They are therefore attempts at the systematisation of popular subjectivity rather than being objective scales which could be employed to explain that subjectivity. Of course it can be claimed that it involves a ranking by society writ large, that they are the product of the normative order but this merely raises issues about interests and the normative order.

Another criticism of employing occupation as the basis for the discussion of social class is that occupations merely refer to the technical division of labour, making no reference to the social division of labour (Poulantzas 1975). Thus the difference between mental and manual labour cannot be understood in terms of general descriptive criteria but rather should be understood as 'the form taken by the political and ideological conditions of the (production) process within the process itself' (Poulantzas 1975:235). To focus exclusively upon occupation is to ignore the antagonisms between groups which is an inherent feature of the capitalist class system.

In some respects Labov's work seems to encompass a Weberian class system. For Weber the analysis of class was rooted in the market, with access to scarce goods and services within the market being particularly important. Market power determines life chances which determine class position. A class becomes an aggregate of individuals who share a similar position. While agreeing with Marx that property was an important criterion in conferring advantage within the market, Weber emphasised that the skills, abilities and educational qualifications of people of the propertyless classes will also be important in influencing their market power. He also viewed class distinctions as being reflected in 'differences in the size of one's purse'. This seems to generate the possibility of an infinite number of market (income) positions so that the differentiation becomes a matter of individual rankings rather than social classes. That is, occupation and income measure different dimensions of inequality. This is one of the problems associated with Labov's attempt to establish a composite class system based upon the four different dimensions referred to above. Weber sought to avoid this dilemma by maintaining that it could be empirically established that only four social classes existed within capitalism. This empiricism has been echoed by the majority of sociologists in the USA who agree with Page's observation that Weber's approach '"fits" the realities of American social life more neatly than does what often seems to be the one-dimensional class approach of Marx and his followers' (Page 1969:xvi). What is overlooked is that the objective is not necessarily to discover a conception which fits neatly with reality but to recognise the relationship between a particular conception and the discourse that it is located in. Furthermore, among the deficiencies of Weberian class theory is its weakness as a theory of class relations and class boundaries, and the fact that Weber's identification of four social classes is merely descriptive, since no explanation for the existence of the class boundaries that separate them is offered. This vagueness with reference to class boundaries is perfectly compatible with the emphasis upon individual social mobility associated with enterprise and effort – the inherent features of individual liberalism. Parkin discusses the social differentiation perspective thus:

> Sociological ingenuity is directed to mapping out the social contours of a territory in which a truce has been declared in the *omnium bellum contra omnes*. Social differentiation within a given class, moreover, is analysed by reference to conceptual categories that generally do not correspond to existentially based groups with the capacity for mobilisation; even less could they be said to constitute social collectivities engaged in mutual competition for scarce resources.

> (Parkin 1979:30)

It is evident that Labov has resorted to a specific conception of social class and that he has uncritically assumed the limitations associated with that conceptualisation. These limitations will become apparent when we turn to a consideration of Labov's broader explanatory framework. However, we should first of all briefly consider his conception of ethnicity.

For Weber ethnic groups were status groups which cut across class lines, being drawn together by a shared life style. This being the case it would appear essential to discuss the relationship between the status group and the constituent social classes, that is, ethnicity and social class should be discussed in tandem. Labov ignores such issues, merely treating the ethnic groups as given. This is not surprising since one objective of Labov's work is to establish relationships in statistical terms between the concepts as variables. None the less, such an omission, while characteristic of the tendency to limit the sociological discussion to a minimum, does have the effect of raising far more questions than are answered.

In considering the broader aspects of Labov's analysis it is clear that his empirical work allows him to single out features of speech which appear to co-vary with the social dimensions he considers and also to identify other features of speech which do not demonstrate any correlation with social factors. This presents him with two problems. First, he has to explain the role of the social in the aspects of speech which are subject to change and, second, he must explain or account for the non-significance of other aspects of speech to his claim that language mirrors society. The second issue is not very satisfactorily resolved in the claim that while all aspects of language are subject to change only some features acquire social value and can thereby be consciously dealt with by social actors so that they assume a social meaning. 'Only when social meaning is assigned to such variations will they be imitated and begin to play a role in the language' (Labov 1972:23). The other features of language, those that do not achieve such meaning, may or may not be dealt with subconsciously. That is, only some features of language mirror some features of society, and we are offered no satisfactory explanation as to why this should be the case. Evidently the second issue is implicated in the first since it is a feature of the explanation of the nature of the relationship between social and linguistic change. It should already be evident that a central assumption of the explanation is the existence of rational actors consciously acting in accordance with some principle or other in relation to a set of social values. These values are a manifestation of a social norm which includes the conception of speech as a structured set of norms. Thus the model of change is based upon assimilation to the norm which implies a general consensus *vis-à-vis* that norm. Yet what is interesting in Labov's discussion of social norms is that he appears to see it as a feature of power rather than merely being something which permeates society without any visible agency. Thus he refers to the manner in which 'members of the high status group in the speech community . . . control various institutions of the communication network' (Labov 1972:179), while adding reference to 'those who set the social norms' (Labov 1972: 295). Unfortunately we are not told any more about this interesting relationship between agency and norm. Yet such a view of norm as a feature of social interest and control is at odds with his concept of social class where the issue of social control is absent.

Once social norms are associated with speech features the latter are transformed into stereotypes and have an impact upon human consciousness so that rational actors act in accordance with their explicit evaluation. Labov claims that in so doing within interaction the actor is telling the listener something about him/herself and his/her state of mind. It is, simultaneously, an expression of identity in that it is an expression of values and an orientation to specific reference groups. This in turn bears a relationship to social norms, since, as an expression of group membership, it expresses conformity with the norms of the group. Behaviour becomes a covert expression of in-group norms manifested in speech.

One of the main features of the evaluation of speech forms within this conception of linguistic change is the conception of such forms as prestigious or stigmatic. Labov claims that the future prospects of the stereotype depend upon the fortunes of the group that it is associated with:

> If the group moves into the mainstream of society, and is given respect and prominence, then the new rule may not be corrected but incorporated into the dominant dialect at the expense of the older form. If the group is excluded from the mainstream of society, or its prestige declines, the linguistic form or rule will be stigmatised, corrected and even extinguished.
>
> (Labov 1972:320)

We are told little in theoretical terms about how new forms emerge. However, in his Martha's Vineyard study it is explicitly related to external influences. This is consistent with the influence of community studies upon his sociological interests. Such studies have been criticised for treating the community as a closed entity subject to change only as a consequence of contact with the outside world. It is also consistent with the tendency for Labov to see change as the consequence of urban–rural diffusion.

Neither are we told much about how a groups moves in and out of 'the mainstream of society'. However, we can assume that, given his assumptions about social prestige and status, it relates to economic success and the social evaluation of that success or failure, that is, it seems to relate to collective upward social mobility. Given his discussion of social differentiation it would appear that the rational behaviour involved in accepting the prestigious form involves optimisation in status terms. Most of the time Labov claims that assimilation is to the prestigious form, simultaneously involving the removal of stigma and the seeking of status, but always within the context of the norm of the speech community. In this respect it seems that the contribution of social class analysis to the discussion is in terms of asserting the importance of upward social mobility, thereby contributing to change in the speech norm through drawing upon the prestige of the upwardly mobile group which is marked through specific speech forms. On the other hand, his empirical data suggest that linguistic behaviour does not always follow this pattern and he is obliged to look elsewhere for an explanation for the linguistic behaviour in which the stigmatic form is retained. That explanation involves drawing upon the work of Ferguson and Gumperz (1960) and Trudgill (1971) who claim that among the working class there exists a covert value system which relates to an in-group norm different from the norm of the wider society. Despite referring to an opposition of values Labov fails to tell us much about this alternative set of norms and values and his class conception, with its inherent consensus orientation, obliges us to exclude the most obvious explanation whereby not only values but social classes are in conflict, with speech being a manifestation of this conflict. On the other hand, there are numerous problems with such a suggestion if one adopts a normative argument. Since such an argument fails to make any suggestion concerning agency, the nature of the agency for the alternative normative order is missing, as also is any suggestion as to whether it is a normative order separate from the predominant normative system or whether it is a subsystem of the predominant form. Whichever the case, the nature of the relationship between the various systems should be discussed if we are to come to terms with the significance of the claim for relative normative systems, and especially if the dynamics of the relationships between the normative orders are to be understood. The only suggestion we have concerning the generation of the normative order is the conventional one which refers to socialisation, and especially peer group socialisation.

From this brief summary of Labov's theoretical argument it would appear that his account of language change fits neatly into the structural functional perspective on society. Change is viewed as a series of stages within which new forms are evaluated by rational actors and diffused in accordance with the principle of status optimisation. All of this occurs within a class structure which affords the enterprising individual every opportunity for maximum social mobility. The system is held together by a series of social norms which are acquired through socialisation. The only feature of the conventional argument that is missing is that of social roles. These roles are replaced in Labov's framework by the social variables such that rather than occupying role positions the individual is seen as a feature of the various social variables which are a manifestation of his/her very being.

When Labov moves from the specific discussion of linguistic change to broader generalisations we encounter a discussion of the role of adaptation in social evolution. One of his central questions in discussing language change is that of the relevance of adaptive diversity. This is precisely the question which we would expect in any functionalist conception of society that incorporates a vision of evolution as progress. Adaptation becomes the driving force of progress. Despite expressing a reluctance to become embroiled in the issues of nineteenth-century evolutionism he does conclude that the most evident feature of language change is increased diversification which, he claims, has a positive value in human cultural evolution, with the possibility of cultural pluralism being a necessary element in the human extension of biological evolution. That is, the idea of unilinear progress is accepted as a feature of evolution and the role of language in this evolution is retained as a functional prerequisite despite the claim that 'any advance in the analysis of the mechanisms of linguistic evolution will contribute directly to the general theory of social evolution' (1972:121). What is ignored, of course, is the argument that if language is a reflection of society, then the increased linguistic diversification must also involve social diversification, and if social differentiation or inequality is a feature of that social diversification then the language diversification which Labov praises is possible only as a consequence of increased social inequality. Thus social differentiation is not viewed as an unnecessary evil but rather it becomes a necessary and beneficial feature of human evolution.

LANGUAGE AND GENDER

One area of sociolinguistics which, more than any other, has sought to escape the limitations of structural functional analysis is that of gender and language. For various reasons those interested in this topic have placed far more emphasis upon Marxist, semiotic or the *pouvoir–savoir* theoretical perspectives than they have upon the conventional sociolinguistic perspective on society. This is hardly surprising given that most of the researchers in this particular field are actively involved in the feminist struggle and that such perspectives lend themselves to the interpretation from the subordinate position, notwithstanding that Marxism is inherently a male discourse. None the less a considerable amount of the work on language and gender does fit into the theoretical perspective which we are focusing upon. Much of that work is correlational in nature, involving the observation that women's speech is different from that of men, and then seeking an appropriate means of explaining this difference in social rather than biological terms. Feminists and non-feminists alike have, time after time, emphasised the manner in which sexual differences are trans-lated into gender inequality. Since the emphasis in this translation is upon the social nature of sexual difference it is not surprising that sociolinguists have assumed the reflection thesis in emphasising that gender inequality is evident in language. In the following discussion the emphasis will be on the manner in which the relationship between language and gender is 'explained', rather than upon the differences between the speech of males and females.

Cameron (1985) has discussed the problem from a feminist position, arguing that most of what has been produced within the structural functionalist perspective is akin to a male discourse. She emphasises that what she refers to as 'sex difference research' carries the implicit assumption that the norm that is referred to is a male norm from which women deviate. Furthermore, in common with most discussions of deviation, female speech is subject to denigration simply on account of being different from male speech. Of course, for many feminists this is no more than a manifestation of the dominance of patriarchal norms. However, it is also a consequence of the tendency for sociolinguists to establish patterns on the basis of the statistical concept of difference. That is, differences in speech behaviour between the sexes are established on the basis of statistical frequency distribution. The method of which this tendency is a part is comparative, involving treating one variety as the norm from which the other deviates; an apolitical difference is transformed into a political deviation. Cameron maintains that this is a major contribution to stereotypification, both in terms of findings and interpretation. Clearly this must be true of all subordinate groups – the inability to deal with difference in terms of power and conflict is a consequence of the explanatory perspective adopted by the sociolinguist.

The supposedly objective findings concerning sex speech differences are interpreted variously in terms of viewing women as illogical, insecure, non-competitive, non-innovative and prestige seeking. This dichotomous series should be familiar in that it is evident in the distinction between state languages and stateless languages, the difference involving the dualities emotional/rational, modern/traditional, artistic/scientific etc. These differences are translated into social praxis within education where women are directed towards the arts, and if used at all in education, stateless languages tend to be restricted to the teaching of the arts with science as the language of reason being left to the languages of reason (Williams 1988b:8)!

This suggestion among sociolinguists that middle-class male speech constitutes the norm involves ignoring the issue of the oral standard. It is conceivable that middle-class male speech is the oral standard, but the unfortunate tendency among sociolinguists is to measure speech behaviour against middle-class male speech rather than an established oral standard. That is, the problem lies in the process of legitimisation of the oral standard rather than in sociolinguistic practice. This is not to deny the sexism implicit in such practice but rather to claim that the problem lies in the power aspect of standardisation. It may be that sociolinguists would claim that the social norm is an objective issue, being the expression of society. But surely this merely ignores both the sexist nature of society and the tendency to treat social norms as apolitical rather than as the product of specific interests within society. As a consequence the deviant is explained in terms of the norm rather than vice versa. That is, there is a tendency to substantiate the norm through comparison. It is the deviant that requires explanation, the norm being regarded as normal or unremarkable.

One of the problems confronted by feminists and those involved in minority language struggles alike is that the tendency to marginalise by treating speech forms of certain social groups as deviations from a norm prevents these 'deviations' from being treated as an integrated system in its own right. This is, of course, a feature of subordination – the deviant is treated as an articulated, inferior, feature of the dominant, standard form. Cameron (1985) makes the point that women, as members of a subordinate group, tend to be treated as an adjunct of men with reference to history and culture. That is, there is an absence of a historical and/or cultural context for the explanation of speech difference. In this respect the situation of women is quite different from that of minority language groups which tend to be marginalised as a consequence of holding a distinctive culture. In this respect women may not be at such a disadvantage since it leads to discussing minority language groups in cultural rather than social terms, thereby displacing the problem. At least gender must be treated as a social issue even if the manner in which the social is conceptualised becomes the site of struggle.

As mentioned above, one of the findings of empirical research on speech variation is that women are more prone than men to be involved in passing or striving for prestige. Unlike ethnic passing, where the tendency is to imitate the dominant language in passing, women are obliged to compensate for their subordinate position by passing in class terms. According to Labov (1972:303) this is particularly prominent among lower-middle-class women. He interprets this feature of sex speech difference as involving greater innovation among women since, he claims, women transmit models to their children. Again his account relates to the structural functional claim that the social norm is transmitted from one generation to the next through socialisation, with children learning roles through imitating the role models of parents. What is interesting is Labov's suggestion that the mother is the dominant force in this process. Labov is not alone among sociolinguists in placing the emphasis on socialisation. Many claim that the different varieties of male and female speech are a consequence of different patterns of socialisation. Within structural functionalism the tendency is to relate these different patterns to different gender roles and identities as well as to different features of the normative structure. This, of course, is consistent with the view that sex language differences are merely a manifestation of this entire process. Cameron (1985:52) refers to this view as a 'subcultural' view of sex difference. This raises numerous questions, apart from the obvious ones of the conceptual nature of culture, the nature of the relationship between subculture and culture and the relationship of subordination to the subcultural form.

The existence of a gender-based subculture rests on the claim that the sex varieties of language reflect contrasting socialisation patterns, intra-sex interactional patterns and separate speech and behavioural norms which derive from the existence of feminine identities and gender roles. Malz and Borker (1982:215) state 'the rules for interpreting conversation are, after all, culturally determined'. This view of culture reminds one of the criticisms of the anthropological view of culture and also of Durkheim's view of culture made by Parsons which we came across in chapter 2, an example of the limited understanding of even the sociology of Parsonian structural functionalism among sociolinguists. It is also claimed that different types of interaction associated with the respective sexes lead to different ways of speaking, implying that culture derives from behaviour learnt through interaction while still seeking to retain a distinction between social and cultural behaviour. The claim is that socialisation teaches men and women to do different things with words and conversations. In common with Harding (1975), whose work they build upon, Malz and Borker appear to be arguing that role separation associated with sexual separation of activities is reflected in speech patterns. It seems therefore that culture is akin to behaviour or way of life, but this merely raises the question of the relationship between culture and subculture. Presumably within any contemporary state it is inconceivable that citizens who hold a subculture are not simultaneously members of the dominant culture of the state. However, even if this is the case, the consensus nature of the culture concept makes it difficult to conceive of the subculture in question as oppositional in its relationship to the mainstream culture. Indeed it would suggest that the subculture merely feeds into the subordination which is a feature of that mainstream culture.

Often the stereotypical denigration of women is adopted as part of the explanation for sex speech differences. Thus the class passing among women referred to above is interpreted in terms of 'women are more sensitive than men to the social meaning of speech' (Cameron 1985:48). This sensitivity is part of the greater emotional nature of women. Similarly the tendency for some researchers to see men as innovative and women as conservative in terms of speech implies, within the discourse on modernity and progress, that innovation is desirable while conservatism is a hindrance. Lakoff (1975) accepts that socialisation into female roles leads to an inability to be assertive while Labov (1972) emphasises the insecurity of women. The psychological conditions which are a consequence of the subordinate position of women are highlighted and speech becomes a feature of personality which is a consequence of sex-role requirements. There seems to be an inability to treat sex-differences in speech merely as different without drawing upon the features of denigration and certainly without reference to power distinctions.

One of those who does seek to discuss gender language in terms of power is Pamela Fishman (1978). She argues that power is embodied in the sex-role definition as it relates to speech. Power is obscured in sex-roles but is active in the norms which specify what is appropriate behaviour for the respective sexes. Being a 'woman' in the conventional sense is incompatible with asserting control and, as a consequence, women contribute to their own subordination. Power ceases to be a conspiratorial feature of male behaviour, becoming instead a feature of the normative order. The social order is thereby constructed out of female subordination. Fishman, despite dealing with power, does so within the structural functional perspective which sees power as a function of system equilibrium. In common with Parsons the argument seems to be that moral values shared by men and women contribute to the stability of cross-sex relationships. The possibility of power differences being conducive to differences in moral values is never considered so that the underlying stability of relationships cannot be considered.

Neither is the evolutionary theme of structural functionalism absent from the discussion of speech and gender. The argument is made that if gender language is a consequence of sex-role differences the more distinctive the roles the greater the differences in gender language. In societies where stratification is weak and where sex roles are weakly defined it is claimed that differences in gender language will be correspondingly less (Wardaugh 1986:311–12). Presumably if we assume a relationship between evolution and progress the increased differentiation associated with capitalism is akin to progress and this, seemingly, will be accompanied by increased sex-language differentiation!

CONCLUSION

In this chapter I have sought to demonstrate that much of the work on speech variation is merely an extension of structural functionalism. The focus is on the manner in which language is an aspect of the social norm which sets constraints upon individual action. Such norms are the product of socialisation into fixed roles within the overall role structure of society. Yet, even within this framework of constraints the individual is not entirely fettered since language is, simultaneously, a feature of the rational expression of the individual expressing a social identity. If language is part both of the normative structure and of individual expression then the individual must also be a willing participant in the creation of a normative order which restrains him/her. It is as if the social structure is a product of individual decisions. Even within feminist studies, an area which has been subject to considerable theoretical innovation, this perspective has been retained by many of those studying gender language as a source of variation.

Despite employing concepts such as social class, ethnicity or gender, which are explicitly related to domination and subordination, as independent variables within the empirical framework, the conflict that is implicit in such dimensions is missing as a consequence of the structural functionalist orientation. The emphasis on normative consensus as the guiding force of individual speech results in the legitimisation of standard forms and the parallel marginalisation of non-standard forms. I would now like to consider language contact, an issue which, in the view of many, carries an even more explicit conflict element, involving the struggle over language in multilingual contexts.

4 Language contact

My objective in this chapter is to consider the relevance of the concepts of domain and diglossia which continue to be of considerable importance in sociolinguistics and the sociology of language. I will show how these concepts derive from an extremely conservative problematic thereby limiting the nature of the debate about what is, for many, a highly emotive subject. As typologies they relate to a perspective, not merely on language, but also on society, and it will become evident that a central ingredient of this perspective is evolutionism. I have already implied that evolutionary theories inevitably result in denigration and this example is no exception. I conclude that there are numerous reasons why these twin concepts should be abandoned.

There are three fundamental weaknesses in the line of enquiry which will be considered below. First, it involves the construction of typologies which are not only of limited analytical value but, in working inductively, which can lead to explanatory misconceptions unless great care is taken with reference to the assumptions that are built into the basis of the typological differentiation. Second, the central theoretical ingredient involves structural functionalist role theory with all of its Comtean and Durkheimian implications. Many of the criticisms of the two concepts appear to have accepted the typologies and then modified or added to them (cf. Calvet 1987, Haugen 1962), these criticisms merely involving statements about the typology's proximity to 'reality'. Others (cf. Kremnitz 1981 for review) have undertaken the much more important task of revealing the consensus nature of the perspective and the associated limitations on the discussion of power and conflict in language contact. This is the line of enquiry which I will seek to pursue.

FERGUSON ON DIGLOSSIA

The forerunner of Ferguson's seminal paper (Ferguson 1959) was the work of Weinreich (1963). Much of his work involved employing contrastive linguistics to investigate the manner in which structural linguistic factors of interference were associated with language contact. The relegation of this phenomenon to a technical, non-social problem was partly redressed by a consideration of social and cultural factors involved in language contact. Characteristic of the sociology of its time, Weinreich's work at times lapsed into listing the relevant variables that hypothetically might be relevant for language contact and, as such, once again appeared to reduce the problem to a technical apolitical problem. Yet his discussion of language shift in relation to social value, that is, to status, and the prestige of languages, was an important contribution which has received insufficient attention.

The issue raised in Weinreich's work that was seized upon by Ferguson involved two functionally different language varieties in a speech community. Here he is addressing, on the one hand, regional dialects and, on the other, a standard form and the relationships between them. The standard form is used for writing and, more often than not, in formal speech situations. It tends to be learnt in a formal educational setting and carries high prestige. The regional dialect is employed in quite different social and institutional contexts and tends to be acquired through socialisation in the home and the community, and it lacks normative control. In contrast to most of the linguistic work prior to Weinreich this approach demanded focusing attention upon the relationship between linguistic varieties. Weinreich maintained that this shift must involve the subdiscipline of dialectology despite its tendency similarly to restrict its attention to heterogeneous speech phenomena with reference to regional dialects.

Ferguson's paper on diglossia was epitomised by the unfortunate tendency to refer to the respective varieties as High (H) and Low (L), hardly neutral terms of reference. The basis for this differentiation is the functional distinction where there is a 'standardisation where two varieties of a language exist side by side throughout the community, with each having a definite role to play'. In referring to each variety having a definite role to play he is unambiguously referring to function. This functionalism is made more explicit by reference to the 'specialisation of function for H and L' with only H being appropriate in 'one set of situations' and only L in another set, the overlap between the two being slight. Now it would appear that the logical next step is to move from the principle that language is a manifestation of the social by considering the nature of the social groups which employ different varieties in different contexts. This, however, is played down and we are given an explanation for the variation in terms of a pre-established normative consensus which results in 'incorrect' application being subject to ridicule, that is, behaviour is referred to in terms of a normative 'typical behaviour'. It is this distinction, established by observation, which serves as the basis for a language typology and it is well to recognise the limited analytical value of such typologies.

We learn that a subjective evaluation is placed upon H and L by members of the community, with the H forms being regarded as superior. Notwithstanding the problems associated with the use of the concepts of prestige and status in sociolinguistics (G. Williams 1979) there are numerous problems associated with this assertion. While on the one hand Ferguson denies that he is dealing with standard and non-standard forms of a language it does seem that if standardisation is treated as a politically implicit labelling process this is precisely what is at issue. It is clear that he regards standardisation as a matter of information rather than as a political issue involving legitimisation and institutionalisation. We find that the two varieties have different grammatical structures, with those of L being 'simpler' than those of H. This difference is translated into superiority by reference to grammatical rather than political features with H reflecting 'inflational systems of nouns and verbs which are much reduced or totally absent in L'.

No reference is made to reverse presences and absences. He comes dangerously close to the evolutionist argument concerning linguistic superiority and cognition. Certainly, when he discusses the differences in terms of a superposed variety and a regional dialect he is on grounds similar to the political distinction between language and dialect, with grammatical forms being employed within a linguistic purity framework.

In this respect it is interesting to note the reference to 'national' language which seems, by inference, to be the converse of 'community language'. We are told that diglossia becomes a problem when community members express a 'desire for a full-fledged standard "national" language' (Ferguson 1959:19). Unfortunately, even when the relationship between the respective uses of H and L is related to social context this is not related to the political and to the manner in which contexts represent manifestations of power. Thus, even when the argument appears to move in the direction of power and conflict it fails to mature into anything more than the descriptive.

The apolitical nature of the discourse is further evident in the reference to normative consensus as the basis for the consolidation of the H/L distinction. The only reference to the source of this consensus is that the acquisition of L is through the family whereas the H variety is reproduced through formal education. Thus we have what amounts to a free-floating norm, substantiated by subjective evaluation and ridicule – with no source of origin nor derivation, and certainly devoid of any reference to power and materialism and without any reference to who benefits from such a norm. Of course it is highly unlikely that this last issue would be discussed since Ferguson's perspective on language is not unlike that of Durkheim, with language being a spiritual phenomenon that transcends the individual and historical society in unifying a culture from which individuals establish institutions of collective communication. As a consequence of the failure to address the differentiation of status between H and L in terms of power the relationship between the two varieties is reduced to one of difference. This is accentuated by Ferguson's claim that H could become the universal variety if it was adopted as the family language – the role of H in relation to power and differentiation is entirely overlooked.

This typological description is elaborated by relating the functional distinction between H and L to other dichotomies including local/universal, formal/informal, urban/rural, etc. This dichotomous proliferation could be extremely interesting but in Ferguson's work it remains a descriptive exercise and the manner in which such a conceptualisation, either in the sociolinguist's mind or in praxis, relates to aspects of power is entirely ignored. Ferguson arrives at his definition of diglossia by induction without any consideration of its relationship to the theoretical problematic. Indeed he appears to be ignorant of the implicit theory behind his typological and conceptual formulation. We are left with a descriptive format which is of limited analytical value and it is little short of amazing that this concept has received so much attention among sociolinguists over the years.

FISHMAN'S ELABORATION

Shortly after the publication of Ferguson's paper on diglossia, Joshua Fishman, who, more than anyone, has been responsible for the development of the sociology of language, sought to elaborate the concept. In so doing he claimed that diglossia could refer to any degree of linguistic difference from the most minute stylistic variation within a single language to the use of two totally unrelated

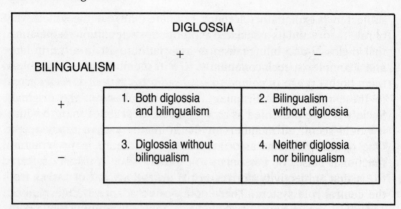

Figure 4.1 Fishman's typology of diglossia and bilingualism.
Source: Fishman (1967).

languages. Significantly the defining criterion was the *functional* feature of linguistic differentiation. Evidently he is discussing both what Ferguson referred to as diglossia and what is customarily referred to as bilingualism. In developing his argument his theoretical reference point is much clearer and less ambiguous than that of Ferguson. Yet we find the same Durkheimian claim that linguistic changes are the result of changes in society. This results in a highly mechanical process involving a degree of inevitability as a consequence of which conflict is absent. He presented his typology in schematic form as in fig. 4.1.

In developing this typology Fishman distinguishes between diglossia seen as sociolinguistic in the sense of relating to the use of different linguistic forms within society; and bilingualism seen as psycholinguistic, involving as it does the capacity of the individual to use more than one language, leading to a consideration of the linguistic attitudes of the individual when confronted with more than one form. Fishman's objective was to discuss diglossia at the 'national or societal level', and its relationship to 'psychologically pertinent considerations'. In so doing he sought to extend the concept to encompass specific languages rather than varieties of a single language. All of the types in the resultant typology refer to a situation within specific speech communities which he states can 'comprise an entire nation', a statement which begs various questions concerning the relationship between community and nation to say nothing of the relevance of the state. Again the inductive method is employed, drawing upon situations to exemplify the various cases.

The associational variations between bilingualism and diglossia are subject to an explanatory account. It is here that we witness the advent of role theory and its associated evolutionary orientation. It is claimed that diglossia and bilingualism in association exist in a 'fairly large and a complex speech community, that its members have available to them both a range of *compartmentalised* roles as well as *ready* access to these roles' (J.A. Fishman 1972:96, emphasis in the original). Society is here presented as a rigid, mechanical set of roles to which, it would seem, all members of the community have ready access. One of the problems associated with role theory in its structural functional guise, or Parsonian role theory as it is usually referred to, is that subjectivity derives not from the actor, but rather from the central role system. There develops an adaptive, deterministic, and often unconscious, psychological concept explaining why people should conform to the external, objective, normative and cultural systems. This removes the subjective and conscious intentionality from the analysis of human activity. It is no longer necessary to know why people do things from their point of view, which means that the concept of action is rejected and also, as a consequence of the internalisation of external constraints, the actor's action is merely adaptive and orientated to these external constraints in a never-ending process of interaction. Once the social system, seen as a system of roles, is conceived, the concept of the actors and the reason for their actions become largely irrelevant. Explaining the reality of action by external determinism links the individual with the social structure in terms of institutional expectancies which are themselves patterned according to 'cultural systems'. It need hardly be said that any theory which derives explanation from culturist standpoints is inherently conservative.

Perhaps more important is the criticism which is aimed at role theory for its inherent evolutionary orientation. This is evident in Fishman's typology. As stated above, diglossia and bilingualism are claimed to exist in 'complex' speech communities, this complexity being reflected in the range and compartmentalisation of roles. Furthermore, Fishman states:

> If the role *repertoires* of these speech communities were of lesser range, then their *linguistic repertoires* would also become more restricted in range, with the result that one or more separate languages or varieties would become superfluous.
>
> (Fishman 1972:96, emphasis in the original)

Thus there is a relationship between the complexity of society and linguistic repertoire through the mediation of social roles, with the nature of roles existing as a measure of social complexity. Furthermore, linguistic diversity, either in terms of varieties of a language, or of the number of languages, depends upon, or is a product of, social complexity. Language is drawn into the evolutionary schema through its relationship to the evolutionary nature of society. In this respect, there is an implicit claim that the elimination of minority languages is a natural, evolutionary process which makes struggle irrelevant.

This evolutionism, and also the rooting of the perspective in the philosophy of individual liberalism, is evident in the following statement:

> were widespread access not available to the range of compartmentalised roles (and compartmentalised languages or varieties) then the bilingual population would be a small privileged caste or class (as it is or was throughout most of traditional India or China) rather than a broadly based population segment.
>
> (Fishman 1972:96–7)

The evolutionism that is evident in the comparison with 'traditional India or China', that is, the counterpoising of 'modernity' with 'traditional', despite their temporal coexistence, is not the main thrust of this quote, neither is the apparent claim for a classless speech community in the form of a 'broadly based population segment'. Rather, the main thrust involves a conception of society as an open system where individuals have equal access to all social roles. It is only among the 'extremely upper and power levels of complex societies' that there is no engagement in this range of roles. Furthermore, 'powerful social institutions and processes', 'encourage or facilitate access' to these roles. Here we do have reference to power, but in terms of 'institutions and processes' rather than in terms of social groups in opposition.

Languages or varieties of languages are separated by norms associated with social roles which, in turn, are separated by, among other things, distinctive values. In effect, norms tend to be equated with values which are implemented in terms of social roles. We are again reminded of the Durkheimian emphasis upon how the creation of normative patterns and moral obligations force action to be cooperative and society to be organic and cohesive. Also, in suggesting that varieties of a language will eventually become languages, Fishman is locking language into the explicitly evolutionary framework: 'varieties not yet recognised as constituting separate languages' (Fishman 1972:97). This is not surprising given that linguistic change is tied to social change and social change is seen in terms of an inevitable process of evolution towards a never-ending 'modernity'.

The explicit modernisation thesis which sees society as evolving from a 'traditional', undiversified form to a 'modern', complex, form measured by role diversification is activated by Fishman to explain variations in language *use*. The activities (roles) of actors are differentiated by context, with the hearth and home being counterposed with the 'formal institutions of education, religion, government or work sphere' (Fishman 1972:97). A restricted and simplistic conception of socialisation as occurring within the home is drawn upon to explain this differentiation, and the political/power contrast between the polarised institutions is totally ignored.

If we now turn to Fishman's discussion of diglossia without bilingualism, it is conceivable that the difference between this 'type' and what has been discussed above will reveal the 'cause' of bilingualism. The first point to note is that this 'type' involves more than one speech community, one involving ascribed status, and the other achieved status – the archetypical distinction between mechanical and organic solidarity within the structural functional perspective. The two speech communities are characterised by role specialisation which, in turn, limits the linguistic repertoire of each. Also, the two speech communities are separated by the absence of interaction across the boundary which separates them. Thus the speech community is defined by reference to linguistic features and interactional patterns. It is these patterns, together with the narrow range of role repertoires, which accounts for the absence of 'widespread societal bilingualism'. Clearly, if the modern end of the evolutionary continuum is characterised by a range of roles which are complex in nature, then what is discussed under this 'type' is closer to the 'traditional' end of the continuum. However, we do learn that political and economic factors link the two speech communities, or, rather, the members of the respective speech communities, into a unit in the form of class differentiation. Thus the social classes are bounded which means that it is impossible to envisage class in terms of mutual antagonisms as in the conflict model – they merely exist as a reflection of political and economic difference. Furthermore, this situation is held to prevail in 'polities that are economically *underdeveloped* and unmobilised, combining groups that are locked into opposite extremes of the social spectrum and therefore groups that operate within extremely restricted and discontinuous linguistic repertoires' (Fishman 1972:101, emphasis added). So here we have it – lack of development involves rigid role and interactional separation, with economically defined classes being socially distinct which restricts linguistic features from emerging, thereby preserving bilingualism. Presumably the converse also applies – modernisation facilitates communication and thereby eliminates bilingualism. We have the classic liberal model of modernisation being for the benefit of all humankind in that it is associated with a form of universal communication which serves to unite everyone into a homogeneous harmony. Conflict and struggle are absent. Furthermore, language problems derive from the effect of 'industrialisation, widespread literacy and education, democratisation and modernisation' (Fishman 1972:102), with persisting disunity being brought to the surface and the disadvantaged, as an undifferentiated whole, demanding language (but not economic) equality. This theme of development through communication is legitimised by depoliticising the dominant language through labelling it as a 'language of wider communication'. As such it becomes the benevolent carrier of all that is good in the form of modernisation as progress; it is the key to the door of the good life. Any notion of dominant as the converse of subordination, or of language as an agency of social control is impossible to envisage within this discourse.

Fishman's third 'type' is that of bilingualism without diglossia. Given that bilingualism refers to 'individual linguistic versatility', and diglossia to 'the social allocation of functions', if there is an evolutionary association then we should witness an interesting shift from function to individual versatility. Indeed, it is the evolutionary which highlights the discussion of this 'type'. One set of controlling norms is abandoned and another set consolidated. The intervening period is seen as one of social unrest, that is, we encounter the characteristic structural functional reference to change in terms of stages rather than process, with adaptation to new functional interrelationships being emphasised. Since the end result is always the reassertion of order, albeit in a new form, it is this which makes the discussion of conflict so difficult within the structural functional problematic. One period of cohesion and institutional balance is replaced by another. The conflict which intercedes is seen as constructive in that it leads to, and precedes, the new consensus. Conflict is adaptive. Bilinguals operate as individuals in the sense that they lack the 'widely accepted social consensus' which constitutes the norm, implying that bilingualism is, in some way, non-harmonious and non-cooperative, since these are the very types of behaviour sustained by the normative consensus. Indeed, it would not be too far-fetched to imply that, within this context, bilingualism is implied to be the converse of social order.

The ensuing struggle between language groups tends to be reduced to a situation where 'formal institutions tend to make individuals increasingly monolingual in a language other than that of hearth and home' (Fishman 1972:102). The agency here involves formal institutions as a neutral, abstract, entity and the affected becomes the individual rather that the language group. The 'success' of this process seems to have nothing to do with power and conflict, rather, we are presented with an image of consenting *individuals* bowing to a superior status separate from any causal agency:

> Ultimately, the language of school and government replaces the language of home and neighbourhood, precisely because it comes to provide status in the latter domains as well as in the former, due to the extensive social change to which home and neighbourhood have been exposed.
>
> (Fishman 1972:102)

Evidently the achievement of status is a 'natural' and expected orientation of everyone and overlies any other form of affiliation – the achieving society is the norm! In fairness, Fishman does relate industrialisation to a language/cultural division of labour, but the appearance of the Marxist concept of means of production in the middle of a structural functionalist discourse is more confusing than revealing. Furthermore, the reference employed in this part of Fishman's thesis is to the work of Karl Deutsch (1966) whose argument relies upon an evolutionism which advocates the erosion of traits such as language, which are associated with the 'traditional past', through the external imposition of 'new' forms which will facilitate social mobilisation in the interest of modernisation and development. It is from this particular perspective that the idea of state formation, of which language planners are so fond, derives. Not only are the dynamic forms external to the minority language group, but the patterns of modernisation are imposed from above; tradition must inevitably bow to modernity. The problem is one of overcoming 'stubborn resistance' in order to produce states modelled on the western European and North American systems. The subordinated systems are incapable of independent 'development' because of their own internal inadequacies, while modernisation is seen not merely as progress but as capitalist progress.

To return to Fishman's argument, he claims that the 'needs' of rapid and massive industrialisation and urbanisation, a conception devoid of action and loaded with inevitability, led the proletarian speech community to adopt the language of production 'earlier than their *absorption* into the sociocultural patterns and privileges to which that language pertained' (Fishman 1972:104, emphasis added). The process is one of voluntary assimilation followed by an uncomplicated absorption into the privileged group, that is, we have the conventional thesis of individual social mobility for the compliant and industrious individual. No mention is made of the relationship between production and the dominant language such that a failure to assimilate linguistically results in exclusion from employment and even from survival.

The imbalance referred to by Fishman is held responsible for the lack of structure that is characteristic of bilingualism without diglossia, but it only occurs in 'speech communities of the lower and lower middle classes' (Fishman 1972:104). It is claimed that random speech behaviour derives from the 'massive dislocation of values and norms' (104). Thus, within the evolutionary schema 'bilingualism without diglossia tends to be transitional' (105). The absence of 'separate though complementary norms and values to establish and maintain functional separation of the speech varieties' (105), means that the 'language or variety which is *fortunate enough* to be associated with the predominant drift of social forces tends to displace the others' (105, emphasis added). Not only is this couched in such a way as to exclude the inherent conflict in difference between 'language or variety' on the one hand and 'others' on the other, but there is a reification of language so that language becomes 'fortunate enough' while social forces 'drift' as if separate from agency and control.

Finally the 'type' involving neither diglossia nor bilingualism is restricted to the 'very small, isolated, and undifferentiated speech communities' (Fishman 1972:106). The adjectives in themselves are interesting, especially in their interrelationship. They convey the arrogance of the superior. What is presented is the archetypical mechanical solidarity deriving from frequent face-to-face interaction and the absence of role differentiation. It resembles the 'primitive' as presented by western anthropologists. The regulating force is self-sufficiency, the converse being dependency, a concept which is absent.

Several themes emerge from this important contribution of Fishman. There is the theme of social order and the relationship of language or languages to this order. Perhaps more evident is that the four cells which encompass the typology are presented as an evolutionary continuum. The dynamic force associated with this continuum is political and economic order which opens closed systems which are subsequently integrated into a harmonious whole. Yet the political is strangely silent. We are referred to the community, and it is indicated that such a community is merely part of the 'nation', but the dynamics of the relationship between them is unproblematically missing. There is an allusion to the creative force of humankind, but the edifice that is created takes on something of a life of its own, with the result that the evolutionary process assumes an element of inevitability and bilingualism becomes merely a transitional phase, prior to the inevitable progress towards monolingualism.

The continuum is unable to refer to process since each one of its constituent parts is a stage which, through adaptation, precedes a subsequent stage of equilibrium. In this respect the typology is remarkably static. Thus, what we have is an account of the features associated with each stage, these being presented as 'types'. While these stages are represented in linguistic terms by reference to diglossia and bilingualism as defining criteria, the more important features are the different role structures associated with different social forms. It is here that the principles of the theoretical perspective become most evident. The greatest debt owed by Fishman is to Parsonian role theory and it is as well to recognise that Parsons first derived the concept of role from anthropology. It is hardly surprising therefore that it is integrated with the evolutionism of classical sociology which, through its relationship to the comparative method and ethnography, became the cornerstone of social and cultural anthropology. Its main ingredients involve the dichotomisation of the social world into civilised/barbarian, modern/traditional, etc., and the superimposition of these as the polar extremities of a continuum which is premised on the idea of progress. Inevitably, anything other than the civilised/modern end of the continuum will be denigrated and subject to both benevolence and rejection. Once language is associated with this model, as was predominantly the case with both early comparative linguistics and the Babel thesis on language, we are faced with the perennial struggle of minority language speakers to justify and legitimise their mother tongue. This is nowhere better presented than in the work of Achard (1980) and Calvet (1974) with reference to the languages of the French polity.

The section of Fishman's four-fold typology which has received most attention is that which involves bilingualism without diglossia, involving what Fishman referred to as one where:

> bilingualism is essentially a characteristic of individual linguistic versatility, whereas diglossia is a characteristic of the social allocation of functions to different languages or varieties.
>
> (Fishman 1972:102)

One study which comes under this heading which has had considerable attention is that of German–Hungarian bilinguals in Austria, written by Gal (1979). Her work follows that of Fishman but also departs from it in several respects. Thus, for example, she looks to ethnomethodology, and network analysis as a solution to some of the theoretical and methodological problems which she encountered. Since these are all topics which will be discussed in considerable detail in subsequent chapters I will do no more than consider their relevance for Gal's work in passing. The essential point that must be made, however, is that while they may appear to resolve some problems, they derive from the same theoretical grounding of structural functionalism and are therefore unable to resolve the fundamental problems of that approach.

Before proceeding to a consideration of Gal's work there are one or two points which should be made about Fishman's observations on this particular phenomenon. The first is that change in the fate of the respective languages in contact is uni-directional involving an increasing trend towards dominant monolingualism, or an alternative condition of stability or 'maintenance'. Not only is it a uni-directional process but it is also uniform, leaving no room for minority language resurgence. Of course, if languages are conceived of in terms of dominant and subordinate or minority, with the power dimension of the relationship being central, it is impossible to conceive of the minority language becoming a dominant language. None the less, some degree of minority language resurgence is conceivable and the failure to accommodate it in the schema suggests a model of language contact in which bilingualism is seen as more beneficial than the continued separation of the two languages, since bilingualism then becomes the basis for increased communication and the associated diffusion of ideas. Communication, here, once again, fails to consider the power dimension and focuses instead upon the conception of individuals resolving problems rationally through interaction.

Others, most notably Aracil (1977), disagree strongly with this conception of bilingual society, arguing that a conception of bilingualism as involving a free choice between two languages unfettered by aspects of power is simply not possible. They emphasise that bilingualism is merely a stage in the demise of the minority language. It is emphasised that any conception of language group relations must have power as central and must be devoid of unilinear inevitability. The possibility of shift in both directions must also be a feature of the dynamics of language change. Only then can we begin to consider the nature of the forces involving language group relations as they relate to language change. It need hardly be added that those who make this point tend, inevitably, to be those actively involved in minority language struggles rather than detached academics!

It should be evident from the preceding quote by Fishman that there is the additional problem of the reification of language by ignoring reference to language groups, there being no difference between a language group and a social group. This weakness derives partly from the insistence of structural functionalist theory that a social institution, just as society itself, must be conceptualised as a system of roles, with groups playing a secondary, consequential role in the schema. It is the fact that people are in roles that makes it possible for them to exist as a group, indeed, for them to exist at all. Placed side by side with the tendency for structural functionalism to see the trend of history as being towards an ever greater 'universality', with an increasing application of the same rules to all individuals, it is not surprising that this leads to an image of uniformity as the product of free individuals acting rationally.

It is not surprising therefore that Fishman sees language shift as emanating from the rational choice of individuals who seek to emulate the more prestigious members of society and thereby stand to gain in 'economic, political and cultural status'. This concept of status is Durkheimian in nature and fits neatly with the conception of society as the consequence of individuals taking or refusing the opportunity that is offered them via the educational system, which includes the opportunity to gain access to the dominant language. Of course, failure is a consequence of the individual's failure to take advantage of the opportunity. Furthermore, the social differentiation implicit in the uneven availability of status is a consequence of social change which generates social complexity. We are not told precisely how language shift can generate upward economic mobility, and we are left with the confusing impression that what is available to the enterprising individual is a status mobility through imitation.

In common with Parsons, Fishman is reluctant to restrict his discussion of language shift to social mobility and seeks to emphasise that the good life has its psychological concomitants. The emphasis here is on the manner in which personality is integrated into the social system through the consistent satisfaction of needs and the manner in which reliable cooperation with others is achieved. Roles, although seen as mechanisms by which persons are integrated into systems, never demand total involvement; while the system must be maintained, a measure of functional autonomy is reserved for the individual who is, thereby, never exposed to unlimited obligations. Thus language shift becomes a gratifying act associated with the gain in status achieved by the enterprising individual. Thus it involves 'the relationship between degree of change (or degree of stability) in language usage patterns, on the one hand, and ongoing psychological, cultural or social processes, on the other hand' (Fishman 1972:109). Rational choice in terms of language has its concomitant rewards in psychological and other terms.

Despite the claim that bilingualism refers to 'individual linguistic versatility', Fishman persists with his concept of domain of language use or the 'clustering of characteristic situations or settings around a prototypical theme that structures the speaker's perception of these situations'(Appel and Muysken 1987:23–4), such that different languages are used in different situations. Notwithstanding the problems associated with the normative nature of this concept, since it is conceived in terms of individual choice conditioned by normative consensus, there is a tendency to ignore the importance of power in structuring language use while simultaneously giving the impression that the processes of language shift and maintenance are totally divorced from power. The focus upon the individual speaker *vis-à-vis* domains inevitably means that structural concepts such as prestige are relegated to the consequence of the whim of the individual: 'language prestige is not a unit trait or tag that can be associated with a given language under all circumstances' (Fishman 1972:134).

Rather, the prestige of a language varies from context to context for the same interlocutors and from one speech network to another. This view only becomes possible through a reification of language and its separation from social group since we are not discussing the linguistic equivalent of esteem but rather, to return to Weinreich's definition (Weinreich 1963), the value of language for social mobility. Even if we accept that social mobility is a feature of the individual, it is not divorced from the concept of social class in group terms unless we adopt an essentially Durkheimian view of social class as involving the material ranking of individuals, in which case it loses most of its sociological essence. It seems that this is not too far from Fishman's conception of society and that prestige refers to a 'social-psychological system of attitudes in which superiority and inferiority are reciprocally ascribed' (Mayer 1955:54). If this is, indeed, the case, then it is little wonder that Fishman's discussion of maintenance and shift is so devoid of reference to social structure and power.

One further point concerning Fishman's work requires elaboration before moving on to consider Gal's work. He makes the claim that language shift is more common in urban than in rural settings and in so doing implies that this is a manifestation of the difference between urban and rural societies. This is a consequence of the same perspective that regards rural society as homogeneous, involving mechanical solidarity as opposed to the diversified nature of urban society with its organic solidarity. The focus on social roles reflects this difference, the role differentiation between urban and rural society reflecting the different qualities of solidarity. Once established, this dichotomy becomes the basis for establishing further dichotomies involving modern/traditional, cosmopolitan/parochial, innovative/conservative, etc. which then tend to be overlaid with diffusionist arguments relating not only to different forms of society but also to different languages. Such a perspective can do little more than denigrate and does little to clarify, let alone explain, language group relations. It should be evident that this merely serves to create a false dichotomy since there can be but one society. To argue otherwise is to claim that the basic feature of society, be it social class or some other dimension, differs fundamentally in urban and rural settings respectively. Rather than claiming the existence of fundamentally different societies, and employing this difference as the basis for explaining variation in language phenomena, it is necessary to consider the ownership and control of economic forces in the respective settings before relating this variation to power as it relates to the respective languages.

GAL ON GERMAN–HUNGARIAN BILINGUALISM

The confusion of theoretical approaches in Gal's work makes a close reading of her opening chapter on theory essential. She begins from the criticism that the conventional distinction between stable and unstable bilingualism is devoid of any conception of process. What she overlooks is that this is a feature of structural functionalism in general. This is a consequence of the biological analogy in which society is seen as a series of functionally integrated parts which must always strive towards equilibrium or order. Consequently, social change tends to focus upon the role of adaptation in terms of the reassertion of equilibrium. Change tends to be seen as a series of stages as opposed to process. Since the main focus of studies of language maintenance and shift is either the change in the composition of various language groups, or the change in the use context of the respective languages, some conception of social change is essential. However, even if the issue of social process, or the lack of it, is resolved, there remain a number of other problems associated with Gal's adoption of variations of the structural functional problematic.

Language use surveys are, by now, fairly common. They involve large-scale surveys of a carefully sampled target population and will focus upon attitudinal as well as self-report data on language use. A central problem associated with such research which Gal quite rightly criticises, is the tendency to seek explanation through correlation between social factors and linguistic use, and she claims that 'whatever the social measures, correlations in themselves reveal little about the processes that bring about, maintain, or change these correlations' (Gal 1979:13). What she fails to recognise is that this is not merely an empirical or methodological problem, but rather it is a problem of theory, and her solution of adopting a different theoretical proposition merely displaces the problem. None the less, Gal's study was valuable in that it sought to integrate the collection of survey data with participant observation over an extended period of time in order that the survey and the observational data could be related. Her objective is one of describing the social process that maintains synchronic linguistic heterogeneity. As such, the emphasis upon description makes it very much an ethnographic study, whereas there is also an attempt at explanation. Such long-term participant observation data also has its limitations in that it is restricted to a limited population universe and it is difficult to generalise from the single location to the entire universe of speakers as one does with survey research. What is possible, however, is to identify the main factors associated with, for example, language shift, and to suggest that the process is a universal one within a general range of variables.

The town which Gal studied lies on the Austrian–Hungarian border within the Austrian state and until recently, it seems, Hungarian was the predominant language in most activities. Gal implied that the shift away from Hungarian to German derived from economic restructuring and sought to discover by 'what intervening process does industrialisation, or any other social change, effect changes in the uses to which speakers put their languages in everyday interaction?'

(Gal 1979:3). In considering this question she distinguished between the shift in the domain context of the respective languages and the different use of languages by the same speakers in the same context. In this respect she is seeking to address both the macro problem of socioeconomic process and the micro or interactional problem. This may well be possible to achieve if they are treated independently, but to try and relate them is difficult on account of the different levels of generalisations involved. She discovered that the changing fortunes of what she refers to as a 'peasant economy' obliged bilinguals to seek employment outside agriculture and that, as a consequence, and not surprisingly, the prestige value of Hungarian declined. Of course German was not only the state language, and thereby the dominant language, but was also the language of industrial activity. Within such a bilingual context prestige is a relative matter and, as such, the language of low prestige tends to become astigmatic, the stigma deriving from its relationship to the symbolic features of those who speak it. At the interactional level she discovered that it was possible to predict the language used in context by different interlocutors with a high degree of reliability. The main intervening variables were generation or age and the nature of the social network. Indeed she went so far as to claim that a thoroughgoing analysis of domains was unnecessary, and that she could determine the use of language simply on the basis of knowing who was involved in the verbal exchange. This may well be true in terms of observation but, as we shall see, it creates further problems when the investigator is faced with the problem of explaining or interpreting the empirical data. Now these are not surprising findings within a bilingual community but what is interesting is the nature of the explanation for these findings and correlations.

One of the factors at issue is the reconstitution of the domain context of a language and how this is institutionalised and legitimised. This is a manifestation of the choice of language among bilinguals. In seeking to explain the empirical patterns which she has established by survey and observation, Gal draws upon numerous theoretical perspectives and methods, including the ethnography of communication, ethnomethodology and network analysis. Despite the apparent innovativeness of Gal's work associated with this theoretical eclecticism, it remains firmly grounded in the assumptions of structural functionalism about the nature of society. However, before proceeding to a consideration of the theoretical issues in Gal's study I would like, briefly, to summarise her main findings and the explanation which she offers for these findings.

Prior to the recent economic restructuring of the capitalist economy in this part of Europe, Gal claims that in the area which she studied there existed two parallel groups, each with its own value system and each with its respective language – German and Hungarian. The two languages symbolised distinctive group values and were also symbolic of different identities. In objective terms each group was socioeconomically differentiated into social classes as is inevitable within any capitalist economy. However, deriving from the contrasting value systems, each group had its own status orientation and ranking system, a system consolidated by normative consensus. Thus the objective system of stratification could be reinterpreted through the subjective system of each group. It appears to resemble Fishman's category of bilingualism without diglossia where separate communities exist side by side.

Gal claims that the advent of industrial employment, wage work and the related values changed this parallel, dichotomous system, and led to a universal evaluation of German as a high-status language and of Hungarian as an astigmatic, low-status language. The two languages were, subsequently, brought within a single conceptual system and ranked with respect to one another: 'Hungarian and German came to represent not mutually exclusive ethnic and class groups but rather different statuses . . . ranked by them in terms of income and prestige' (Gal 1979:162). In order to achieve status and deny stigma, individuals opted for the German identity and rejected Hungarian and the associated life style. The peasant value system is abandoned in favour of one based upon materiality.

The preceding quotation suggests that the groups constituted ethnic groups representative of different language groups but that they were, simultaneously, class groups. However, with social class conceptualised as different from status, it seems to involve the subjective evaluation of individuals in terms of wealth and prestige. Evidently this raises numerous problems. First, it is difficult to conceive of different social classes having contrasting value systems since the relationship between them, which is implicit in any system of social differentiation, would be meaningless. Second, without a detailed account of how what were once separate social groups came to be fused into a single entity we are obliged to accept the prior existence of the two separate groups, something which appears to contradict the logic of conventional analysis of class systems. If prestige is treated in its conventional manner as a sociopsychological category, it means that prestige rankings must be recognised by everyone and are conveyed in terms of deference. Hence the existence of status differences depends upon awareness of prestige rankings. The only way in which sense can be made out of Gal's statement is to infer that the language groups are not class groups but status groups in the Weberian sense and, furthermore, that what she is dealing with is a local assessment of prestige rankings of status groups. However, within such a situation there seems to be little difference between esteem and prestige and the subjective nature of the evaluation exercise can only be sustained by referring to a common value-system which is the basis of such an evaluation. More importantly perhaps is that such a heavy emphasis upon the subjective nature of social differentiation, as we shall see, places severe limitations upon the manner in which inequality can be discussed in the ensuing analysis.

Fasold (1984:220) paraphrases Gal in stating: 'To take advantage of these new opportunities it was necessary to become a real Austrian, rather than to remain a local peasant who speaks Hungarian primarily, but happens to live in Austria.' This unfortunate description may well reflect Fasold's prejudice but none the less it is interesting in itself. Industrial employment is presented in terms of 'opportunities' implying a very specific gift-like quality within the context of capitalism as opportunity. Furthermore this opportunity was not available to anyone but a 'real' Austrian and evidently 'peasants' who spoke Hungarian were not considered to be qualified. This intolerance of bilingualism belies a dogmatic view of language contact. Hungarian must become secondary. There is a conception of bilingualism in terms of a very strict opposition between citizenship and parochialism, between modern and traditional, and between industrial and peasant, between rural and urban. Involvement in one involves exclusion from the other. Yet the binary oppositions are not conceived of in terms of struggle, with German being seen as the language of the state and Hungarian the language of the community, with state and community locked in struggle. The main reason for this is that the languages are not related to their social constitution, that is, they are not related to language groups as social groups, and the entire issue is discussed in terms of individual identity. Without the concept of struggle the entire process becomes normative and it is presented as a natural phenomenon. The main driving force is the desire for status on the part of rational individuals. Since German is the prestigious language and Hungarian stigmatised, the shift from German–Hungarian bilingualism to German monolingualism is seen as a natural process and makes the retention of Hungarian an aberration. It all becomes an issue of identity and self-conception:

> More recently the two languages have become symbols of two ethnic identities . . . . The two identities co-exist and compete; so do the two languages. As a result, to the extent that an individual thinks of himself as a member of the Austrian social and economic system, to that extent his use of German increases at the expense of Hungarian. An individual who conceives of himself as a peasant will maintain Hungarian to a greater extent.
>
> (Fasold 1984:221)

Persisting to speak Hungarian is akin to language treason. Now this may well be the conception of the situation among some of the actors, and even by the state, but sociology involves more than a mere phenomenological exercise. It is necessary to consider how such prejudices are created and how they become implemented as ideology, who benefits from such developments and how such views relate to tension, struggle, power and domination. It is such prejudices which contribute to the paranoiac view that those who speak Hungarian in the presence of German monoglots are being 'deliberately rude' (Gal 1979:196), a view which Gal feels obliged to defend by claiming that this is not the speakers' intention. Surely it is the prejudice against bilingualism that needs attention and not the act of speaking Hungarian. Otherwise it merely becomes a manifestation of the view that monolingualism is somehow more natural and desirable than bilingualism.

The second issue – the variable use of language among bilinguals – of course derives from the explanation for the first, since it is a manifestation of what happens in society at large. She draws heavily upon the concept of communicative competence, a feature of the ethnography of communication which draws upon established patterns of communication within any particular speech community and which are known to the members of that community. In so doing it involves a system of shared beliefs, values, attitudes etc., which constitute the social norm, much in the same way as in conventional structural functionalism. These are the 'rules' which Gal refers to in relating linguistic variants to particular types of speakers and environments. That is, what we have is the conventional exercise involving the establishing of co-variation between language and context, and the employment of a specific theoretical perspective in order to explain this correlation. Within the ethnography of speaking the speaker is seen as exercising choice in a systematic way, the assumption being that the range of linguistic possibilities is open to the speaker. Communicative competence involves the socially appropriate and interpretable ways of speaking which draw upon an implicit knowledge of what is appropriate and inappropriate in which social context. This concept relates both to the structural functionalism of sociology and to the culture concept of North American cultural anthropology. 'Appropriate' behaviour constitutes a social norm and Gal (1979:6) refers to 'appropriate language use' in terms of 'cultural knowledge'. It is the absence of this cultural knowledge rather than the technical ability to speak a language that is claimed to make it difficult for an outsider to comprehend what is said.

Thus the main polarisation is not between objective social categories such as social class, but between the community and the outside. We have communities constructed not out of locality, but out of networks of interaction and identity: 'networks of informal social interaction in which speakers are enmeshed and through which, by pressure and inducements, participants impose linguistic norms on each other' (Gal 1979:14). These social networks, she claims, exert a greater influence upon language use than do objective social criteria. She begins from a uniform speech community involving frequent interaction without reference to any socioeconomic or political basis for such action. She then proceeds to identify different uses of language and creates parallel communities on the basis of the social networks involved in such behaviour. The respective social networks, and the languages that they represent, are dichotomised on the basis of a worker/peasant distinction. The emphasis on subjective status evaluation and social networks, Gal claims, is essential since it 'allows the analysis of the processes through which speakers in interaction exercise control over each other through language choice and hence maintain linguistic diversity' (Gal 1979:131). It seems therefore that power relates to control and that in choosing the use of one language or another individuals exert control over each other. Thus power is a feature of the individual rather than of the social structure. How it operates is not clear and we are obliged to surmise that the use of one language or another obliges the presentation of self to be couched in terms of the relevant value system. Thus we are told that the status which a person can symbolically claim in speech depends as much upon the nature of the social network of the speakers as on factors tapped by traditional status indices. That is, one derives status from one's circle of contacts as well as from the status system that is related to that circle. If this is correct then the argument depends upon the existence of parallel status-related value systems, a view at odds with any sociological perspective.

Another feature of the distinction between the language groups is the peasant/Austrian urban worker dichotomy. The 'peasantness' of the Hungarian language group is based upon the extent to which the raising of cows and pigs is part of the household economy. Yet this emphasis upon economic activity is not employed in terms of social class or occupation. Rather it draws upon the work of cultural anthropologists such as Foster, Diaz and Potter (1967). Once again we recognise that this work places heavy emphasis upon the importance of culture as life style involving specific values, and is almost entirely divorced of any class conception and the political ramifications of economic inequality. It fits neatly into the modernisation thesis of structural functionalism in which peasantry is defined as one end of a continuum of which the modern industrial society is the other. Peasantry involves subsistent economic activity which does not contribute a surplus for reinvestment, and it is precisely this sector of the population in the Third World which is claimed to be a deterrent to 'progress', until such time as they can be transformed into farmers. This pejorative connotation and the associated stigma is implicit in Gal's work, and in the manner in which she constructs Hungarian speakers as peasants and claims that a commitment to the life style of peasantry entails a commitment to Hungarian community values. That is, to speak Hungarian one must be a peasant, but one is a peasant as a consequence of choice, a choice that is, since it is the converse of economic optimisation, irrational. Thus, it is a measure of stigmatisation as encountered in the community and, as such, it is a feature of the power relationship between language groups. However, it is not presented in such terms by Gal. Indeed her only reference to power involves the observation that formal speech forms are employed in prestigious contexts, and the informal in non-prestigious contexts. From this observation she claims that formal varieties convey power while the informal convey solidarity. No attempt is made to elaborate upon this very interesting binary opposition which tends to be treated in terms of mutual exclusivity.

Having established the existence of interactional language groups she proceeds to claim that they have an essence in terms of identity. It is not difficult to see how an emic approach must rely upon some cognitive explanation since the objective is to seek to 'explain' people's self-conception *vis-à-vis* behaviour, with the self-conception being an expression of a psychological condition. She claims that German and Hungarian have become symbols of distinctive ethnic identities which are claimed to coexist and to compete. Identity is conceived of as how a person feels about him/herself so that:

> to the extent that an individual thinks of himself as a member of the Austrian social and economic system, to that extent his use of German increases at the expense of Hungarian. An individual who conceives of himself as a peasant will maintain Hungarian to a greater extent.

(Fasold 1984:220)

People are what they feel themselves to be. However, identity is conditioned and constrained by social networks through the imposition of norms.

Social norms are discussed in terms of their derivation from participation in social networks involving members who employ pressures and inducements in order to impose the norms on one another. Again rational choice is evident with norm being seen as a product of the rational actor operating in harmony with other actors. Thus, if the rational actor opts for the status accruing behaviour associated with the use of German, then the norm which determines language choice must also have changed, but we are not told how this norm shift came about. Of course this is not surprising since the general conception of social norm within structural functionalism is of a free-floating entity which derives from socialisation. We have seen that the sociological concept of group seems to have been replaced by that of networks of interacting individuals. However, this is countered by a strange form of reasoning in the claim that if speech is social activity then norms of language use must also be partly social, but if social network differences can account for the process by which differences arise in people's norms and expectations then social networks can be employed to help explain differences in linguistic expectations. The social and the network seem to be taken to be one and the same and this is only possible if 'social' is interpreted as interactional, with the consequence that the explanatory model becomes interactional. In this respect the work is reminiscent of the forerunner of network analysis – the psychometric work of social psychology.

Equally interesting is the claim that norms derive from interaction within networks – an essentially behaviourist conception of norm, particularly in the reference to pressures and inducements. The norm leads to 'expectations' of linguistic behaviour, that is, it is the norm which conditions behaviour, and, presumably, the associated rationality and identity. This would suggest that rationality is not an equally distributed attribute, there to be employed by any person within an equal environment, rather it is differentiated as a consequence of involvement in interaction. Participation in social networks thereby conditions access to social status. Consequently, the irrational behaviour of those who reject the status that derives from optimising economic behaviour is explained away through a self-imposed norm deriving from socially conditioned interactional choice.

Throughout the discussion of linguistic variation there is the image of conscious and meaningful or rational actors:

> Listeners use their own knowledge of linguistic norms and expectations to try and create sensible interpretations in which the combination of the choice, however, unusual, within the context, can be understood as an expression of the speakers intent, attitude, personality or social background.
>
> (Gal 1979:10)

Thus even the inappropriate switching of language form represents indicators of the speaker's momentary attitudes, emotions and communicative intents. She draws upon ethnomethodology in order to elaborate upon such inappropriate switching and particularly the manner in which this perspective claims to make the unusual, obvious, in striving to comprehend the basis of the speaker's rationality. However, since her allusion to communicative competence implies that such rationality is culturally conditioned in the sense of not being accessible to the outsider then the investigator must become an insider, hence the emphasis upon ethnography. Her work, taken as a whole, involves a mixture of such ethnomethodological and Weberian principles mixed with the culturist orientation of North American anthropology. Such a mixture only makes sense when we recognise the link between Schutz's phenomenology and Weberian theory on the one hand and of ethnomethodology with structural functionalism on the other.

Two problems stand out in the interpretation of Gal's data – the issue of separate communities with contrasting value systems within the same society, and the relevance of social class for the analysis. I will treat each of these in turn.

There is a suspicion in Gal's work that induction is prominent, with theory being applied to the already gathered data in order to make sense of it. Thus in order to sustain the argument that the two language groups have different evaluations of what carries status and what does not, and, as a consequence, how different identities are sustained, it is essential to posit the existence of distinct groups with distinctive value systems. Furthermore, this becomes an essential feature of the need to explain why, if language shift is a consequence of rational action *vis-à-vis* socioeconomically derived status, there remains an allegiance to what, within these terms of reference, would be astigmatic and irrational. The existence of different value systems serves to explain this allegiance in terms of contrasting evaluation of what is and what is not stigmatic. Now while this may be very useful in terms of resolving some of the empirical and conceptual dilemmas in Gal's work it does present other problems. It means that, in effect, two societies exist side by side, separated by language and, as we shall see below, social class. Yet we are not told how this is possible, how two populations living in the same locality, and sharing at least some institutional and cultural contexts can, simultaneously, be conceived as separate, other than in terms of interaction. That is, the separate existence is explained through physical separation. It also means that society is a feature of culture since the values that separate these two societies derive from distinctive cultural and value orientations. Thus the independent variable is culture and socioeconomic differentiation becomes a subjective category. Inevitably any explanation that derives from such an orientation must be culturist and conservative.

There is evidence throughout Gal's monograph that the language groups are also ethnic groups and class groups and that the separation of the language groups as social groups is, in effect, a matter of social class. We are told that the vast majority of the bourgeoisie are either newcomers or local monoglot German speakers, and that all peasants are almost exclusively Hungarian speakers. Language appears to be a marker of social class. However, she also claims that 'peasants' and 'workers' do not constitute a ranking *vis-à-vis* one another because both carry the same degree of prestige. Notwithstanding her tendency to confuse status and prestige such a statement is possible only within a conception of social class in terms of status ranking rather than power. We are not told whether this status ranking is merely a local feature, in which case it becomes a local subjective system of differentiation with no wider relevance, so that it has little conceptual relevance, or whether it is a universal system applicable throughout Austrian society. The limited discussion which she does devote to related issues suggests that what she calls the 'emic' or subjective local evaluation is her point of reference. If, on the other hand, class was conceptualised in terms of relationships of production, workers and peasants would constitute quite distinctive social classes. Of course, such a conceptualisation must involve a conception of society as involving socioeconomic groups in conflict, with language becoming a source of struggle. Yet if we are to recognise the relationship between language groups and social classes there is no reason why such an analysis cannot be undertaken. This being the case it would appear that Gal has systematically chosen the consensus orientation which she has adopted, unless the possibility of class analysis has been overlooked.

Despite Gal's claim for theoretical innovation in her work what we have in this study is little different from the work of those whom she criticises. This should not be surprising given the overall theoretical perspective from which the study derives. Indeed, some ten years after publication the work appears remarkably outdated and it is clear that criticisms of sociological theory, current at the time of the study, were not considered in its implementation.

What we have is the modernisation thesis involving a peasant–industrial or traditional–urban continuum. Within this thesis the class dimension is continuously played down while culture as way of life becomes an explanatory force. The undeniable forces of industrialisation as inevitable progress are claimed to intrude on the integral integrity of a peasant tradition. Two separate value systems, presumably deriving from different cultural traditions, are merged into one as a consequence of industrialisation. What remains is the residual of the dichotomy, with the deviant, who is conversant with both value traditions, selectively delving into one and the other. The dominance of the modern, industrial, society obliges a change in the normative structure, a change that becomes possible through the assumption of a common value system which leads to a consensus *vis-à-vis* the normative, since norms are held to be expressions of values. Language shift becomes a smooth adoption of consensus marred only by the few who stick resolutely and irrationally to 'tradition'. Associated with this traditional–modern continuum is the inevitable relationship to role structure, the claim being made that role relationships constrain speech forms within the process of rational choice, and, since industrialisation leads to change in role relationships, ethnographic work is essential in order to discover how this occurs.

Within such a vision of society the emphasis is, inevitably, on the individual as rational actor. The rationality is based upon the constant striving for social status through consumption in its symbolic form. A failure to strive for such status must therefore be seen as irrational and traditional and, as a consequence, the retention of the minority language must also be seen as irrational.

Conflict and struggle are systematically excluded from such an argument. Despite an awareness that the social networks which

Gal makes the focus of her study could well be replaced in terms of composition by an analysis in terms of diametrically opposed social classes or language groups, these dimensions are peripheral to the study. Indeed when social class is discussed it is in terms of social status and occupation – the technical aspects of class, rather than in terms of relations of production or groups locked in struggle over economic resources. Similarly, language groups are not conceived of as social groups but rather as aggregates of individuals in interaction, albeit individuals who share a sense of identity.

The inevitability of the transition from tradition to modernity implicit in the continuum means that features of each end of the continuum are subject to a similar inevitability of change with reference to direction. While the traditional must bow to the modern so also Hungarian must bow to German, however, unfortunate this may be. Its demise is a feature of evolution. This is despite the citing of evidence for the manner in which political change can reverse the process of language shift.

Within the analysis the state is presented as benign and neither German nor Hungarian are seen as state languages, a feature which would clarify the power aspect of the dominant–minority language group relationship. Indeed the Austrian state is portrayed as paternalistically benevolent in its protection of privileges through law – the state becomes a manifestation of the will of the people. Under such circumstances it is inconceivable that the state can be seen as an arm of oppression, even in terms of its language policies, either in conspiratorial or non-conspiratorial terms. Yet Gal is unambiguous in her historical account of the manner in which the relative status of German and Hungarian as dominant and minority languages depends upon their respective roles as state languages. Clearly a conception of the state as an oppressive force is incompatible with the view of the role of the individual as a free agent exercising rational choice.

In short, despite Gal's claims to the contrary, there is little that is new or different in her study. It retains the basic assumptions of structural functionalism. Consequently, it fails to see language shift as part of a struggle over language.

CONCLUSION

In this chapter I have argued that the main orientations in the study of language contact have tended to involve typologies and perspectives which set great limitations upon what can be said about the inherent conflict between language groups that is a feature of language contact.

The work of Ferguson and Fishman, in the form of the concepts of domain and diglossia, have become axiomatic in the sociology of language, when, in my view, they tend to be more of a hindrance than a help in analysing language contact. They both express an evolutionary continuum which depends upon highly questionable assumptions about the nature of modernity, tradition and progress. Within this expression about the nature and direction of social change there is a highly conservative orientation which is embedded in the various concepts. This has the consequence of marginalising the minority languages while also making it virtually impossible to express the anger and frustration experienced by members of minority language groups confronted by the process of language shift. The main reason for this is that the perspective adopted by most writers on this issue is inherently consensual in nature and plays down conflict while ignoring power.

When we do consider a characteristic study of one of the types of language situations in Fishman's typology we find a reassertion of the emphasis upon rational choice associated with the discourse of individual liberalism. Such a perspective involves the projection of language contact through language shift to 'language death'. Rationality and bilingualism are incompatible.

Furthermore, the problem of explaining the persistence of non-optimising behaviour which we encountered in Labov's work re-emerges, and is explained away as an aberration. This emphasis upon the contrast between language choice, seen in terms of a rationalism involving economically motivated individual social mobility, and a language choice which rejects this rationality re-emerges again in chapter 8 when we consider the work on social networks. In the meantime I would like to consider the applied aspect of language contact under the heading of language planning.

5   Language planning

LANGUAGE MODERNISATION

Shortly after the second world war the ideas of Parsonian structural functionalism were put into operation in a variety of applied contexts associated with what became known as modernisation. It was an exercise in systematic social scientific engineering whose objective was a form of social evolution. It was argued that the reasons for the lack of economic development in the non-western world derived from the absence of the cultural and social features which were evident in the 'modernised countries', and that if a systematic programme of social and cultural change was applied then economic development would result. Manicas (1988:85–6) has pointed out how this represents a rationalisation of imperialism in the name of 'modernisation' masked as scientific neutrality. As such it is the converse of Herder's rejection of Eurocentrism in the philosophy of evolutionism and progress that rests in his claim that all nations are important, a view expressed in his linguistic patriotism. Yet it is from this climate that language planning appeared as the practical side of the linguistic endeavour. Clearly what passes as language planning is not that new and, as we shall see, the idea that language can be planned has a long history. However, its emergence as an academic subdiscipline of some force derives from the past thirty years. Its objective was to influence directly the various social and cultural factors which were held to influence language change. Clearly what language planners seek to do will therefore derive largely from how they perceive language change. It is here that sociological theory becomes important, since the understanding of how and why language changes must, in the end, be influenced by the theory that informs such an understanding. Yet most planners involved with language planning have seen their task as ideologically neutral, whereas the politicisation of language in multilingual settings has increasingly drawn attention to the relationship between language planning and wider political issues.

Language planning tends to be divided into two streams – status planning and corpus planning, the first involving an understanding of how social factors relate to language in terms of status, while the second is associated with the linguistic features of a language, mainly in relation to some form of standardisation of one variety over another. I will try to show that there is no need to treat these two aspects of language planning separately since there is a direct link between language status and language corpus. First, however, I would like to consider the conventional approach to both aspects of language planning.

The idea of language status presents a problem in that there is a tendency to reify language, claiming that status derives from the language itself rather than from those who use that language or language variety. When we consider the concept of status one thing is evident – the tendency to interchange the two concepts 'prestige' and 'status'. Furthermore status is a relative and comparative concept and therefore any reference to status planning in language terms must involve reference to more than a single language or language variety. This much was evident in the early discussion of language planning.

As I have already indicated, language planning emerged side by side with the theory of modernisation which not only was closely integrated with a specific theoretical perspective – structural functionalism – but also involved a specific conception of the world. This world view involved dividing states into the modern and the traditional. A typology of states was established by resorting to the various features of 'modern', invariably the features of the western states to which the sociologist or anthropologist belonged, and asserting that those which did not have these features must, as a consequence, be 'traditional'. Language was included among these features and there emerged a discussion of language in terms of degrees of modernity. Often language was regarded as an aspect of culture, something that was divisible into high and low culture. Thus for many of the early, and not so early, practitioners of language planning, languages were subject to modernisation, involving

> being consciously expanded in vocabulary and standardised in spelling and grammar so that they can increasingly function as the exclusive language of government and of higher culture and technology.
>
> (J.A. Fishman 1974:1630)

Recently Eastman (1983:31) has described this as 'languages . . .

seeking entry into the modern world'. This patronising attitude towards the languages of the 'traditional' societies was denied in the argument that modernisation was an altruistic approach which sought to present the benefits of economic development to the less fortunate, a view which, in sociology, was to be shattered by the criticism from the so-called dependency theorists but which has yet to penetrate the field of language planning. The 'modern' which Eastman referred to was not a temporal meaning since both it and its converse exist at the same moment in time, but rather it was a 'modern' in terms of the difference between the social, cultural, political and economic features of one state *vis-à-vis* another.

Implicit in this drive for modernisation is a faith in communication and in English as the 'language of wider communication' as it is called. Again I turn to Eastman:

> For economic development to take place, it is necessary to set up a type of 'linguistic infrastructure', so that in areas where many vernacular languages are in use a 'common language of wider communication' is also available.
>
> (Eastman 1983:66)

This is akin to the search for a form of communication which can transcend impure thought and reasoning which we encountered in the opening chapter. The thinking associated with the link between ideas about economic modernisation and language are expressed by Eastman (1983:117) as follows:

> it also became clear that languages that are to be politically sanctioned in the interest of development need to be purified, reformed and modernised in order to keep pace with the nation's development.

That is, although 'modernisation' may precede language 'development' the two are inherently related and, presumably, a 'developed'. language can be adopted as a language of wider communication in place of the impure 'native' form! Evidently these views on society, world development and language carry in them the ethnocentrism that was so evident in nineteenth-century thought on the same issues.

The sociological theme of modernisation is also evident in another respect. Lambert (1967) argued that there were instrumental and integrative motives for second language learning. The former involved those who learnt the second language in order to seek pecuniary gain whereas the latter were involved in the goal for social or cultural integration. The two are regarded as incompatible, that is, language motives cannot be seen as drawing upon integration in order to seek pecuniary advantage. This is merely another expression of the Durkheimian principle of mechanical and organic solidarity, with the individual becoming increasingly important with the increase in the division of labour associated with economic 'development'. The literature of the 1950s and 1960s is full of such manifestations of the predominant perspective on society of that period. Subsequently they became uncritically adopted as the basic principles upon which subsequent developments in LP should be built.

Perhaps the most explicit expression of this argument is to be found in Fishman's study of the correlation between economic wealth and states which are linguistically homogeneous or heterogeneous (J.A. Fishman 1968). The assumption is made that economic development is rendered more possible in ethnically homogeneous states. Thus states which lack ethnic, religious, class and linguistic variation, are held to be economically more successful than those in which the converse is true. The reasoning behind this argument is that communication facilitates economic development and that a single language facilitates communication. Similarly the other features of heterogeneity – religion, social class, and ethnicity – are held to generate conflict which hinders 'progress'. These assumptions tend to be uncritically adopted and often derive from an inductive approach in which the link between homogeneity/heterogeneity and some measure of economic 'development' is established and the features of homogeneity then explained within the terms of this correlation. Reminiscent of Parsons' discussion of evolution, J.A. Fishman (1968:60) claims that linguistic homogeneity tends to characterise states that are 'economically more developed, educationally more advanced, politically more modernised, and ideologically-politically more tranquil and stable'. That is, more like his own USA. This is consolidated in his claim that homogeneity also characterises

> the state in which primordial ties and passions are more likely to be under control, cultural–religious homogeneity and enlightenment are advanced . . . and in which the good life is economically within the reach of a greater proportion of the populace.
>
> (J.A. Fishman 1968:60)

A clearer expression of the nineteenth-century view of social order, and the shift from the organic solidarity of the primordial society to the mechanical solidarity of the 'modern' state, together with the bias associated with such a view, could not be desired. The failure to realise that the correlations which he has established merely display an empirical relationship and do not explain that relationship accounts for the nature of the conclusions at which he arrives.

Thus if we are to achieve the good life then we should eliminate, or marginalise, among other things, all but the language of wider communication since economic growth is best achieved within monolingual states. Any subsequent argument in favour of bi- or multilingualism must be seen as a concession and even as a sacrifice! This argument appears to have become dogma among language planners, having become associated with the claim that communication between, and within, states encourages group cooperation and is therefore an inherent good, with the interests behind such a conception of commonality remaining unspecified. The vehicle for such communication is a single language, which is depoliticised by being referred to as the language of wider communication rather than as the specific dominant language. Furthermore, this occurs within a world system based upon a conservative conception of equality, with equal states competing on an equal basis within a world economic order.

The criticisms levelled against the modernisation theory within sociology and economics during the late 1960s had quite a different conception of the world order. Needless to say they have not been taken on board by the proponents of LP. It was argued that the lack of what was referred to as economic 'development' derived not from the absence of western traits or homogeneity but rather from the exploitative nature of the relationship between the dominant, economically developed states and the subordinate underdeveloped states. As a consequence of this dominance the latter lacked the power to determine their own destiny. Within this perspective it requires only a little imagination to realise that what is labelled the 'language of wider communication' is little more than an agency of ideological control which facilitates world domination. It also leads to an awareness that all social systems exist within the same temporal framework and that the variations of these social systems is a consequence of integration, rather than of temporarily disassociated stages in some abstract 'developmental' process, as the modernisation thesis maintains. As a consequence the dichotomous referents of modern/traditional, advanced/traditional and even rural/urban are merely ideological supports for the modernisation thesis and, as such, have to be discarded, together with the associated typological constructs. This is as true of language as of any other societal feature – languages are not in need of modernisation any more than difference can be conceptualised in terms of modern/non-modern.

Equally conservative and utopian is the belief that: 'something could be done to language to avoid or solve language-related social and political problems' (Eastman 1983:108). This is the kind of reasoning that derived from an awareness that the pattern of language use correlated with behaviour and context. It served to displace the political nature of social and cultural problems and to replace it with a reified conception of language. It was merely another expression of the theological faith in behavioural study as science, a science which, in being objective, excused the investigator from investigating his/her own involvement. This is clearly expressed in an introduction to a recent book on language planning by Cobarrubias (1983:6):

> It is understandable that language-planning issues relate to value judgments. However, a theory of language planning qua theory, has to take a stand on value judgment. . . . Although theories may show different forms of theoretical and methodological commitment, no theory, to my knowledge takes, as part of its own task, a stand on value judgments.

He proceeds to state 'we should not saddle the theory with ideological considerations'. While arguing that a theory of language planning *per se* is not possible the debate in this chapter is firmly based upon the recognition of the ideological nature of theory.

What we have in LP as it developed and, indeed, as it now stands, is an expression of the evolutionary theme of modernisation. Languages are dichotomised into modern/non-modern, European/non-European and developed/less developed. Modernisation theory is invoked to legitimise this procedure by dividing the social and cultural world into civilised/barbarian, modern/traditional, Great Tradition/Little Tradition. The most important of the diacritica of such a typology are literacy and writing, and what is referred to as graphisation is essential before a language can be 'modernised'. Thus one of the functions of literacy involves the ability to denigrate the illiterate! This is a clear expression of the Parsonian thought on evolutionism and its relationship to language.

PLANNING, SOCIAL POLICY AND LANGUAGE

What is suggested in the preceding discussion is that the prevailing philosophies of the dominant states pass as objective reasoning associated with theory. It is not surprising therefore that language planners are accused by members of minority language groups of merely serving the interests of the state and thereby being agents of sociopolitical dominance. They are told that it is only by changing their language or, indeed, other aspects of their culture, to the point where it resembles the 'modern' that they can escape the pejorative connotation of being 'traditional', and in so doing, of course, they cease to exist. The ideological or hegemonic nature of this argument should be clear.

Planning is an integral feature of policy in the sense that its function is to seek to formulate and/or administer policy. It is also important to realise that policy is the product of social and political factors, even though the orthodox philosophy views policy as action on behalf of, rather than in the interest of, the public body or society. Thus it is evident that policy involves policing on the one hand and politics on the other (Corrigan and Corrigan 1979). It is also clear that planning and policy relate to the state while having a direct influence on civil society. This, in turn, leads to an awareness of political power, function, interests and social change and to ignore these factors is tantamount to treating a lack of policy as policy.

Within the contemporary state conformity is achieved through legitimising the state and its power. This is achieved through the process of separating the individual from the law in such a way that within political relations individuals obey the law rather than one another. Although law is the product of the state the two tend to be related through what is referred to as 'the public democratic process' which, together with individual liberalism, is a central element in the process of legitimising the state. It is consolidated through the relationship that exists between the concept of the citizen as one who obeys the law on the one hand, and the idea of 'democratic country' on the other, with the individual being portrayed as part of the state through his/her rights to participate in the political process as 'free' individuals. The concept of individual is lent meaning within law by implying that individual rights, obligations and functions constitute the very nature of the relationship between the individual and the state. No reference is made to group rights. Furthermore, these rights, obligations and functions are presented in terms of the state's authority over the individual. On the other hand, the citizen holds rights within public life that cannot be trespassed upon by the state's institutions. Thus it would appear that the citizen is independent of the state while contributing to its order.

It should be evident how the philosophy of individual liberalism is an important ingredient of state legitimacy. As such it has served as the basis for the predominant theory in those disciplines which purport to 'explain' the nature of society. It is this individual liberalism which has been to the forefront in the modernisation thesis as criticised above. Evidently a contrasting argument must bring the state to the forefront rather than leaving it as a neutral entity which, as a consequence, appears to be more of an onlooker than an active participant.

There is also room to be sceptical about the suggestion that one feature of LP involves the state's desire to sustain minority languages (Apple and Muysken 1987). Certainly there is a limit to which this can be true and I would be very sceptical of any suggestion that a state voluntarily adopts such an altruistic attitude towards minority languages within its territory. The tendency is for such activity to involve concessions deriving from a protracted struggle.

When we do encounter discussions of LP within a single state we find the same theme as that identified with reference to a conception of the world order. There is an unquestioned equation of the state with the nation. The nation is, in turn, presented as undifferentiated and united, with a 'national language' existing to serve the entire population of that state. Nation is counterposed with region in the characteristic state discourse which refutes minority nationalism, this merely revealing the shared interests of LP and the state. This being the case, it is difficult to envisage LP as serving the interests of the minority language group or, at best, it can do so only insofar as the state or dominant language is not challenged. The minority cannot be seen to be gaining at the expense of the totality which the state represents. The unity of the state and its citizens is threatened by the very existence of a medium of communication which is not universal and the resultant conflict potential is seen to derive from linguistic rather than economic differentiation. This displacement of the economic or material base as an explanatory phenomenon is, of course, the ingredient of most conservative perspectives on society. Within the state the citizen is presented as an unconstrained actor operating as a rational being which means that any resistance to the process of unification through linguistic unification is undeniably irrational. As a consequence it is not surprising that LP is presented as a means of alleviating oppression and subordination much in the same way as the 'progress' of the modernisation thesis is presented in the economic model. There is an implicit assumption that the benevolence of the state permits members of the minority language group to attain the prerequisites of upward social mobility as well as both economic and social integration with the wider society, thereby reducing discrimination based upon language while simultaneously guaranteeing altruistic responses on the part of the state to the demands of the minority. The net result is that, rather than being discriminated against by the dominant society, the boundary is created by the members of the minority language group's tendency towards self-categorisation. Thus, for example, Allardt (1979) implies that the shift from 'tradition' to 'modern' generates psychological needs which cannot be met by modern society and that the diacritica of ethnicity, including language, are heightened in order to compensate for the loss of primordial attachments which, hitherto, were the hallmarks of 'traditional' society. Implicitly, the only social boundaries which exist in 'modern' society are those created by the actors rather than those which are imposed! It is difficult to accept that the relationship between power structures and psychological correlates are this simple, there being no indication as to why a shift should occur except that it is a consequence of the change from tradition to modernity. Again the teleological nature of the argument is evident. Of course, the claim that increased integration through education and the associated 'opportunity', together with the picture of an open society, is part of the consensus denial of the role of institutions in the perpetuation of discrimination. Rather, opportunity, being presented as the prerogative of the gifted or striving individual, simply denies the existence of structurally persistent inequalities.

Concentrating on the power and control implications of majority–minority relationships raises critical issues regarding viewing language or culture – or both – as the handicap(s) which impair individual mobility. The tautology of 'explaining' the concept of minority, within the context of its subordination, by the failure of individual members of the minority to achieve because of the 'disadvantage' of their knowledge of the minority language and/or culture, is then brought into focus. Inequality is explained in culturist terms of language rather than being viewed as related to social structure. If inequality is culturally derived, then it is hardly surprising that the egalitarian thrust of liberalism should seek to alleviate this inequality via programmes of cultural compensation and the associated education schemes. It is through the agency of such programmes that minority group members are 'educated' to a standard sufficient to enable them to interact with dominant group members and thus reap the 'benefits' of being a dominant language speaker. The evaluative assumption of the inferiority of minority languages, and thus of minority language speakers, is clear.

The fallacy of this argument is demonstrable on three grounds. We should recognise first, that social mobility within capitalism is in itself ideological, focusing as it does on the individual without changing the social structure; second that education is part of the process whereby the social structure is reproduced; and third, that minorities are defined by reference to their lack of power, which is a corollary of their generalised low position within the cultural division of labour. Consequently, bilingual education will inevitably be seen as a means whereby the minority is functionally integrated into the system of production without presenting any threat to the state and its system of domination. Individual mobility is simply a meaningless by-product, albeit one which has tremendous ideological potential.

The conventional view of minority problems reflects the ideological position of the power-holders in society – a position characterised by the minority language, which thus implicitly entails a denigration of the minority language in order to legitimise the institutionalisation of the majority–minority power relationship. This position also results in the problem being viewed as the prerogative of a uniform minority, and its solution the responsibility of the individual. However, it does not preclude the minority being allocated 'rights' within a liberal democracy, since these may serve to guarantee the power of the majority insofar as the concessions granted to the minority do not threaten this power. Such rights are granted by the power-holders, whose power is thereby confirmed. An associated concept is that of 'discrimination' which conveys the impression of an unfair condition of inequality and implies the existence of some abstract form of rights within a democratic framework. It also suggests the existence of a preconceived plan constructed by some unspecified force. If we accept that discrimination in this sense is a manifestation of the power relationship between dominant and subordinate language groups, then any rights associated with it are themselves ideological – being part of the process of language planning conducted by power holders on behalf of the minority. The problem is expropriated from those to whom it is claimed to pertain. It is within this context that a discussion of LP should be located.

It is difficult to accept an argument which suggests that the state willingly and ungrudgingly responds to the demands of the minority. It is naïve for sociologists such as Allardt (1979) to assert that such a response involves the power-holders asking themselves whether or not 'granting recognition to the minority will serve to improve their living conditions' if, as he implies, the conflict between minority and majority involves a conflict over resources. Given the nature of the hegemony of the dominant group, one does not need a conspiratorial theory to recognise that the dominant group is unlikely to subscribe to enhancing the situation of the minority without, simultaneously, guaranteeing or strengthening its own position. If the state is so benevolent, and if boundaries are not imposed but created, it is difficult to envisage why minority language groups persist. Experience clearly shows that concessions to minority language groups on the part of the state are the result of long, protracted struggles on the part of the minorities, these concessions being relatively small compared both with the needs of the situation and the amount of energy expended in the struggle. Furthermore, even where such concessions are made, one has the sneaking suspicion that they involve strengthening rather than weakening state control over language and ideological production and reproduction.

I do not wish to consider in detail the manner in which ideology is produced in and through language and how this particular perspective serves to eliminate the criticism of ideology as conspiratorial (see G. Williams 1988a). However, there is a need to emphasise that the expropriation of LP away from the community to the state is by no means ideologically neutral. The survival of minority languages invariably depends not upon some abstract process of 'modernisation' involving linguistic exercises, but rather upon the ability to shift the language into new domains of language activity. This involves not displacing the dominant language, such a process being inconceivable in most situations, but rather striving to establish some semblance of coexistence. This invariably involves reinstitutionalising and relegitimising the domain context of the minority language. Such processes invariably rely upon the support of the state and what passes as LP is a feature of such support. While, on the one hand, this domain extension can serve to enhance the status of the minority language, it does so at a cost in that the very institutions which are largely responsible for the reproduction and production of that language are increasingly within state control as opposed to the control of the community. In some cases there is an explicit control on what can and must be said within these agencies of language production and reproduction. More often the process of state control is much more subtle, involving ideological processes beyond the control and knowledge of the rational actor. None the less its effect is profound and it leaves the minority language group with the choice between the survival of its language and the survival of its culture, the latter being seen as the conception of the world conditioned by ideological forces.

It is at this point that I wish to move to a consideration of corpus planning. However, before so doing I would like to make one or two concluding remarks about status planning. It should be evident that I wish to see several changes in the orientation of language planners and that these changes involve a shift from viewing the situation from the perspective of those who activate LP to that of those who are the subjects of such activation – a shift from the perspective of the state to that of the minority language community. The commitment to the antidotal effect of communication must be questioned. Surely the research which has thus far been conducted into language and society indicates that a shared language is accompanied by social division rather than integration. This, of course, is what is to be expected if we recognise that language is merely one feature of an internally divided socioeconomic order. No extent of communication will alleviate the social differentiation which derives from the economic order. On the contrary, it will merely facilitate and extend that differentiation. Most of those who write about LP seem to be blind to this issue. Such a blindness must be an issue of central concern.

Two of the most evident aspects of status planning, those aspects which are self-evidently most effective in increasing the status of a language are legislation, and the domain extension of the language, especially into the world of work. Again these are not mutually exclusive processes for the state can legislate in such a way that the domain extension of the minority language is the consequence – it is axiomatic that the state language will already exist in all domains of activity. In the remainder of this discussion of status planning I would like to consider these two processes and to suggest that both have consequences which can be detrimental to the minority language.

An example of an attempt to legislate with reference to a minority language is the Welsh Language Act of 1967 (G. Williams 1987). There are one or two immediate points which have to be emphasised. First, that this Act was, in some respects, the consequence of a struggle on the part of members of the minority language group and that, in this respect, the government of the time was responding to this struggle. However, the extent to which this involved a 'concession' on the part of the government and the state was extremely limited. Of course the official discourse involves the assumption that concessions to minority groups are possible and even desirable but only insofar as they do not prejudice the nature of the dominant/minority relationship. Furthermore the manner in which such concessions are granted are based not upon any conception of group rights since this would contradict the fundamental nature of the individual liberalism of the legal system, but rather on the basis of the 'rights' of individuals without reference to their group affiliation. Yet there must be an implicit reference to group since language is one means whereby group boundaries are highlighted. Thus, within this particular constitutional context, the state is obliged to legislate in a manner which does not challenge the rights of the dominant language group while also making the individual rather than the group the point of reference. This is the manner in which the discourse of politics determines what can and must be said within legislation. The manner in which these objectives are achieved within the British state involves legislating English as the language both of the state and of the community (Williams 1988a) while, simultaneously, ensuring that any legislation relevant to Welsh, or indeed any language other than English, does not trespass into areas which can in any way diminish the effectiveness of English as the language of power within the context of individual behaviour. In effect, legislation within the context of the Welsh Language Act involved the legitimation of Welsh as a minority language and in this respect there is a strong argument that having no status was preferable to being granted the status of a minority language within Wales. Furthermore, by ensuring that English is both the language of the state and the language of the community, in the latter sense being no different from any other language used within the state's territory, the state makes a knowledge of English inevitable while simultaneously respecting the 'democratic' principle within which English is subject to the same constraints as any other language *vis-à-vis* individual behaviour. This seemingly contradictory position is what has the effect of making English appear to be subject to the constraints affecting all minority language speakers while ensuring that power, even within Wales, is firmly located in the dominant language group of which, of course, everyone must be a member!

It should be evident from what has been said above that the most important feature of status is the economic and that this feature of social status which pertains to individual attributes – esteem – is relatively insignificant from a sociological perspective. It should also be evident that the relationship between dominant and subordinate language groups relates to the extent to which the respective languages exist within different domains of activity. Furthermore, it is no simple matter to extend a minority or subordinate language into new domains of activity. This is not merely because of the behavioural tendencies of individual bilinguals or multilinguals as many sociolinguists would claim but rather because of the manner in which languages are institutionalised and legitimised *vis-à-vis* domains. It has recently been claimed that:

whether and how a language gains legitimacy, and how language plan or policy may serve other political ends, can only be understood in terms of the interlocking imperatives of the economic, political and sociocultural systems. In order to gain legitimacy, or mass loyalty, acceptance and actual use, a language must indeed have apparent value and use within the cultural traditions of the latter sphere: it must serve a political structure; and it must be congruent with the economic imperatives of the economic system in question.

(Luke, McHoul and May, forthcoming)

Evidently to reconstitute the domain context of a minority language is no simple matter once the power ingredients of language group relationships are recognised, and it must involve struggle, a struggle over language. This is particularly true of the world of work within the liberal democracies which claim to operate on the basis of equal opportunity and individual excellence (G. Williams 1987). It is the distinction between work and non-work languages which is the most significant aspect of the difference between state and community languages referred to above.

It is no coincidence that the class varieties of minority languages are far less developed than those of the dominant languages. It is my claim that this derives from the contrasting domain contexts of the production and reproduction of the respective languages. Being constrained, the minority languages tend not to be related to the very institutions which are responsible for social reproduction, particularly the economic domain and more specifically the world of work. In contrast, these languages tend to be produced and reproduced within contexts which cut across class lines and the context of their production and reproduction relates more to status-group rather than class contexts. If this is the case then the extension and reconstitution of minority languages in what are, for them, new domains, will have consequences for varieties of that language, that is, for the corpus of the language.

CORPUS PLANNING

The tendency to separate status and corpus planning derives from the work of Kloss (1969) and this false dichotomy has tended to be universally adopted by those involved in LP. It leads to a failure to discuss the inherent relationship between the two issues. This weakness is partly a consequence of viewing language change as a natural phenomenon on the one hand, and of the adoption of a specific area of sociological theory to account for linguistic change on the other. The relevant theory derives from Durkheimian evolutionism within which 'modernisation' is exemplified by urbanisation, industrialisation and associated diacritica. This process of modernisation involves a shift from mechanical to organic solidarity involving increasing social complexity which is reflected in linguistic diversity. Thus the relative lack of linguistic diversity of minority languages inevitably relegates them to a position outside of 'modern'. Furthermore the relationship between evolutionism, racism and language-group relations has an air of inevitability about it. It leads to the claim that change is 'natural' and that linguistic diversity is an essential correlate of a natural social development devoid of human agency – it is the consequence of 'progress'. It is this kind of argument which leads to the implication that a language can be 'modernised' by tampering with its corpus.

The most evident feature of the reconstitution of the domain context of minority language relates not merely to the status of that language but also to its prestige. Rubin (1968) drawing upon the earlier work of Weinreich (1963), refers to language prestige as the relative value of one language over another in social advancement. She maintains that

> the more difficult it is to move from one social class to another, the more significant the association between language and social class will be and the greater the prestige of one of the languages.
>
> (Rubin 1968:7)

This conceptualisation of language prestige has become widely accepted and therefore obliges us to distinguish it from language status even though it does, clearly, influence language status.

However, it is necessary to realise that with reference to any language not all forms are of equal prestige. Thus, within a dominant language, class varieties carry different degrees of prestige. Similarly, the domain extension of a minority language, when associated with increased prestige for that language, does not necessarily mean that this prestige value is open to all speakers of the minority language. It is here perhaps that the struggle within language becomes most evident. If the value of the minority language for social mobility relates merely to one economic sector, or to a single class or class fraction, then there is a danger that language will become a feature of class struggle as opposed to language group struggle – the emphasis shifts from a struggle over language to a struggle in language. While increased prestige seems to be an essential prerequisite of increasing the status of a minority language it can lead to factionalism within the minority language group and the scene of the struggle shifts.

The phenomenon which is often associated with such developments is that of language purity. It is here that we are obliged to address the one feature which tends to be the cornerstone of the discussion of corpus planning – language standardisation. Eastman (1983:153) states: 'Language planning is defined by many scholars almost exclusively as standardisation.' In some respects the standard form of a language holds the same position with reference to corpus planning as the language of wider communication holds with reference to status planning and with similar political connotations. It is argued that in order for a language to be 'modernised' it must develop a writing system – graphisation. In order that it can be employed in formal universal education, it must be modernised that is it must be subject to 'the development of expanded vocabulary and ways to communicate "about contemporary civilisation" so that the language can be used in all necessary situations' (Eastman 1983:71 referring to Karam 1974:114), and standardised in order that it becomes 'a common form of language that speakers of varying dialects learn to read and write both formally and informally' (Eastman 1983:71). Once again it is evident that the debate hinges upon the evolutionary theme and that judgement is passed upon one language or language form *vis-à-vis* another.

The preceding reference to dialect suggests that the function of a standard language is to overcome the 'hindrance of dialects'. This reflects the manner in which the discussion of standard/non-standard has derived from dialectology. The shift away from a preoccupation with the spatial mapping of lexical items in order to demonstrate the existence of regional dialects has given way to a preoccupation with linguistic variation associated with social rather than spatial phenomenon. Francis (1983:195) claims that the most relevant work with reference to dialectology is that which systematically describes linguistic variation and its significance for language structure and language change. This emphasis upon description as opposed to explanation is reflected in the methodological approach which tends to be inductive, involving as it does a search for social and spatial patterns before resorting to some theoretical framework in order to 'explain' these patterns. The tendency is to establish patterns through correlation between speech patterns on the one hand, and social categories on the other. We have already discussed the limitations of this methodology. The new orientation of social dialectology has involved a preoccupation with the relationship between speech pattern, geographic location and social class and gender above all else. The predominant polarisation involves the contrast between standard and dialect forms.

It would appear that the definition of the standard is a simple matter in that it is what regional dialect is not. Yet it seems that things are not this simple. Trudgill (1984:32) who, among sociolinguists, has contributed most to this area of study, gives the following definition of Standard English (SE) as 'typically used in speech and writing by educated or highly educated . . . native speakers'. It seems that the defining criteria are being a native speaker and having been exposed to formal education. Yet there is no reference to what role education plays in standardisation and if, as suggested above, societal features are central to any understanding of the difference between SE and regional dialects then this definition is inadequate if only because of its lack of reference to the social. On the other hand, education may be an indicator of social class and/or social status. If this is the case then it locates the definition within a particular theoretical perspective on inequality. Having thus established a definition all that remains is for Trudgill to establish what kind of language is spoken by 'educated or highly educated . . . native speakers' and SE is established.

On the other hand, Cheshire (1984:546) is more specific in her discussion of SE stating:

> The term 'nonstandard accent' is used here to refer to a regional pronunciation of 'General English' . . . it refers, that is to say, to an accent that is NOT Received Pronunciation.

That is, oral SE is RP. This seems to be a step forward in the sense that it is a definition which identifies linguistic features which are known to correlate with social class, that is, even though the definition purports to be a linguistic definition it is simultaneously a definition of social dialect.

Cheshire here seems to be focusing exclusively upon an oral standard whereas Trudgill's definition involves both oral and written forms of language. The written standard or Standard English as it is often referred to involves lexis and grammar whereas the oral standard also involves accent. The distinction between the written and oral standard is encapsulated in the following statement:

> Accent and dialect are words which are often used vaguely, but which can be given more precision by taking the first to refer to characteristics of the medium (i.e. speech) only, while the second refers to characteristics of language as well.
>
> (Abercrombie 1967:19)

For this reason alone it is necessary to distinguish between written and oral standard. In addition of course the processes of institutionalisation and legitimisation of each will be different even though there may be similarities within the relative processes. The legitimisation of the written standard is much more clear cut in that it relies heavily upon dictionaries and grammars to a far greater extent than is the case for the oral standard. Furthermore the agencies of this legitimisation, involving education and the media among other agencies, are also more formal in nature than are the agencies of legitimisation of the oral standard which tends to be legitimised as a consequence of its relationship to the social class of those who use that standard. It is generally claimed that the speech style of the dominant class is reproduced and diffused through normativisiation and here again the media is of central importance (Dittmar 1976, P.M. Fishman 1978). However, this view is misleading, not only because it is normative rather than descriptive or analytical, but also because it ignores the political dimension of such a process. I shall return to this issue later, but for the moment let us return to a discussion of the nature of the oral standard.

We have reached the point of establishing that the oral standard is the speech of the dominant class – in RP Britain. Gimson refers to RP as 'a form of pronunciation that has been considered more correct, desirable, acceptable or elegant than others' (1984:45). Yet he also states that it is no longer possible to define RP by analysing the speech of an appropriate sample of 'well bred (preferably upper class) Londoner(s) educated at a public school' (1984:46). This confused and indirect reference to the social aspect of RP is followed by an attempt to define RP, not in social but in linguistic terms: 'The description thus arrived at will constitute a definition of RP without reference to social class or education' (1984:48), as if this were a desirable achievement! It is this uncomfortable relationship between sociolinguists and sociology that is so disturbing in the field at large.

It seems that the oral standard relies largely upon accent but that it is also accompanied by the lexis and grammar of the written standard. In this sense it is the written standard with an added ingredient and therefore it must involve something in addition to the institutionalisation and legitimisation of the written standard. That is, the oral standard assumes the existence of the written standard as the prerequisite of its existence. Trudgill (1984) claims that it is restricted to a limited number of speakers, the majority of whom occupy upper-class places. Furthermore, within these upper-class places these speakers occupy places which reflect considerable power within key institutions. The reasons for this are not difficult to find once we recognise that social mobility into this class fraction is limited, and membership, as a consequence, is not only hereditary but is also related to specific educational processes and establishments. That is, RP seems to be reproduced through the family which tends to be endogamous with reference to class, through the public schools and allied educational spheres where the peer group is an important agency of legitimisation. It is the manner in which it is produced and reproduced which explains the other marked feature of RP – its universal nature in terms of not being restricted to any specific geographic location or region. In this sense, it reflects a part of society which, while it is universal in geographic terms, is simultaneously restricted and in that sense it constitutes the speech of a fraction of the ruling class within the British state. As such it serves as the only oral standard against which all other speech varieties are measured.

The preceding discussion has tended to treat the standard in static terms. It is, of course, essential to recognise that society is not a static entity, and if the central assumption of sociolinguistics is that the social is never absent in either speech or language, then the social dynamic will involve speech dynamics including the dynamic nature of the standard. This may involve changes in the extent of the RP or even a reassessment of what constitutes a standard. Trudgill (1984:43) states:

> judgment about what is standard and what is not have changed and are changing just as notions about what is BRITISH English (rather than North American English) have changed to keep up with the developing situation, and just as the linguistic forms themselves change.

However, this statement is devoid of agency and 'developing situation' is hardly sociologically explanatory. Indeed sociolinguists appear to be unable to handle any discussion of social change even if it is so important to their central concern. While recognising the importance of social change it is also the case that the power structure of society is the most resistant to such change. Indeed it can be claimed that social change operates quite effectively in preserving the nature of the power structure. Furthermore, the legitimisation process relates to this persistence since, in the long run, it is power and domination that are legitimised and other aspects of social change, including the changing class structure, can well be seen as an integral part of this legitimisation insofar as it does not redress the location of power.

An important agency of legitimisation of SE is the mass media which simultaneously operate as an ideological force and play an important role in language standardisation. Leitner (1980) has discussed this role in some detail. He states: 'State or party-political influence over the BBC has always been minimal', a claim which ignores the hegemonic effect of the state which serves to obscure its role while also making any discussion of the issue difficult by appearing to confuse the difference between government and state. He proceeds to assert: 'But . . . the BBC has been under a strong social-class influence', which merely emphasises the role of the state. The early objective of the media was to educate and to propagate 'high culture' (Smith 1974), including the cultivation of 'good' language. At first this involved the exclusive use of RP and even the accepted range of variation of RP was strictly controlled. It seems that a central objective was the 'establishment of a standard form of English pronunciation for all educated people' (Leitner 1980:86), believing that raising speech standards would raise social standards! That is, if people spoke like the upper class they would behave like them! Of course it is not that the relevant committee of the BBC was seeking to generate social equality through language but that the emphasis was on the link between language and behaviour. In this sense it saw itself as an adjunct of the educational system, claiming that the BBC should avoid 'the lapses of the uneducated, and the affectations of the insufficiently educated at both ends of the social scale' (quoted in Leitner 1980:88). In this respect it was preoccupied with a conceived link between speech and writing, believing that the oral standard reflected the written standard. Perhaps more relevant is that this belief stems from a discourse which saw culture as a general process of intellectual or spiritual development, an idea that was prevalent in eighteenth-century social philosophy. To be cultured or civilised was to be cultivated, and language was the means whereby this state could be achieved. Heath and Mandebach (1983:99) refer to it in the following terms: 'English teachers have claimed that ethics and aesthetics are transmitted through the "laws of language" and correct grammar has close connections with "correct thinking".'

The English language and culture, in their most pure form, were the gifts of a civilising force which would lead the denigrated citizen into the fold of progress and away from barbarism. The means of denigration were presented as the means of self-liberation. This theme of language as the prerequisite of social standards was a feature of BBC objectives as recently as the 1930s. Thus these statements constitute an attempt to civilise the unruly masses. Evidently the role of the media was seen as to employ language as a means of introducing the masses to 'high' culture rather than being a means of the creation and transmission of 'popular' culture.

Whatever its limitations the work of Bernstein and his associates (Bernstein 1971–5) has served to demonstrate the role of the education system in producing and reproducing the written standard, They show how this involves denigrating the regional dialect which, of course, is referred to primarily in oral terms since the role of the written standard is to formalise written correctness in such a way that errors or 'mistakes' do not have a regional referent but rather exist as a universal lack of correctness.

It should be clear that the converse of the oral standard is largely established by that which it is not, as the converse of RP. Thus it is its converse not simply in linguistic terms but also in terms of its class constitution and its spatial extension. Regional dialects constitute the speech of the proletariat no matter what their geographical location. Why is it that there is so much variation in regional dialects within Britain when RP, as the language of the dominant class displays such uniformity? Again the answer must lie in the agencies of production and reproduction. Evidently the family is again important and class endogamy again evident. The main difference between the production and reproduction of RP and regional dialects is that the latter lack the institutions and organised activities which cut across space in an integrated state-wide manner. Wakelin (1972:5) claims that SE is treated as 'the sort of language used when communicating *beyond* the family, close friends and acquaintances, whereas dialect is nowadays often kept for intimate circles'. That is, in a sense SE serves as the language of wider communication. Even though he is referring to individual use of language rather than the overall configuration of standard/non-standard forms the contrast which he claims to identify is important with reference to demonstrating the relative status of the two forms. That is, in a sense, corpus planning can be seen as a form of status planning since it merely serves to retain the relative status difference between SE and the regional dialect. French sociologists interested in language (Calvet 1974, Achard 1980, Balibar 1985) have long been aware of this, noting that French was regarded as the language of reason as a consequence of its written codification and its use for legal and other state matters, with all other languages and varieties within the boundaries of the state being relegated to standing beyond or outside of reason, that is, to the level of *patois* or dialect.

It has not been my intention in the preceding discussion to seek an exhaustive explanation for the institutionalisation and legitimisation of the difference between SE and regional dialects. Such an exercise is hardly possible within the confines of the present chapter and involves a process which is far less conspiratorial than that suggested above. Rather my objective has been to establish that British English tends to be produced and reproduced in terms of a continuum, the respective ends of which are SE and regional dialects; to emphasise that the important feature of these varieties is their class dimension, involving the power fraction of the dominant class on the one hand and the proletariat on the other; and to establish that the legitimisation of the hierarchical distinction between these two 'types' is not politically neutral. The tendency to discuss the RP/regional dialect dichotomy in terms of a continuum inevitably means that the intervening forms will tend to be discussed in terms of a mixture of the features of the two polar forms. It also leads to obscuring the relationship between the respective ends of the continuum. Thus the intervening forms should be regarded as concrete types and the fact that they may include linguistic features of either RP or regional dialects does not necessarily mean that they must be regarded as features of either, rather they must be treated as manifestations of social structure rather than language. This being the case, then the nature of the relationship between RP and regional dialects largely depends upon the conception of social structure that is employed by the sociolinguist. It should be evident that if structural functionalism and its conception of inequality is employed then the discussion of the relationship between language varieties will inevitably involve a consensus perspective devoid of any discussion of power, domination and conflict. It is hardly surprising therefore that the predominant argument concerning SE and regional dialects involves a normative argument which contrasts with what has been claimed above.

What has been hinted at above is that the dichotomous relationship between standard and non-standard is a lot more involved than the sociolinguistic argument would suggest. It involves a number of dichotomous relationships involving:

STANDARD	NON-STANDARD OR DIALECT
DOMINANT CLASS	PROLETARIAT
STATE	COMMUNITY
STATE	REGION

This is no coincidence and it is essential to consider how these polarised concepts align in the discourse on standardisation. It becomes clear that standardisation is not a passive process deriving from social consensus in the form of normativisation but that the state is heavily implicated in the production and reproduction of the standard/non-standard distinction. It is also clear that in determining that the standard shall be the class dialect of the dominant class it is legitimising the standing of that particular class in contrast to all other classes. In this respect, standardisation is part of the legitimisation of inequality. Once an integrated state is created there is a tendency to equate state with nation with the consequence that the territory of the state is only divisible into geographical zones or regions rather than, for example, being seen as a confederation of nations. Thus to speak of a universal standard and regional dialects is to consolidate the territorial integrity of the state. This is also true of the state/community dichotomy with the state being presented as an amalgam of communities. The two are seen as being in a condition of mutual support and harmony, with a single language being the basis of cohesion even though that language need not be uniform in nature. This is the basis of dividing distinctive forms of the same language into different types which are related to state and community in distinctive ways. The regional dialect, as a collective term, represents the national community, with nation being equated with the state in the sense of being a nation-state, while also being the sum of its constituent parts, the geographical regions. The civilising role of correct language involved the basis for a moral order which lay in the custody of the state but which was open to the entire community, and thereby the source of moral order has been displaced. In this sense the issue of standard/non-standard derives from a discourse located at a particular historical conjuncture. It should now be clear how in the legal discourse of the Race Relations Act (G. Williams 1987), English becomes both the language of the state and a community language whereas all other languages spoken in Britain are restricted to community status. It is this which allows English to be included in the Act thereby conveying the impression that all languages are equal in standing in the eyes of the law.

The most interesting feature of Gimson's remarks quoted above (p.140) relates to what seems to be axiomatic among linguists – that there is no reason why any variety of language is preferable or superior to another in linguistic terms. This being the case, then his definition of RP makes the evaluation of it subjective in nature, a position which must, in some way, be justified. I wish to emphasise that this justification, and with it the justification of the regional dialect as non-standard, involves a political process of legitimisation rather than being a social process described in terms of normativisation. A somewhat similar stance has been adopted recently by some social dialectologists wishing to assert the respectability of regional varieties of English. However, their approach systematically fails to recognise that the problem lies in the adoption of a particular theoretical perspective in the conventional discussion of standard and non-standard language. This much should be evident once the issue of normativisation is considered.

The reluctance of sociolinguists to conceptualise standardisation in other than normative terms is clear. Much of their conceptualisation of standard derives not from theory but rather from a descriptive basis of linguistic features and their subsequent relationship to some social category which suits the arguments of that particular analyst. Thus Trudgill's (1984) treatment of SE as the speech of educated native speakers lacks sociological precision but does allow him to accommodate varieties of SE beyond the confines of the British state and thereby succeeds in making the social dimension virtually meaningless. It should be clear that I view standardisation as a socio-political process involving the legitimisation and institutionalisation of a language variety as a feature of the sanctioning of that variety as socially preferable. However, if we maintain that language is itself social then this process is also part of the ideological aspect of social differentiation. We cannot discuss issues such as standardisation or language purity without simultaneously discussing social class. It is important to recognise this ideological feature of standardisation since normativisation, as the perceptual evaluation of speech forms, does not simply appear as the structural functional perspective would imply, but is the product of an ideological system which conditions our perception of the social, and thereby linguistic, world. This view of standardisation is significantly different from that which defines standardisation in terms of codification or normativisation which not only involves consensus sociological perspectives but also denies any political context. Even if one of the consequences of standardisation is normativisation, it is inadequate to adopt this descriptive assessment as a defining criterion since it is a consequence rather than a cause of standardisation.

CONCLUSION

I would like to conclude this chapter by referring to the relationship between status planning and corpus planning and in so doing I would argue that to treat them as separate activities is to create yet another false dichotomy. One of the points I have sought to emphasise above is that the state is implicated in both status planning and corpus planning and that the issue of status is implicit in both. While status planning tends to refer to the relative status of state language and minority language, corpus planning refers to varieties of a single language, to the relative status of the state variety and the regional dialect. This difference constitutes a difference involving what I would call the struggle over language and the struggle in language. The former involves Weberian status groups which cut across class and this may well be a feature of the second as well, as in the case of gender language, but by and large the struggle in language involves social class struggle.

The most evident feature of any attempt to increase the status of a minority language is that it involves the reinstitutionalisation and relegitimation of its domain context. Whenever the minority language enters into new domains it has repercussions for its corpus, not necessarily because of any 'deficiency' in that language but because of its social reconstitution. One feature of minority languages is that they tend to be systematically separated from those domains which are crucial for social reproduction, domains such as work, administration, etc. In this respect they tend to be seen as 'community' languages. Any entry of the minority language into these domains of direct social reproduction leads to the emergence of class varieties which hitherto were non-existent. That is, change in the corpus derives from change in status. This in turn leads to a focus upon standardisation. If a minority language becomes a state language as a consequence of political change its status is at a maximum and the emphasis must be exclusively upon standardisation and other features of the corpus.

It is more difficult to envisage changes in the status of the non-standard language for the simple reason that, as a manifestation of the class structure, it can only be subject to such profound change if the capitalist system which is the basis of the class structure is eliminated. None the less neither the corpus nor the social structure is static. New features of the corpus may be legitimised and accepted as features of the standard partly as a manifestation of the increased status of a particular class fraction and even as the consequence of the displacement of another class fraction.

6 Conversation analysis

The three preceding chapters have focused upon the use of structural functionalism as the theoretical basis of sociolinguistic analysis. That discussion suggested some of the limitations of the perspective. The ensuing chapters will focus upon approaches which have sought to resolve some of these limitations. I will endeavour to discuss the nature of these efforts, and the extent of their success, and I will also seek to demonstrate that even where these efforts have resolved what they claim are deficiencies in structural functionalism, they have retained many of the problems as a consequence of retaining the fundamental philosophical orientation of the theoretical problematic. The discussion will begin with a consideration of ethnomethodology and the role of conversation analysis within it.

ETHNOMETHODOLOGY

In some respects ethnomethodology is a new force in sociology deriving from the 1960s. In other respects it derives from a long tradition, having inherited aspects of Parsonian structural functionalism, the phenomenology of Schutz and Husserl and some of the philosophical tradition of Heidegger and his predecessors. As an aspect of interactional sociology the majority of those who are actively involved in conversation analysis are sociologists who are very much aware of the social philosophy which underlies the practice. This is in contrast to the majority of sociolinguists whose main allegiance is to linguistics or anthropology, and who seem to adopt the sociological features of their work mainly as an adjunct to their linguistic interests.

It cannot be said that ethnomethodology asserts a very great influence on sociology, and certainly the number of practising ethnomethodologists is relatively small. However, the dedication and belief in a common sense of direction is quite striking and their assertion that they are giving a new direction to sociology irritates many other sociologists. This is partly because a rejection of what is often axiomatic in mainstream sociology is demanded before their work can be fully appreciated, and partly because of the claim that ethnomethodology constitutes a radical shift from conventional conceptions of social reality. However, as Atkinson (1988) has recently shown, there is considerable variety within ethnomethodology and the claim for an internal cohesion is somewhat misleading.

The main preoccupations of ethnomethodology are the analysis of rationality, practical reasoning, the way in which reality is constructed out of common sense, moral assessments and categorisations and inter-subjectivity. At a more general level they ask the question of how sociologists and non-sociologists know that the social world has a real character. If it is consciously and unconsciously constructed, sustained and altered by human actors, then

> the cement that holds society together may not be the values, norms, common definitions, exchange payoffs, role bargains, interest coalitions, and the like of current social theory, but people's explicit and implicit 'methods' for creating the presumptions of social order.
>
> (Turner 1986:390)

Clearly this is quite a large shift from the assumptions of Parsonian structural functionalism. In some respects the goal of the respective approaches to society are quite different in that the ethnomethodologist would claim that the construction and recognition of social activities by the actors is preliminary to any theory of social action and to any form of sociological investigation. It also denies the neo-Kantian distinction between rationally based knowledge on the one hand, and falsity or ideology on the other, in that it is claimed that it is insufficient. In the same breath it dismisses both the rational actor and the non-rational, but normatively determined, action of structural functionalism, and more specifically, the entire theory of action. This is the inevitability of challenging the idea of error. For the ethnomethodologist knowledge is socially constituted and this, in turn, raises questions for the epistemological nature of sociology as a scientific endeavour which is superior to everyday knowledge. As such it challenges the profession of sociology and it is hardly surprising that this has dismayed some sociologists.

The phenomenological input derives, of course, from the work of Husserl who argued, among other things, that scientific knowledge had been divorced from the everyday experience and activities in which it was grounded. This is similar to the argument which ethno-methodologists made *vis-à-vis* structural functionalism. The central assumption of Husserl's work was that the world of living subjects only existed in consciousness or in people's heads. The objective of phenomenological work was to uncover the structures and workings of human consciousness. It is not that the external world is denied, as in the *pouvoir–savoir* perspective, but rather that this external world only assumes meaning through people's consciousness of it. In this respect it also contributed to the field of symbolic interactionism which, some would claim, ethnomethodology draws upon. Meaning assumes centre stage and norms, values, beliefs and so on are seen as meanings.

Husserl challenged the empirical sciences by refuting the naturalistic method in which the tendency to generalise from induction fails to guarantee the future and where the rules of logic fail to stipulate their own grounds for why any rules established should be as they are. In his quest for a universal form of reasoning Husserl abandoned the naturalistic method and in its place established a new method, which, he claimed, should yield absolutely certain results in every case. This method he named phenomenology. The basic principle of this phenomenology involved discovering the essences which are prior to all experience. This quest for the true essence of things does not rely on empirical evidence but rather involves what Husserl referred to as 'epoche' – taking the contents of consciousness as they appear while suspending judgement as to whether it is true or false. Experience becomes a form of consciousness. Subjective structures are actively involved in the constitution of the objects of experience. The objective experience and the subjective structures which bring them into consciousness should not be dismissed through reference to psychology or cognition as explanation but have to be carefully described. Consciousness is primordial. Husserl distinguished between what he referred to as the 'natural attitude' and the manner in which such an attitude is phenomenologically reduced. The former involves the framework necessary for the manner in which we mundanely perceive, interpret and act upon our immediate environment. It excludes or suspends the idea that things may not really be the way we see them – things are the way we conceive them, so that, unless there is some counter evidence to the actor, his/her understanding of the situation is correct and if previous interpretations have been correct or adequate then these will also be true in the future. Meaning becomes something that is constructed in the act of consciousness. In contrast to empirical reality which refers to particulars, Husserl emphasised the importance of universals and his objective was to establish all of the pure essences which constituted the absolute structure of the universe. From the method of 'epoche' absolutely valid laws could be established. Clearly, if possible, this would be a tremendous undertaking and the necessary dedication is one of the features of the ethnomethodologists who have adopted features of Husserl's work.

Thus the essence of Husserl's work was that we know about the world only through experience. Therefore society, in the form of other people, norms, values and physical objects, is always mediated by experience as it relates to people's conscious awareness. Direct contact with reality is, thereby, impossible, since the human mind mediates between subject and object. Humans operate in a taken for granted world which, for them, is reality. Rarely is this reality the topic of reflective thought but, none the less, they act on the assumption that this reality is shared by other humans. If our consciousness is structured by this implicit life-world, how is an objective knowledge of a so-called 'real' world possible? Husserl's answer was to concentrate upon the basic processes by which this 'reality' is mediated, that is, he focused attention upon consciousness. However, this process had to suspend or bracket out any assumption about 'an external social world out there'.

In some respects what I have outlined above of Husserl's contribution is not too dissimilar from Weber's seminal work on *verstehen* or sympathetic introspection into an investigator's own mind. However, the link between Husserl and Weber is clearer in the work of Schutz who also had a more direct impact upon the foundations of the ethnomethodological enterprise.

The starting point of Schutz's work is Husserl's claim that human reflection is grounded in the *Lebenswelt* or the mundane world of lived experience which exists in the unreflecting awareness of ordinary people. The ordinary actor constantly constitutes and reconstitutes this world of mundane events and institution without even being aware of it. In this respect Schutz was involved with the theory of action which we have seen in Parsons' work but he focused upon the feature which Parsons omitted – the knowledgeable nature of the actor's activities.

Schutz was also involved in detailing what, in his view, Weber should have pursued in his method of *verstehen*. Indeed his first work of substance involved an attempt to take to task Weber's methodological synthesis of the competing claims of science and subjectivity by drawing upon phenomenological concepts in order to analyse the meaning structures underlying the social world. He insisted that the social world is interpreted in experience as meaningful and comprehensible by human actors. For Weber, of course, any social science must comprehend social reality at the level of meaning, and, therefore, it must delve into how people view, define and conceive the world. His method was that of *verstehen*, or sympathetic introspection. Part and parcel of any investigation, empirical or otherwise, must involve the ability to enter the subjective world of actors. Schutz' advance on this position was to investigate why, and through what process, actors come to share common meanings. This is the problem of inter-subjectivity. It is the point of contact involving the preoccupation with the question of social order. It was this feature of Schutz' work which was grafted onto the assumptions of Husserl about the nature of the social world. He insisted that observation had to replace the radical abstraction of Husserl's work, and this led to the possibility of an empirical rather than philosophical input into phenomenology.

Turner (1986:328–9) claims that Schutz must have been influenced by the symbolic interactionists and especially by the analysis of role-taking which shares some commonality with the concept of inter-subjectivity. Particularly important is the process whereby actors anticipate each other's roles and employ this anticipation to evaluate likely behaviour. He derived his concept of 'stock knowledge at hand' from Husserl's concept of life-world. This stock knowledge is akin to people's reality which is the essential ingredient of all social events and the basis for their pragmatic relationship with others. Despite this reference to pragmatism the stock knowledge was treated by Schutz as a taken for granted phenomenon, and as something that was learnt through socialisation. People also assume that others share this stock knowledge thereby facilitating a 'reciprocity of perspectives'. Evidently there is a sense in which the world is the same for everyone and this is the basis of social order. One feature of this presumption is that people categorise one another through mutual typification. The emphasis is very much upon the manner in which actors create a sense of a shared world.

Evidently any discussion of meaning and inter-subjectivity must address the issue of rationality. While Schutz saw rational action as involving choice in terms of goals and the means for achieving these goals, his awareness of the incomplete nature of the actor's knowledge in a situation of action meant that distinguishing between rational and non-rational action was futile. None the less rational choice is a reality for Schutz and involves means and ends or goals. However, there are severe limitations upon what can be known with reference to reaching a decision, especially with reference to other actors who may be a part of that decision. Consequently, Schutz concluded that it is impossible to construct a form of scientific rationality against which any course of action may be measured. Rather it becomes necessary to establish the nature of the information that is available to the actor, together with the associated criteria of choice and evaluation which might be applied.

It is this perspective on society which the ethnomethodologists have adopted from Schutz. It focuses upon the manner in which social order is constructed out of the shared experience of social actors. As such it challenges the assumption that social order derives from values, norms, common definitions, role structures etc. The interactionist element of the field involves establishing how meaning is created by actors in and through interaction, the emphasis being upon the process of interaction. However, it is more than this in that the focus is upon Schutz's analysis of the life-world and the manner in which people construct a sense of a common perception and understanding of the world. In so doing, the idea that there is an external social world is suspended or bracketed, as also is the related issues of norms, values, roles and beliefs. Thus they 'have chosen to ask not how order is possible, but rather to ask how a sense of order is possible' (Mehan and Wood 1975:190). The emphasis shifts from a concern about the scientific nature of sociological knowledge about social order to the actors' creation of a sense of social order. As Turner (1986:394) has emphasised, the important element in ethnomethodology is not the nature of rules, definitions and values but how people see, describe and assert that rules and definitions exist. A central feature of such an objective is reflexivity, involving how people in interaction maintain the presumption that the world is guided by a particular reality. Indeed much of ethnomethodological research focuses upon the question of how reflexive interaction actually occurs. However, such reflexivity relates to context and the concept of indexicality is employed to refer to the relationship between indexicality and context. Within interaction ethnomethodologists maintain that actors constantly seek to convey a normal form or situation to one another; they try and assure one another that they would have the same experiences if they were to change places; they 'fill in' information that is necessary in order to 'make sense' of another's words or deeds. Where there is failure to agree on such interactive techniques interaction will tend to be disrupted and much of the recent work of the sociolinguist John Gumperz, who assumes much of ethnomethodology in his work, involves demonstrating how such miscommunication occurs (Gumperz 1982). Such miscommunication would, presumably, be interpreted as a breakdown of social order. Before considering some of the specific work pertaining to language which has derived from this perspective let us consider the manner in which this perspective differs from that of Parsons.

The most eminent of the ethnomethodologists is Harold Garfinkel who was one of the first graduate students in the Department of Social Relations founded by Talcott Parsons at Harvard University. Indeed his doctoral dissertation was supervised by Parsons himself. Not that he abided by the theoretical reflections of his mentor; in many respects he challenged them.

While the Parsonian actor is related to a set of objects which she/he can know with reference to, and in comparison with, scientific accuracy, Schutz focused far more attention upon the inner self of the actor. The domains of consciousness which involved imagination, theorising and dreaming as well as the 'real world', all had a reality in their own right as well as logic relating to experience. These are the very things which Parsons tended to relegate to the world of non-logical sentiments or attitudes while Schutz's understanding of the social world encompassed a vast range of universes of meaning. Bloor (1976) suggests that this claim on the part of Schutz rejected the 'sociology of error' which derives from establishing a privileged status for social science constructs of social reality. It is this which obliges Parsons to distinguish between rational knowledge and non-rational orientations. The difference between the two orientations is profound in that Parsons, on the one hand, is obliged to opt for the superiority of social scientific methods or, in Heritage's words (1984:68), 'the cognitive superiority of science', which becomes the basis for explaining the supposedly non-rational action. Furthermore, if behaviour is non-rational, how is it that social action is effective. In the view of the ethnomethodologists any answer to this problem must involve not merely the assertion of the superiority of social science, but also an ignoring of the knowledge and judgement of the actor in question. Perhaps the most common means of avoiding this problem is by reference to the concept of culture which we will encounter in chapter 7. For Schutz, on the other hand, the problem does not arise because the distinction between rational and non-rational action is absent since there is no claim that the actor's point of view is somehow defective.

Whereas Parsons claimed that knowledge and language existed within an institutionalised and internalised manner, Schutz claimed that shared understanding was also relevant. Furthermore, he maintained that there is a need to investigate how inter-subjective knowledge and understanding is achieved. It is no longer sufficient to rely on an unspecified, free floating social norm as the essential guide. Indeed, for Schutz, norms play no role whatsoever in constraining the actor. Similarly, for Garfinkel normative rules could never determine behaviour while inter-subjective knowledge could not be founded on such rules. Yet it is clear that ethnomethodology, in pursuing the issue of the common-sense construction of reality, represents a neo-Durkheimian notion of rules which organise 'externally' as it were, the behaviour which occurs within the social setting. That is, 'rules' which specify appropriate behaviour in particular settings are regarded as external to the settings, at least in the sense that their existence is independent of, and extends beyond, the particular setting and its participants.

Heritage (1984:34) claims that the main point of departure between the work of Garfinkel and Parsons involved Parsons' displacement of the common-sense world from a position of any importance in the analysis of social action or social organisation. For Parsons, the idea of ordinary actors selecting courses of action on the basis of practical considerations and judgements which made sense to others within a common-sense world bore no relevance to his theory of action. On the other hand, for Garfinkel the theoretical choice between 'rational' and 'normatively determined' action was inconceivable since mundane conduct was based on 'reasonable' considerations related to contexts of uncertainty which are entirely resistant to scientific calculation. The crux of the disagreement revolves around one of the central issues of nineteenth-century German philosophy – the nature and methodology of the social sciences.

The Parsonian view of social life focused upon a system of action operating in relation to rewards and sanctions. Such a world can only work if it is assumed that the actors share a normative orientation to rationality. This rationality, for Parsons, involved the Weberian means–ends thesis, allowing actors to understand one another, to share conceptions of situations and to come to similar conclusions. It is through rationality that the actor comprehends his/her situation. The sharing of expectations is, in the view of ethnomethodologists, dismissed by the reference to a shared culture as its source of origin. The non-rational actions were implemented by institutionalised norms of conduct. Social organisation, involving stable patterns of activity, derives from the internalisation of normative patterns as need-dispositions. Thus, as a consequence, social actors consciously come to conform with what the institutionalised normative patterns require them to do. The rejection of the centrality of the normative order involved a denial of the Durkheimian basis of social action as involving the relationship between the individual and society. Instead we have an individualist and indeterminate conception of social life in which any form of 'external' determination is opposed. Human actors are free to constitute their own situation in the sense that they determine action while also generating their own social world through their subjectivity. The centrality of the disagreement involves the Kantian conception of free will and the indeterminacy of the human realm.

It is not that there is no sense of social organisation but, rather, that it is seen as a product of the coordinated 'accommodative work' (Garfinkel 1963:187) whereby the social actor establishes and reproduces extended courses of action. Parsons confronts the problem of the maintenance of the organisation of action in terms of 'moral' rules which operate both externally and internally *vis-à-vis* the actor. The separation between external and internal is akin to the distinction between moral and cognitive, and what Garfinkel succeeded in doing is to integrate the two so that the moral is akin to the manner in which mundane actors deal with one another's action through choice. Action becomes the product of accountable moral choice. Social organisation is reduced to a matter of interaction. Consequently, some of the central concepts are also modified. Thus the concept of role is no longer the static, mechanical concept of structural functionalism but involves the momentary construction by the actor out of his/her definition of the situation. Patterns of interaction are made stable by this process. The claim that roles are learnt early in life through child socialisation such that they become so predictable that they have an automatic and unreflective quality to them is denied. Ethnomethodology maintains that the stable, rational, intelligible, reasonable, understandable, justifiable features of a situation are a practical and continuous accomplishment of members throughout the course of their daily life. Social roles are one feature of the manner in which social structure is mutually produced by actors as a feature of everyday activity such that social order is constantly created and re-created. The task of ethnomethodology is to describe this process and to show how it works.

Having established the subjectivist nature of ethnomethodology and shown how the premise that human actors are not merely acted upon by social facts or forces, but rather are constantly shaping and creating their social world in interaction with others, constitutes a critique of structural functionalism and the associated positivistic model which claims that the truth of a scientific statement lies in its correspondence, however indirectly, with facts derived from sensory experience. I would now like to turn to consider the importance of language in ethnomethodology. In so doing it is as well to recognise Atkinson's (1988) claim that ethnomethodology is not a uniform endeavour.

CONVERSATIONAL ANALYSIS

For Schutz, language *per se* pertains to the inter-subjective world of the 'natural' attitude and, as such, 'obstinately resists serving as a vehicle for meanings which transcend its own presuppositions' (1972:233). This implies that thought is something other than language, the former being private and the latter public:

> From the outset, we, the actors on the social scene experience the world we live in as a world both of nature and of culture, not as a private but as an intersubjective one, that is, as a world common to all of us, either actually given or potentially accessible to everyone; and this involves intercommunication and language.
>
> (Schutz 1962:53)

As Torode (1984:28) rightly points out, this presents problems for social science in that the possibility of any language other than that of everyday life is denied, and the writings of the social scientist must take the form of the 'natural attitude'. Hindess (1972:21) claims that 'relationships between the provinces of history and of social science exist only in the consciousness of the knowing subject – or in books or papers that he may have written', describing Schutz's position as deriving from 'psychologism'. He was referring to Schutz's claim that:

> The finite provinces of meaning are not separated states of the mental life in the sense that passing from one to another world requires a transmigration of the soul and a complete extinction of memory and consciousness by death. . . . They are merely names for different tensions of one and the same consciousness . . . experiences in various provinces can be remembered and reproduced. And that is why they can be communicated in ordinary language.
>
> (Schutz 1962:257–8)

However, Schutz's position in this respect is perfectly consistent with his belief in scientific production as a basis for study and is reflected in the ethnomethodological claim that the investigator is him/herself a feature of the production of meaning. Perhaps the link is most explicit in the manner in which Garfinkel refers to everyday language 'from within' in the context of Schutz' claim that – 'language – any language pertains . . . to the inter-subjective world of working, and therefore obstinately resists serving as a vehicle for meanings which transcend its own presuppositions' (1962:261). Garfinkel's objective was not to transcend these presuppositions but rather to reveal them.

Schutz operated upon the principle that language is inadequate to communicate everything that can be known and, as a consequence, language is inherently typifying; it is a 'treasure house of ready-made pre-constituted types and characteristics all derived and carrying along an open horizon of unexplored content' (Schutz 1962:14). Thus language is incapable of coming to terms with the infinite uniqueness of each situation and state of affairs. Features of language generalise in the sense that in describing they express the commonalities across states of affairs. That is, there is an element of approximation between language and that which it seeks to describe. Thus, following Husserl, Schutz claimed that mundane common-sense type terms are not fixed but can be elaborated and extended as experience and circumstance requires. This in turn means that, if precise definition is not possible, a process of 'contextualisation' must occur on the part of the listener in interpreting a description. The description in language presents a context which is then elaborated upon through contextualisation. Evidently, from the standpoint of much of semantics, this would suggest that language is defective, but ethnomethodologists would claim that this is erroneous since it is a mistake to separate language from the contextual, and it is here that we evidence the link between language and society which is the defining criterion of sociolinguistics. Perhaps this is best exemplified in the work of Cicourel.

In referring to Cicourel within the context of ethnomethodology it is necessary to state that in the view of some ethnomethodologists his emphasis on cognitive competence departs from the mainstream of the subdiscipline (Atkinson 1988:443). The departure derives from Cicourel's belief that Garfinkel is wrong in claiming that interaction and verbal accounts are the same process (Cicourel 1973). Such a position would mean that language is not a reflection of society, as structural functionalist sociolinguistics maintain, but that language is society – a position fully compatible with what we have expressed about ethnomethodology. In contrast, Cicourel maintains that people sense, see, and feel much that they are unable to communicate with words, and that verbal accounts are merely crude and incomplete translations of what is communicated in interaction. His objective, therefore, is to discover the universal 'interpretive procedures' whereby humans organise their cognitions and give meanings to situations. Such interpretive procedures are held to be an inherent feature of all humans through which they create a sense of social structure and manage to organise action. The continuity with, and the departure from, the ethnomethodological endeavour should be obvious. Also it would seem that, for Cicourel, the objective of society is to create a coherent sense of social order which sustains the status quo. None the less his reference to transformational theory is revealing.

Cicourel's main interest is in the use of generative transformational theory as a theoretical resource. He builds upon Chomsky's claim that language is creative, that is, it is free from external stimuli and internal drives. The source of this freedom is in the basic mechanism of language production, or its 'deep structure', which consists of a finite set of propositions (subject–predicate form, grammatical relations, functions and categories). The elements of the deep structure are manipulated by processes called transformations (obligatory and optional additions, deletions and rearrangements), to produce what we perceive as utterances (surface structures). In this generative model, behaviour (language) is produced through the use of a finite set of processes. Cicourel sees his own notion of interpretive procedures as forming a generative model for assigning infinite meaning to the social world.

Linking interpretive procedures and surface rules presumes a generative model in the sense of Chomsky's work on generative or transformational grammar: 'The interpretive procedures prepare and sustain an environment of objects for inference and action *vis-à-vis* a culture bound world view and the written and commonly known surface rules' (Cicourel 1973:52). Chomsky's distinction between surface structure and deep structure is employed by Cicourel to call attention to the incomplete nature of the sociological normative model. Normative theory provides descriptions of the rules (deep structure) but tells us nothing about the interpretive work people do to decide their meaning and application in concrete situations. He treats norms as 'surface rules' which have an open structure that results in multiple interpretations. He views the problem of semantic interpretations of sentences as similar to that of deciding the meaning and applicability of a rule. The meaning of rules and sentences is not obvious and objectively fixed for all occasions. Rather, meaning tends to vary from occasion to occasion so that people must continuously construct anew the meanings of rules and sentences. Just as deep structure forms the ability to produce surface sentences, interpretive procedures constitute the basic ability to assign meaning and decide the applicability of sentences and rules. Socialisation produces the articulation of a general rule or policy (norm), with a particular event or case said to fall under the general rule, but there are no surface rules which guide how the articulation is to be made. Rather people must acquire the competence to assign meaning to their environment so that surface rules and their articulation with particular cases can be made. That is, linguistic and social rules always require some recognition for their meaning and applicability. Interpretive procedures are part of a person's social competence in performance.

Cicourel refers to the manner in which the linguist elicits ethnographic detail from an informant in establishing the syntactic rules of a language which he does not 'know'. This ethnographic detail forms a context for understanding both the language and the syntactic rules. However, when the formalised properties of the grammar are presented, the ethnographic details used to derive it are not part of the formal analysis. Yet interpretive procedures are the methods whereby contexts of ethnographic particulars are employed to determine the meaning and existence of rules and sentences. Both the linguist and the lay person must use interpretive procedures to recognise the rules that could fit the sentence and give it meaning.

Cicourel's criticism of Chomsky involves the rule-governed nature of the Chomsky model. He criticises the notion that the semantic content of talk is governed by the rules of syntax. Meaning is located primarily in syntactic rules. Cicourel claims that while syntax plays a part in constructing meaning, it is not the central element used by people. To make sense of an utterance, the person must go beyond syntax and linguistic markers.

Cicourel proposes that a generative model of semantics is needed, based not on a syntactic rule, but on the assembly of contexts that are recalled or imagined to give meaning to utterances. Syntactic rules are consulted by people and used to justify the semantic boundaries placed upon the utterances, but linguistic rules for Cicourel are not causal agents but are interpretive devices used by people to present their meanings as objective and as falling within conventional usage.

Through this critique of linguistics, Cicourel is in effect questioning the theoretical status of norms in sociological theory. Norms have been reified and given an existence in their own right. Situational usage is missing so that the judgemental work of using and recognising norms in ongoing social scenes has been left out of sociological study. The rule-governed theory of such sociology cannot adequately deal with ambiguous utterances and behaviour because it creates a static world where everything has its formal, denotative meaning.

While, for transformational grammarians, the semantic context of utterances is based on the rules of syntax, for ethnomethodologists meaning goes beyond this. Rules are interpretive aids as opposed to being causal agents. It is the account rather than the sentence – a convenient normative practice for teaching rules of language – which is the basic unit of analysis. Pauses, ellipses, features of the setting, sounds and physical posturing become important elements of an analysis because they are used in the situated construction of meaning. For Chomskyan linguists native intuition consists of rules and deep structures that are more heuristic than empirically real. For the ethnomethodologist, on the other hand, the study of nativeness is the study of interpretive procedures. Also, for Chomsky, the sense of social structure is a given whereas for the ethnomethodologist it becomes a practical, ongoing accomplishment that is constitutive of everyday and scientific knowledge.

It is Harvey Sacks who tends to be regarded as the initiator of conversation analysis (Heritage 1984:235). He investigated a number of problems involving the accomplishment of social order in the conversational setting – problems of opening and closing conversations, question and answer sequences and the beginning and ending of stories. In an early paper (Sacks 1963) he criticised both the Durkheimian tendency to develop type concepts by 'averaging', and Weber's idea of ideal types, on the grounds that they lead to ignoring the detail of what is under investigation to the extent that sociological concepts have only a vague relationship to the events in everyday life to which they pertain. This in turn restricts the possibility of a sociology consisting of a cumulative body of knowledge. Evidently he saw ethnomethodology as a continuation of the scientific endeavour, as an additive process of knowledge accumulation. In so doing he seems to be denying sociology's existence as a body of generalisations.

The answer, in Sacks' view, was to establish a method which allows findings to be replicated. His work on speech was an attempt in this direction. Such a view implies what many would deny, that the concrete details of social interaction are organised in such a way that replication can be expected. This view was inherent in Chomsky's tendency to avoid the analysis of speech. It also implies that human conduct cannot be coherent and meaningful unless such a detailed organisation of social interaction does indeed exist.

Two things should be clear from the preceding discussion. First, that the focus is very much upon social interaction, and second, that language or speech is only part of that process of interaction. Thus it is not surprising that the methodology which Sacks developed focused upon the detailed recording of social interaction, including speech. As Heritage (1984:236) has emphasised it also means that research methodologies such as the formal interview, field notes for the gathering of observational data, native intuition and the use of experimental methodologies must be abandoned because of the involvement of 'idealizations about how interaction works'.

Atkinson (1988:443) refers to the concerns of conversation analysis as paying

> special attention to the fine-grained analysis of naturally occurring spoken interaction (and, more rarely, to the coordination of spoken and nonverbal activities) . . . [which] has its own characteristic set of concerns and procedures . . . .

However, the focus is upon competence and in this respect it shares an interest with the ethnography of communication to which we shall turn in chapter 7. The basic assumption is that effective communication in interaction involves the production of language conduct and its interpretation. That is, it involves the manner in which actors draw upon procedures and expectations in interaction. This, in turn, draws upon the assumption that interaction is structurally organised; it involves contextual orientation and the entire process involves finite detail which must be included in any analysis. The structural organisation refers to patterns of stable, identifiable structural features which are social in nature. In contrast to psychological linguistics it is claimed that such structures are independent of psychological or other characteristics of particular speakers. Furthermore, these organisations are known to the actors who employ them in communication, that is, there is a rational feature to such communication, part of which focuses upon what can be discovered through observation. The context nature of the interaction refers to the need to view the sequence of actions of which any utterance is part as an on-going process, with that utterance being interpreted by the hearer in terms of its context, while the speaker creates utterances with context in mind.

The method of conversation analysis claims to focus attention upon the detailed data of interaction rather than 'a priori speculation about the orientations and motives of speakers' (Heritage 1984:243). This is expressed by Sacks and Shegloff (1973:290) in the following terms:

> We have proceeded under the assumption (an assumption borne out by our research) that in so far as the materials we worked with exhibited orderliness, they did so not only to us, indeed not in the first place for us, but for the co-participants who had produced them.

It is also assumed that the regularities are produced and related to as normative, at least in terms of being the basis for further action and inference. Furthermore, it is maintained that the organisation of talk involves a striving for maintaining bonds of solidarity and the avoidance of conflict on the part of actors.

Atkinson (1988) suggests that much of conversational analysis has lost sight of the original intention of ethnomethodology which involved searching for the orderly character of human activity or social action by focusing upon practical reasoning associated with the construction of meaning and the constitution of everyday reality. For some ethnomethodologists the concern with order has focused upon the 'order' in which things occur. The emphasis is upon sequence whether it involves turn taking in conversation or any other form of sequential order. The focus has shifted from the sharing of socially shared resources associated with the construction of meaning and the constitution of everyday reality, to an interest in collaborative conduct involving the orderly sequences of activity. Atkinson claims that this leads to ignoring the issue of motive in social action and, with reference to language, speech is not seen as a medium for intentional, motivated social action. As a consequence there is a tendency to present the model actor merely as the exponent of sequenced activities:

> In the case of conversational analysis, the complex phenomeno-logical and sociological problems of mutual understanding between actors are rendered through the mutual monitoring of utterances for their completions, overlaps and the like.

> (Atkinson 1988:450)

Others (e.g. Heritage 1984:291) deny this form of mechanical and deterministic behaviourism, claiming that conversation analysis does adhere to the principles of ethnomethodology whereby actors are not obliged to conform to normatively organised constraints insofar as their deviance conforms with the commensurate sanctions and accountability. That is, he suggests that despite appearances the reasoning individual is still central to conversation analysis. None the less the sensitivity to the accusation of behaviourism is interesting in itself and appears to involve a purity associated with the origins of the enterprise which is seen as additive rather than diversionary.

ETHNOMETHODOLOGY AND STRUCTURAL FUNCTIONALISM

Garfinkel's (1967) original dissatisfaction with Talcott Parsons' theory of social action involved the manner in which action was treated in terms of retrospective evaluation. The sociologist stood back from the situation in employing the consequences of action before working back to determine the 'necessary causes'. Thus:

> hierarchies of need dispositions, and common culture as enforced rules of action, are favoured devices for bringing the problems of necessary inference to terms, although at the cost of making out the person-in-society to be a judgmental dope.

> (Garfinkel 1967:68)

Parsons discussed routine institutionalised expectations about social conduct in terms of norms of conduct which are internalised as need dispositions of personality. Socialisation creates dispositions for action with the consequence that the actor is unreflexive with reference to these norms, so that he/she is capable neither of selecting from among norms nor of making a moral choice which involves reflection. Garfinkel does not depart from a concern with the moral order:

> For Kant the moral order 'within' was an awesome mystery; for sociologists the moral order 'without' is a technical mystery. From the point of view of sociological theory the moral order consists of the rule governed activities of everyday life. A society's members encounter and know the moral order as perceivedly normal courses of action – familiar scenes of everyday affairs, the world of daily life known in common with others and with others taken for granted.

> (Garfinkel 1967:35)

None the less the critique of the normative consensus of Parsons leads to the possibility of an actor who can rationally select from among alternative courses of action. This is notoriously absent in Parsons' discussion of deviance which he saw as the product of inadequate socialisation. Garfinkel's alternative to the 'judgmental dope' is apparent in the following statement:

> social science theorists . . . have used the fact of standardisation to conceive the character and consequence of actions that comply with standardised expectations. Generally they have acknowledged but otherwise neglected the fact that by these same actions persons discover, create and sustain this standardisation.
>
> (Garfinkel 1967:66–7)

Yet again we find an element of continuity and this is not surprising since the ethnomethodological concern shares a preoccupation with the Durkheimian sense of social order with structural functionalism. Even though it can justifiably be claimed that ethnomethodology has turned the Durkheimian maxim on its head in stressing that the social scientist should treat facts as social accomplishments, the continuity with the fundamental concern of Durkheimian consensus sociology persists. It can be claimed that the concern is more fundamental and involves that of Garfinkel with the Hobbesian factor of trust between people, especially with reference to speech and the ability of people to engage in conversation. While some ethnomethodologists wish to deny the continuity between the work of Parsons and Garfinkel (Heritage 1984:129) the commonality clearly derives from the link back to Weber's concept of *verstehen* even though the phenomenology of Husserl, and more particularly of Schutz, is a dividing force. In a sense it could be claimed that ethnomethodology accepts some fundamental aspects of the philosophical underpinnings of structural functionalism while striving to treat the ends of action in terms of their origins and interrelationships. However, we should also realise that, unlike Parsons, Garfinkel does not claim that social stability or cohesion insists that rules or values be deeply internalised in the actor or the personality. Rather, it relies on a cultural order which, while being fragile, is none the less the basis for interpersonal understandings.

Perhaps the most important deviation from Parsonian structural functionalism involves the Kantian conception of free will and the indeterminacy of the human realm. It was emphasised in chapter 2 that, in contrast, Parsons saw humankind as being subject to constraints associated with the social system. For the subjectivist sociologies, that is phenomenology, ethnomethodology and symbolic interaction, the human actor is free to constitute his/her own situation in the sense that she/he determines action, while also generating his/her own social world through his/her subjectivity. Meanings govern action but these meanings are the product of his/her own construction. In a sense it can be seen as an intellectual version of the 'do your own thing' of the 1960s.

Yet this focus upon free will does not mean that a guiding social structure is missing; rather it is created in and through interaction. The neo-Durkheimian emphasis on rules is found in the emphasis on that which organises behaviour in particular settings. It is these rules which guide participation in social roles which are created in interaction by the actor's definition of the situation, something which stabilises interaction and thereby becomes predictable. Even though the concepts of norm and social role appear both in structural functionalism and in ethnomethodology, it should be evident that they have quite different meanings. In this respect it is fair to state that what Garfinkel recognised as a deficiency in Parsonian structural functionalism has led to a radical reassessment of the problem of social order, and both the criticism and the creation of an interactionist alternative for the study of social action are revealing and constructive. None the less the retention of the broader concerns and the philosophical assumptions associated with them means that whatever its advances over structural functionalism, ethnomethodology remains a consensus orientation which finds difficulty in confronting some issues. Social organisation is reduced to the 'contextual achievements of socially organised common practices' (Garfinkel 1967:33), which involve, more than anything, a drive to establish reciprocal cooperation. The consequence is a highly consensual image of societal organisation.

The interactionist emphasis and the discussion of social structure in terms of the social construction of reality rather than as a 'society' external to individual actors overcomes the problem which Durkheim had about constraint being the consequence of obligations prescribed 'externally' to the actor, but it does not resolve the problem of constraints, no matter how they may be conceived, being quite different from the operations of power. If interaction between individuals relies on understanding which, in turn, is based upon culture and repetition, then social cohesion derives from cultural integration. Cohesion is a feature of rules and social order. Society is built around the idea of a culturally determined cohesion, and power seems to be absent in such a construction. Power and authority seem to be reduced to the issue of rules. In talk, for example, it involves the situated rules of talk which embody the differential distribution of power and authority. Whatever reference power may have to social groups is merely embodied in the interaction between individual members of these groups as a structural feature of everyday life (see Davies 1988). This is not to say that conversation analysts do not make reference to the notion of control, and may even refer to power and domination, but they never do so in a systematic way, partly, one suspects, because such issues cannot be limited to the analysis of talk. Furthermore, the tendency which Atkinson identifies for much of conversation analysis to focus upon sequential analysis of talk means that the identity of the speaker and the power nature of the speaker is played down (Thompson 1984:116). Similarly the assumption that talk focuses upon an overarching need to establish reciprocal cooperation leads to playing down how what conversation analysts call 'trouble' or the breakdown of communication in talk is differentiated in social terms:

> An utterance can be treated as a 'trouble' by lay actors as well as by professional analysts, only in so far as the individual so treating it has some conception of correct or 'untroubled' discourse; and this conception is not independent of relations of power and privilege in the society concerned.
>
> (Thompson 1984:116)

Giddens (1976:53) also claims that dealing with action as meaning rather than as praxis or interests results in ignoring the importance of power.

There is an inevitable silence with reference to the wider social environment with which the practices which are the focus of discussion are articulated. Garfinkel (1967:57) does adopt the conception of the social actor as a member of a collectivity which is central to the work of Parsons and, indeed, to most sociology. Levinson (1979) claims that what he calls institutionalised 'activity types' constrain verbal action and simultaneously influence the hearer's interpretation. Thus, within the inter-subjectivity the actors locate one another in roles which relate to institutional contexts. This, in turn, involves knowledge of specific goals and objectives and the normal routes for achieving them. It would appear that the context is somehow external to the interaction. Heritage (1984:290) seeks to show that it is only through 'the specific, detailed and local design of turns and sequences that "institutional" contexts are observably – i.e. accountably – brought into being'. He claims that it is only within talk that institutions make their appearance. None the less there remains the problem of generalising about society from the micro data which constitute the rules which ethnomethodologists generate. Garfinkel resorts to Parsonian systems theory in order to define the collectivity member. It would seem that such an abstraction is inevitable if a conception of social structure as something revealed through interaction is to emerge. This is not to return to the Durkheimian issue that social life involves the unconscious, neither is it to adopt Goldthorpe's (1973) position that there exists a social world which has an autonomous existence. None the less it would seem that the ethnomethodological tendency to adopt an empiricist position in claiming that it is early days in terms of seeking to deduce a theory of social structure from the available data is merely to avoid the issue.

Atkinson's critique is that: 'in conversation analysis the hermeneutic-interpretive strand has been suppressed in favour of a more narrowly empiricist, even behaviourist element' (Atkinson 1988:460). The argument is that the grounding of ethnomethodology in the phenomenology of Schutz and Heidegger has been ignored and replaced by a mechanical focus upon sequential analysis. This has involved a shift from a concern with social action to a concern with activity, and to an associated emphasis upon relations between activities at the expense of a concern with the meaning of activities. Consequently, the emphasis is upon signs rather than upon the relations between sign and signified which is the embodiment of interpretation. The preoccupation with collaborative conduct to an extent takes motive for granted and the focus shifts to a concern with competence, with meaning and the constitution of everyday reality being very much secondary (Hammersley 1986). As a consequence language ceases to be seen as a medium for intentional, motivated social action and is reduced to a form of mechanical behaviourism. This is not unrelated to the belief that conversation refers to the primordial side of social life, and that social action is similarly organised and orderly, so that if the organisational forms and practices of talk can be identified, it constitutes a feature of the order of social action. This perspective carries much from structural functionalism. Thus competence is seen as acquired through socialisation, almost as if the norms of conversation are a manifestation of social norm acquisition in structural functionalism. One feature of this socialisation is the acquisition of common-sense knowledge which appears to be treated much in the same way as Parsons treats culture. Furthermore, the absence of motives and interests obliges a return to a functionalist form of explanation of social order:

there is a 'bias' intrinsic to many aspects of the organisation of talk which is generally favourable to the maintenance of bonds of solidarity between actors and which promotes the avoidance of conflict.

(Heritage 1984:265)

Evidently ethnomethodology must persevere with an epistemology which sees the rational actor as solving problems in order to create and sustain social order if the critique of structural functionalism is to be sustained. The difference of course is that for ethnomethodologists action is treated as 'rational' only insofar as it is 'accountable', but as Giddens (1976:40) points out this leads to isolating descriptions of acts and communications from purposive or motivated conduct. Interest is denied.

Even though he does not restrict himself to ethnomethodology in the sense of excluding his work from the broader field of sociolinguistics, John Gumperz is one whose work tends often to be included in the ethnomethodological endeavour, an affiliation which he himself acknowledges (1982:4). In a recent work he places the concerns of a phenomenologicaly derived sociolinguistics within the evolutionary context which should by now be familiar. He states:

As Alfred Schutz (1971) and other sociologists after him have shown, typifications reflected in schemata or interpretive frames derived from previous interactive experience are the foundation of the practical reasoning processes on which we rely in the conduct of our affairs. In our modern socially diversified and occupationally specialised urban societies, verbal communication has become more important than ever before in human history. To get things done, we must communicate intensively with individuals whose background we don't know. This means that we must verbalise information which, in small scale, face to face groups could be taken for granted and need not have to be put in words. Thus the volume of communication increases as socio-economic complexity grows.

(Gumperz 1982:22)

He proceeds to state, 'overtly marked social boundaries are disappearing and sanctions compelling adherence to group norms are weakening throughout the known world. Many new options have come to exist so that individuals are freer to alter their social personae with circumstances' (Gumperz 1982:26). This description of the current condition of progress as a reflection of the American ideal of individual liberalism, freedom and identity could not be clearer. It is a rare piece of reflection on the relationship between speech and social structure for an ethnomethodologist whose contention that social structure is created in and through interaction limits such a statement. Indeed, it would appear that Gumperz assumes a functionalist position in the sense that he would appear to suggest that an independently evolving social system demands a response in terms of communication. It is also unusual in that, even though Garfinkel stressed the significance of time as intrinsic to meaning, the work of ethnomethodology is essentially ahistorical. In this respect he contrasts with the *pouvoir–savoir* work of Foucault (1972) who seeks to show how specific definitions of reality prevail at one moment in time while also showing how meaning is the source of struggle. The evolutionism in Gumperz's statement is familiar, being a reiteration of the Durkheimian evolution from mechanical to organic solidarity, with a single society being divided into two, one urban and the other non-urban. His argument further claims that the increasing complexity of an evolving social structure can only function given the existence of 'signalled information about interpretive schemata' (Gumperz 1982:22). This would seem to be an expression of the claim that communication must involve generalisation placed in an explicitly evolutionist context.

CONCLUSION

It can be argued that while ethnomethodology has resolved several of the objections to structural functionalism, it has adopted many of the overriding assumptions about the nature of society. Foremost among these assumptions is that society is consensual in nature, deriving from a form of social contract between social actors. In so doing it is obliged to restrict its discussion of crucial features of society, most notably that of power and dominance.

Earlier in the chapter (pp.159–62) the difference between ethnomethodology and Chomskyan linguistics was noted. Ethnomethodology shares these differences with the ethnography of communication in that the two perspectives are concerned with the study of everyday language as opposed to formal aspects of language. The study of code switching is a case in point since the importance of context in deciding the meaning of talk and action is highlighted. Rather than seeing code switching as the consequence of a deficiency in one of the two languages or codes, it is seen as a means of communicating intimacy, seriousness, a change of status from the formal to the informal. It serves as a cure telling the hearer to employ different background information to interpret what follows. Thus the ethnography of communication and ethnomethodology are complementary in terms of substantive interests and findings. Let us then turn to a consideration of the ethnography of communication.

7 The ethnography of communication

The ethnography of communication derives from what is referred to as anthropological linguistics and, more specifically, from American cultural anthropology. Despite the tendency to regard it as a product of the 1960s, and, in some respects, as running parallel to the emergence of ethnomethodology with which it appears to have much in common, it does have a longer history in that it derives from the language philosophy of Herder and relies heavily on the work of the founders of cultural anthropology, especially Sapir and Whorf.

More than anything, the ethnography of communication can be seen as an expression of the principles of anthropology and, simultaneously, as a rejection of the work of Chomsky. This is best expressed with reference to the perspective's main concept of communicative competence. Whereas Chomsky maintained that competence was a matter of the mastery of grammatical rules, the protagonists of the ethnography of communication, much in the same way as the ethnomethodologists, maintain that there is much more than this to competence. The anthropological ingredient of this argument involves the emphasis placed on the role of culture in the achievement of competence.

In surveying the ethnography of communication I would like to consider the intellectual and philosophical tradition from which it derives. This will then allow an overview of the main concepts and arguments associated with this perspective and its relationship both to ethnomethodology and to Parsonian structural functionalism.

ORIGINS

For many not familiar with the tradition, American cultural anthropology will seem to be an aberration. While it does retain much of the Durkheimian origins which are common to all anthropology, the emphasis upon culture and its role in explanatory analysis marks it off from the older anthropological tradition. In this respect it is tempting to suggest that the functionalism of social anthropology, primarily through the work of Radcliffe-Brown, left a greater mark on sociology and more specifically on Parsonian structural functionalism than it did on cultural anthropology. What is necessary in this chapter is to outline the relationship between the historical tradition, the emergence of cultural anthropology and its input to the ethnography of communication.

Perhaps it is with the work of Herder that we should begin. It is easy to understand why Hymes, the leading protagonist of the ethnography of communication, contrasts what is termed 'Cartesian linguistics' with the work of Herder since it is an expression of his rejection of the work of Chomsky. In his discussion of linguistic competence, Chomsky emphasises the manner in which linguistics after Descartes emphasised the nature of mind as prior to experience (1966). This, in turn, led to the advocation of an analytic, universalising, reconstituting methodology for linguistic behaviour. Hymes (1970) opposes this by drawing on the work of Herder, claiming that his, and subsequent work, discussed language as the constitution of cultural identity. Associated with this perspective was a methodology which emphasised cultural relativity. Evidently this is a somewhat arbitrary distinction, even if it is useful in emphasising Hymes' main focus. Herder's work represented a definite continuity with earlier concerns, even if in nothing more than the tendency to relate different languages to the essence of community and culture, and in the tendency to treat language as a feature of social order and internal cohesion. More importantly, perhaps, it also treated single languages as the unit of analysis and interpretation, with the consequence that linguistic universals tended to be disregarded. However, when we consider the work of von Humboldt, as the inheritor of the work of Herder, it is clear that he was as concerned with universals as he was with differences.

In chapter 1 it was noted that the main concern in the study of language during the nineteenth century was with descriptive theory and a historical analysis which emphasised the relationship between distinct languages. Greenberg (1968:62–3) has argued that it was the emergence of anthropological linguistics which was responsible for the shift away from this approach. He argued that the Boasian emphasis upon the description of cultures through intense ethnographic work made it clear that the methods of descriptive linguistics and the associated explanatory inference based upon historical texts were inadequate with reference to unwritten languages. It is claimed that this led to a revolution in linguistics, a revolution reflected not merely in the work of Saussure, but also in that of the North American anthropologists, most notably Boas, Sapir and Bloomfield. The emphasis shifted to the synchronic study of language, with languages seen as coherent and distinctive wholes, but the descriptive emphasis remained. The aim was to discover the structure of any language which could be 'described in its own right, rather than being distorted by the arbitrary imposition of Western habits of hearing or of grammatical categorising' (Greenberg 1968:64). That is, the anthropological emphasis on the emic, or the objective of seeing the world through the eyes of those who were being studied, was adopted. This apparent allusion to phenomenology will be discussed below (pp.183–7).

The demise of philology and the emergence of phonology, morphology and semantics was claimed to involve entering into the other's frame of reference (Gumperz 1982:13). This was not merely a reference to the emic objective but also involved constructing a framework for linguistic analysis based upon speech rather than grammar. As a consequence, where many features of language had been merely grafted onto the evolutionist assumptions of the analyst the new approach developed a conception of cultural relativity and explained differences in terms of culture rather than primitiveness or irrationality. At first, of course, the approach suffered from the influence of the Boasians with their emphasis upon induction, but the deductive approach was eventually reintroduced in the form of a psychologism which stressed the link between mind and speech. Greenberg (1968:65) has equated this view with behaviourism which was also coming into vogue at that time.

The work of Sapir and Whorf characterises this focus upon language, culture and cognition. In opposing the claim that linguistic reasoning is a feature of universal logical processes which are independent of specific languages and cultures, they emphasised the link between language and world view by claiming that meaning was, simultaneously, culture bound and subconsciously structured. It is this tradition with its focus on language and culture which the ethnography of communication has inherited.

EMICS, ETICS AND ETHNOSCIENCE

One of the concerns which derived from the work of Sapir was the distinction between etic and emic frameworks. The claim for universal phonetic elements and the associated phonological theory meant that it was possible for linguists to agree on the sound system of any particular language without either distorting that sound system by any bias of classification or perception which would derive from the investigator's background. This seemingly neutral and objective basis of language classification and description was known as the etic framework. Concern with the scientific claims of the discourse of professional linguistics was satisfied by the assertion that any study and its results could now be replicated. On the other hand, there was also the belief that each language should be treated separately because of the inherent unique features of different languages. This involved the emic elements and their arrangement. These emic elements involved the subjective dimension of the native speaker's categories underlying his/her perceptions of significance. The emergence of what has been termed ethnoscience among North American cultural anthropologists during the 1960s was an attempt to develop the precision associated with phonology and grammar with reference to ethnographic description and analysis. In a sense it was an attempt to apply scientific principles to the study of culture and behaviour. As such it amounts to a continuation of cultural idealism albeit within a distinctive context associated with the rigour of linguistic science.

The need to learn to see the world through the eyes of the studied has a long history in anthropology. The importance of Kantian and neo-Kantian philosophy in Germany during the second half of the nineteenth century involved focusing upon a compromise between idealism and materialism which claimed that knowledge of external 'things-in-themselves' depended upon sense impressions which are conditioned by moral sense and concepts of space and time. Mind and reality coexist in the production of knowledge. One emphasis deriving from this claim was the emphasis upon a form of mentalism which heralded the cultural anthropological concern with cognitive science. It is evident in Fechner's psychophysics, and in Dilthey's concern with the *Geistwissenschaften* or human sciences and his emphasis upon the importance of articulating a concern for 'lived experience' and 'understanding' with a historical dimension. This concern with the human sciences was also evident in the work of Rickert and Windelband who were tracing a similar concern with neo-Kantian philosophy. This German anti-materialist orientation had a profound influence upon the work of Boas and subsequent North American anthropologists, including Sapir (1917).

Neither was this concern with a subjective orientation missing from the concerns of British social anthropology. Malinowski claims that the ultimate objective of the ethnographer is:

> to grasp the native's point of view, his relation to life, to realise his vision of *his* world. To study the institutions, customs, and codes or to study the behaviour and mentality without the subjective desire of feeling by what these people live, of realising the substance of their happiness – is, in my opinion, to miss the greatest reward which we can hope to obtain from the study of man.
>
> (Malinowski 1961:25)

Evidently this view derives from an intimacy with the work of Durkheim and his student Mauss, and with their influence on the link between individual consciousness and collective representation.

Sapir's claim that emic or underlying structures affect the perception of sound (Sapir 1925) is a reflection of the following claim:

> It is impossible to say what any individual is doing unless we have tacitly accepted the essentially arbitrary modes of interpretation that social tradition is constantly suggesting to us from the very moment of our birth. Let anyone who doubts this try the experiment of making a painstaking report (i.e. an etic one) of the actions of a group of natives engaged in some activity, say religious, to which he has not the cultural key (i.e. a knowledge of the emic system) . . . . He will be guilty of all manner of distortion; his emphasis will be constantly askew. He will find interesting what the natives take for granted as a casual kind of behaviour worthy of no particular comment, and he will utterly fail to observe the crucial turning points in the course of action that give formal significance to the whole in the minds of those who do possess the key to its understanding.
>
> (quoted in Pike 1954:9–10)

A number of points stand out here. First, the emic is equated with the cultural, it is cultural variation which obscures inter-subjective understanding. Also the emic or cognitive categories which the individual holds derive from culture. Second, behaviour is to be understood in terms of a form of normativeness deriving from socialisation into a 'social tradition'. That is, culture is neither behaviour nor the conception of the world itself but that which conditions the *Weltanschauung* and, subsequently, behaviour. It is essentially a feature of mentalism involving purpose, meaning and attitudes. Emic study

> helps one to appreciate not only the culture or language as an ordered whole, but it helps one to understand the individual actors in such a life-drama – their attitudes, motives, interests, responses, conflicts, and personality development.
>
> (Pike 1954:11)

That is, culture constitutes an ordered whole which conditions individual behaviour as a member of the social aggregate which we treat as culture. It would appear that culture seems to be treated as the aggregate of individuals but closer scrutiny makes it clear that culture is treated, at least in part, within the context of the Durkheimian sense of a social totality.

At one level it seems strange that the emic/etic distinction should derive from linguistics. All grammars have derived, in one sense or another, from ethnographic work since they are built up out of the informant's knowledge of the acceptability of any rules or patterns associated with his/her language. Similarly, phonetic distinction relies upon the existence of sound contrasts which are significant to the native speaker. Not, of course, that either the phonetic system or the grammatical rules will necessarily correspond to any analysis which the native speaker is capable of performing. This much is evident in the work of the Chomskyans whose main concern, in stressing the pan-human linguistic ability, is to account for what the native sees as valid relationships among grammatical sentences, rather than describing everyday talk (Gumperz 1982:18).

The association between emic and etic is problematic. Certainly the tendency of ethnographers is not to resort simply to the perspective of the studied but rather to integrate this with a conceptualisation and categorisation which derives from the investigator and his/her intellectual profession. Thus there is an attempt to place emic data within the context of epistemology, thereby establishing the truth validity of interpretation. Thus the etic avoids the premises of the emic.

It is from these concerns that what became known variously as ethnoscience, ethnosemantics and the new ethnography derived in the 1960s. As a form of cultural idealism it sought to commit cultural anthropology to an emic-based orientation. Harris (1968:598) has claimed that this orientation is merely another manifestation of the Durkheimian concern with social order. Its main preoccupation is a mentalism involving the search for patterns in the cognitive orientations of the subject of study. It involves a concern with the logical functions of mind rather than the emotional or irrational. Whereas earlier emic approaches focused upon discovering the unconscious psychological complexes which the investigators assumed underlay ideal and actual behaviour, ethnoscience ignored the premises of psychological science. As such there is a tendency for culture to be conceptualised as a static system of logical categories which is contrasted with a materialist approach:

> The great problem for a science of man is how to get from the objective world of materiality, with its infinite variability, to the subjective world of form as it exists in what, for lack of a better term, we must call the minds of our fellow man . . . . Structural linguistics has, I think, made us conscious, at least, of their nature, and has gone on to convert this consciousness into a systematic method.

> (Goodenough 1964:39)

It would seem that the materialist position is rejected because of the difficulty of it being encompassed within a programme of ethnographic work which must be emic in nature.

The chief aim of ethnoscience is to discover the ways in which members of a community categorise their own behaviour and in so doing to ensure that the analytical categories of the investigator are not superimposed. It also seeks to move beyond mere observation and recording. The referent 'science' involves classification deriving from the claim that aggregation into classes is a general 'characteristic of living things' (Simpson 1964:3). Simpson proceeds to claim that this form of generalisation is essential for adaptation seen as a feature of survival. That is, generalisation is a fundamental principle of being. It is particularly evident in science which classifies and aggregates things in order to minimise chaos and rests on the assumption that nature itself is orderly (3–5). However, the bases of the classificatory systems are by no means uniform across human populations and the prefix 'ethno' infers systems of knowledge and cognition typical of particular cultures, or, 'To put it another way, a culture itself amounts to the sum of a society's folk classifications, all of that society's ethnoscience, its particular ways of classifying its material and social universe' (Sturtevant 1964:99). From this conception of ethnoscience various attempts were made to compile such fields of study as ethnobotany, ethnogeography and so on. While it was a form of protest against the Enlightenment claim for the superiority of science and reason it retained the centrality of rationality even if it was culturally conditioned rationality.

COMMUNICATIVE COMPETENCE

The following statement by Goodenough is an early expression of the principle underlying the concept of communicative competence:

> A society's culture consists of whatever it is one has to know or believe in order to operate in a manner acceptable to its members, and to do so in any role that they accept for any one of themselves.
>
> (Goodenough 1957:167)

However, it is the work of Del Hymes which is generally associated with the relevance of this perspective for the ethnography of communication. Hymes appears to have been involved with ethnoscience from the beginning of his career (Gumperz and Hymes 1972:130–1), and the similarity of his concept of communicative competence to the above statement by Goodenough is striking: 'Communicative competence involves knowing not only the language code, but also what to say to whom, and how to say it appropriately in any given situation' (Saville-Troike 1982:22).

This conception is evidently a reaction to the Chomskyan concept of linguistic competence which rests on the knowledge of all of the grammatical sentences of a language. Hymes (1966) reacted to this by claiming that the cultural and social knowledge of any society is an essential feature of successful communication. Indeed much of Hymes' writing involves the repeated explication of cross-cultural examples from exotic societies which underline this point while simultaneously refuting the Chomskyan position. These examples emphasise that values and *Weltanschauung* vary by culture and thereby underline the overriding importance of culture within any explanatory framework. The main thrust of both his and Gumperz's work is that cross-cultural differences can and do produce conflicts or inhibit communication. Indeed, Gumperz (1982:19) reiterates the emphasis upon communicative competence as an alternative to the Chomskyan emphasis in stating that if individuals are to be effective in cooperation with others they must share a common grammatical structure even if the surface forms which they employ may differ. That is, speakers must understand each other in more than a grammatical sense.

The concept of communicative competence involves the idea of communicative repertoire, or the variety of the language codes of a specific speech community, and includes 'all varieties, dialects or styles used in a particular socially defined population, and the constraints which govern the choice among them' (Gumperz 1972b:217). The individual selects from among these codes whatever is appropriate to the context. However, it cannot be assumed that every individual will be able to produce the entire range, so that different subgroups within the speech community may understand and employ different codes. The extent of knowledge of these codes appears to relate to the social organisation of the group, this social organisation involving not merely the structural features such as social class and the associated social status, but also related psychological conditions such as 'goals of interaction' (Saville-Troike 1982:51). This variation in social structure is conveyed in speech so that when reference is made to the competence to convey meaning it is a social meaning that is involved. Furthermore, the rational aspect of the conveying of meaning involves interactional strategies on behalf of the speaker, strategies which are employed to 'establish, maintain, or manipulate role-relationships' (Saville-Troike 1982:52). These roles are a manifestation of individual social positions which involve rights and obligations and which are marked by language. That is, roles are signalled by speech.

The essential starting point for the understanding and evaluation and even the recognition of this communicative competence is, once again, the speech community. It is essential in order to emphasise that language is a social phenomenon and that the point of departure is social rather than linguistic (Hymes 1977:47). This community is a normative construct involving the shared knowledge of rules of speaking. As such it is a community built up out of interaction, these interactions being a manifestation of identity (Hymes 1977:47). Gumperz defines it as follows: 'A speech community is defined in functionalist terms as a system of organised diversity held together by common norms and aspirations' (1982:24). Not only is it normative but it also involves a shared goal orientation. One of the problems with this conception of speech community surrounds the issue of identity in that identity derives from language, and yet it is a social identity. This dilemma is resolved by claiming that language is a mirror of society. There is an attempt to acknowledge social diversity by departing from any claim that a community is a homogeneous, undiversified entity but this merely confounds the issue of any common goal orientation that derives from social commonality. Evidently there is an attempt, inevitably unsuccessful, to rephrase the conventional understanding of community as interactional, normative, spatial and psychological. Despite the emphasis upon the importance of the social nature of the community it is clear that language remains a central ingredient, and if it is claimed that speech similarity and identity derive from interactional forces which, in turn, are manifestations of social similarity, it is difficult to accommodate the idea of a community built out of interaction which is not homogeneous. Inevitably there emerges a circular argument in which community is socially defined while maintaining that the maintenance of the separate identity of the speech community derives from the function of language. However, the social variation within the community gives rise to different language codes which have a signalling potential in alluding to a shared history, values and mutual obligations, and interaction is seen in terms of the availability of these signals which are claimed to contain culture and society. It is unclear how the variation of codes and, presumably, signals which convey commonality, serve to integrate what is defined as a community unless the integration derives from diversity and even adversity. It would appear that the position advocated, whatever else its limitations, is possible only if language and society are one and the same, rather than language being a reflection of society. The one element that, it would appear, does integrate the community is the 'cooperation' referred to by Gumperz (1982:94), the very ingredient which is essential for successful interactional competence. Interaction is reduced to effective and successful cooperation and becomes the *sine qua non* of community. This argument is, of course, similar to that we have already seen with reference to ethnomethodology, but must also relate to Mauss' insistence upon the universal nature of reciprocity as a guiding force of social behaviour.

To participate in a speech community is not the same as being a member of that community (Hymes 1977:50) since membership depends upon the shared knowledge of rules for the conduct and interpretation of speech. That is, membership is restricted to a matter of competence and it would seem that this, therefore, is the defining criterion even though the reference to participation would suggest the pre-existence of a community, but a community devoid of members would be meaningless. This community is a local unit, that is, it is spatially confined, and involves primary interaction. This interaction involves a series of speech networks which link community members through a shared knowledge of forms of speech and ways of speaking.

Membership of the speech community involves a sharing of the normative system and the question arises of how this is achieved. The answer inevitably involves socialisation. It is claimed that:

Children's intent to communicate arises naturally out of the system of shared assumptions and understandings which result from the regularities and rituals of their early socialisation.

> (Cook-Gumperz 1977 cited in Saville-Troike 1982:210)

It is through these norms that communicative events are judged (Hymes 1977:21) and, as a consequence, competence judgement is established. That is, norm is not equated with competence, but rather competence is a manifestation of the norms.

The issue of where the norm derives from and whose interests it serves is answered by the claim that culture conditions the normative structure. It would seem therefore that we are locked in what is essentially a culturist argument in which culture is the ultimate explanatory force. Certainly culture plays a central role in the ethnography of communication. Hymes rejects the idea of culture as shared behaviour, stating:

> I subscribe to the view that what is distinctively cultural, as an aspect of behaviour or of things, is a question of capabilities acquired or elicited in social life, rather than a question of the extent to which the behaviour or things themselves are shared.
>
> (Hymes 1977:20)

Culture becomes synonymous with meaning associated with social practice and social experience – socialisation. Furthermore: 'The systems of culture are patterns of symbols, and language is only one of the symbolic systems in this network' (Saville-Troike 1982:23). The consequence is that communicative behaviour is symbolic and, in that sense, it is simultaneously cultural behaviour. It is in this sense that culture is defined as what the individual must know in order to be a functional member of the speech community. Thus Hymes (1977:207) emphasises Sapir's account of culture as:

> The true locus of culture is in the interaction of specific individuals and, on the subjective side, in the world of meaning which each one of these individuals may unconsciously abstract for himself from his participation in these interactions.
>
> (Sapir 1932:515)

It would appear therefore that culture is both interaction and that which conditions interaction. Of course this is necessary otherwise it would be impossible to encounter culture through the ethnographic method. As a feature of culture, language, in a context characteristic of Whorf, is held to inform the world view and is, thereby, a metalanguage of culture and a socially situated cultural form. Since culture is an inherent feature of social behaviour, even if it is not conceptualised in a behaviourist mode, our understanding of the concept is enhanced by considering the view of interaction within this field of study.

Since the emphasis of the ethnography of communication is upon the analysis of situated talk, it must, inevitably, be interactionist. The conception of interaction involves the existence of rational actors operating within a goal-orientated framework. Thus interaction is purposive and therefore functional. Communication is seen as orientated towards conveying information in order to trigger a response. Thus language, as a symbolic form, is employed to convey social position and identity. Interaction proceeds through the interactors exchanging signals which contain both culture and society and involve such features as values in a symbolic form. What must be involved here is a conception of meaning and its decipherment and it is, of course, embedded in the idea of a restricted form of competence, restricted through that which it conveys – culture. The rational nature of the activity involves a purposive action interpreted as meaningful, but we have already seen that meaning is synonymous with culture, and therefore the rationality of the action is rooted in the culture of the actor. The anthropological nature of the enterprise and the heavy emphasis upon the need for an emically based ethnography is now clear – it involves the need to probe the rationality of such purposive behaviour. Meaning no longer has the more common conception as deriving from a pan-human ability to reason through logical procedure but is closely tied both to language and culture. It would appear that the emic emphasis that is inherent in this conception of interaction must bear a close relationship to the phenomenological nature of ethnomethodology and it might be useful to outline the differences and similarities between the two schools.

ANTHROPOLOGICAL ETHNOMETHODOLOGY?

On the surface it would seem that the emphasis upon seeing the world through the eyes of the studied has a great deal in common with the phenomenology expressed in the ethnomethodological perspective. Indeed there seems to be a great deal of overlap and we have already seen how John Gumperz, one of those most closely involved in the ethnography of communication, also places himself within the ethnomethodological camp. Similarly, the work of those involved in the ethnography of communication is replete with references to ethnomethodologists such as Garfinkel, Sacks, and Shegloff. This should not be surprising since both perspectives derive from the same country and often involve colleagues working in different departments on the same campus. Yet in the work on communicative competence there is also frequent reference to the work of Goffman, who many ethnomethodologists would claim had very little to do with the ethno-methodological enterprise. What is common to both, and indeed to the ethnography of communication is, of course, the Durkheimian concern with the theory of rituals. Evidently it is essential to consider the extent and nature of the overlap between the two approaches.

Hymes emphasises that the object of study for the ethnography of communication is communication from the standpoint and interests of the community itself; this plural conception is expressed in terms of the singular community being the consequence of community members sharing knowledge and insights (Hymes 1977:8). The reason for expressing this emphasis is to counteract the prevalent tendency for research to be deductive in nature. On the other hand, we find Gumperz (1982:6) stating that the interpretive approach which he advocates makes no assumption concerning the sharedness of rules or oral norms. However, in stating that the norms of interpretation must derive from the purposes and needs of human persons in social action, Hymes (1977:61) would appear to be closer to Gumperz' position than initially appears to be the case.

The explicit reference to ethnomethodology and various ethno-methodologists makes very little reference to either philosophy or theory. Rather the reference is to conceptual similarities between the two perspectives. Thus Hymes (1977:11) claims that ethnographic objectivity is inter-subjective objectivity which is, in turn, that of the participants in the culture. He also makes reference to 'ad hocing' as employed by Garfinkel (1972). Indeed his main link to ethnomethodology seems to be methodological, mainly involving semantic analysis (1977:80). Similarly, Gumperz refers to 'turn taking' and 'referential semantics' (1982:4), while Saville-Troike (1982) relates discontinuous events to 'interruptions', and functional relativity to 'inter-subjectivity', while also making reference to shifting for repair and the assumptions concerning the sharing of interest in the assessment of meaning in communication between the ethnography of communication and ethnomethodology.

Evidently what the two perspectives share is a concern with the interpretation of meaning within what purports to be a phenomeno-logical context. Perhaps it is Gumperz, as I have already implied, who is closest to the ethnomethodologists. He explicitly rejects the empirical positivism of more conventional sociolinguistics such as variable rules (1982:26), and emphasises the fundamental ingredient of ethnomethodology – that social reality is only constituted in and through interaction. The opposition which he develops between variable rules and linguistic competence relies, once again, upon methodological issues, claiming that the survey method is incapable of resolving those issues which involve competence and which require in-depth participant observation. None the less, his statement is more than a statement of preference since he does contest the a priori assumptions associated with aggregate populations while simultaneously emphasising that, for him, the alternative involves a study of how reality is constituted in and through interaction. In this respect he seems to be emphasising the individualism of interactionism as opposed to the Durkheimian concern with the pre-existing, supraindividual nature of society. In so doing he emphasises that individuals are free to alter their social personae as circumstances demand and the objective of study then focuses upon the interpretational nature of human interactional behaviour. Such a speaker-orientated approach focuses attention upon the strategies of the actors and demands an interpretive analysis of verbal strategies. In this respect it would appear evident that Gumperz has approached the study of verbal behaviour, at least in his more recent work, with the same rejection of theoretical statements concerning the nature of society as have his colleagues who founded ethnomethodology. Whereas Hymes is concerned with the interpretation of verbal strategies, Gumperz places the emphasis upon their creation.

Hymes' position is quite different and is, perhaps, more characteristic of the manner in which ethnosemantics inherited the anthropological concern with the view of the actor, but subsumed this within a more conventional approach to social structure and social psychology. While the ethnosemanticists emphasised the need to develop folk taxonomies or classification, they also assumed that the ultimate goal of their work was to translate these taxonomies into the terms of their own society and culture (Conklin 1955). What is emphasised is that this is no simple matter and he stressed, as if paraphrasing the Boasian recipe for the study of cultural traits at the beginning of the century, that before any relevant attempt can be made to abstract any theoretical conclusions from their data, a dedicated approach to the cross-cultural study of folk taxonomies must be undertaken (Hymes 1977:34). As such it is a statement in favour of cultural relativism which carries within it a hidden concern with evolutionism and diversity, a point I shall return to. In this respect they seem to echo the sacrificial dedication of the ethnomethodological endeavour. As a consequence, the emphasis is on the descriptive and Hymes (1977:33) expresses the belief that the exotic nature of the anthropological object of study precludes the deductive approach of social science. This is akin to stating that the emergence of theory is only possible within the context of western society without going so far as to claim that it is a feature unique to western culture.

Where Hymes would appear to depart from the ethnomethodologists is in his persistent reference to a social structure which pre-exists the interaction which he studies, that is, in the rejection of the fundamental concern of ethnomethodology. Throughout his work there is reference to norms of conduct which derive from the speech community and which are a facet of communication (Hymes 1987:223). With reference to a rejection of ethnomethodology, this is expressed in the following:

> Contrary to some writers (Cicourel 1981, Penalosa 1981) values, norms, attitudes and beliefs are a part, both as knowledge and as facets of motivation, including such capabilities as confidence and courage.

(Hymes 1987:223)

For Hymes, behaviour is a manifestation of a deeper set of codes and rules which precede actual behaviour. Thus the speech event is governed by norms of use which, in turn, are shared and are acquired through socialisation. Norms are also conceived of as culturally conditioned and language as a selective metalanguage of culture, or as a socially situated cultural form. Thus culture as a source of meaning expressed in a symbolic form is the ultimate source of guidance of human behaviour. This all seems far closer to the Parsonian argument than the ethnomethodological deviation from it. Once one separates the interactional analysis of the interpretation of meaning from the frame which seeks to account for social action, no matter how rudimentary that frame, the difference between the ethnography of communication and ethnomethodology becomes evident.

Perhaps the reference to Goffman which appears in much of the work by ethnographers of communication affords a key to the difference. Some (Attewell 1974), to the dismay of ethnomethodologists, have sought to lump Goffman's work with that of the ethnomethodologists, but there are clear differences between them. For Goffman social structure came first in the sense that subjective consciousness derives from it. The process of impression management which he emphasises is not equivalent to the structures it creates, sustains or changes, as the ethnomethodological argument implies. This is not to deny that ethnomethodologists are also concerned with the idea of impression management, but that their conception of it is quite different from that of Goffman, whose concern is with Durkheim's vision of a real material world in which rituals are performed through interaction and collective mental representations thereby created. The importance of Durkheim's work for the anthropological concern, especially with reference to the significance and importance of ritual and culture, makes the parallel between Goffman and the ethnography of communication appear appropriate. What is surprising is that those involved in the ethnography of communication persist in talking about Goffman and the ethnomethodologists in the same breath despite the sustained criticism of the latter by Goffman (1974).

EVOLUTIONISM

I have already implied that there is an element of evolutionism associated with the ethnography of communication. It is time to pursue this issue further. That evolution is a concern should not be surprising given the centrality of this concept in cultural anthropology. Even when there was a grave concern with the implication of such a concept as in the debate concerning unilinear evolutionism, it was not rejected but merely reformulated. As we will see, assumptions in the variety of evolutionism presented by the ethnographers of communication are fascinating discourses which reflect much of what has already been said about this topic.

We have already discussed how socialisation is a key factor in explaining how the normative structure is operationalised within society. However, socialisation is also treated as a feature of social order in the sense that it is the means by which people learn 'one's place in society' (Saville-Troike 1982:219). However, the rigidity of such a conception is denied by the claim that people as individuals are creative, and are capable of changing their place in society through self-initiative. This, in turn, is premised on the idea of a society which affords freedom of choice to the individual. Hymes (1977:90) places some constraint on this freedom in stating that freedom is akin to human nature but that societal rules exist to curb freedom, that is, some semblance of social order as constraint is essential. A central feature of this social order involves the concept of role seen as involving the rights and duties which are exchanged through social roles. Thus Hymes argues in terms of a rule-governed creativity. Furthermore, since language is held to reflect society, when he discusses the creative aspect of language as a measure of freedom and diversity, it is an expression of the same qualities within society. This creativity, although constrained by social rules, is essentially individual in nature, and is a manifestation of a belief in individual freedom and diversity.

There is clearly a tension between social constraint and individual freedom in this argument, the Hobbesian problem once again in evidence. While individuals appear to be assigned to social 'places', this assignation is not viewed as a permanent state. Rather, through self-initiative, the goal-orientated behaviour of the individual, within the context of freedom of choice, is capable of changing his/her 'place' in society. The individual is truly responsible for his/her own destiny and a failure to achieve is, presumably, a failure to exploit the available freedom through creativity. One feature of this creativity involves a constant striving for reciprocal cooperation based upon people's communicative competence within the context of rational decision-making. It is true that Hymes, as if responding to criticism concerning the consensus nature of this argument, claims that cooperation cannot be taken for granted as the *sine qua non* of communication, but rather, that 'cooperation is often something to accomplish, not something given' (Hymes 1987:222).

It is here that we encounter the concept of adaptation which is seen as a feature of individual creativity. Hymes claims that a goal of education is

> to enable children to develop their capacity for creative use of language as part of successful adaptation of themselves and their communities in the continuously changing circumstances characteristic of contemporary life.
>
> (Hymes 1977:119)

That is, the goal-orientated behaviour is not seen as inherently selfish since the adaptation which it is a feature of contributes to the benefit of other members of the individual's community. Adaptation can only be a positive quality since everyone will gain from it. Striving for reciprocal cooperation now makes more sense in that, as a feature of individual creativity, such behaviour is also a feature of that which integrates the community within adaptation. Communicative competence now becomes the essence of harmony and solidarity within difference; it is the basis of social order, albeit a changing order which requires constant adaptation. A clearer elaboration of the Comtean conception of functional integration could not be desired.

Perhaps the most interesting feature of the evolutionary argument is the link made between individual creativity on the one hand, and democracy and freedom on the other. We have already had a hint of this relationship in the portrayal of individual creativity as involving freedom and diversity. I have already hinted that social roles are conceived of in terms of rights and obligations with reference to other members of the community (Hymes 1977:203). These features of social roles constitute the normative structure of the society. Saville-Troike (1982:87) has an explicitly functionalist conception of social roles, a conception which relates to the issue of evolution. She claims that societies differ in the rigidity of social differentiation, this rigidity being reflected in language. A rigidly stratified society is contrasted with 'democratic communities' in which roles are open for individuals to assume. Again we find the dichotomous distinction between mechanical and organic solidarity placed within an evolutionary context. Saville-Troike (1982:43) claims that in societies where there is more emphasis upon ritual, and the cases she cites are what she calls closed social groups, there is less freedom and more direct control with social roles rigidly delineated. The alternative is the open society characterised by democratic procedures. Given this contrast, implicit though it may be, it would appear that freedom, as conceptualised within this discourse, is akin to progress. This is followed by a reference to the work of Bloomfield (1927) which contrasts 'primitive' groups and literate societies. The contrast is between groups and societies, a clear reference to the relevance of political systems to the evolutionary argument.

The relevance of language to this argument involves the claim that language reflects society. Not all languages are equal in the sense of their functional potential (Saville-Troike 1982:49) and, it would seem, isolation restricts the potential of language. That is, while language has the potential to serve all functions it is only communication which activates that potential. Once again we encounter the idea that communication is the driving force of progress and the evolution of mankind:

> It therefore remains central to our concerns to describe what a community has made of its language, and why, and how – not only as part of our scientific enquiry, but because one of the responsibilities and motivations of a socially constituted study of language is the welfare of its human speakers.
>
> (Saville-Troike 1982:49)

It would appear that progress and, consequently, democracy, is the responsibility of the community which is the basis of human welfare. Presumably if the community is unable to make much of its language, regardless of the political context, either another language can be imposed or external intervention justified in the name of human welfare seen as progress. Since adaptation as a feature of evolution is dependent upon individual creativity, which is synonymous with freedom, the inability to make much of their language is a manifestation of a lack of freedom and creativity in the speakers of that language.

This argument would appear to be an argument in favour of an evolutionary process which culminates in a single language which constitutes the language of freedom and democracy. Yet we find two arguments which would contradict such a development. First there is the characteristic anthropological argument in favour of human diversity, an argument which we have already placed within an evolutionary context with reference to the work of Gumperz. The plurality of human society is a theme which emerges constantly in the work on the ethnography of communication. One of the functions of the persistent reference would seem to be to emphasise that values, world view, etc., vary by culture, and thereby to underline the importance of culture. The following statement is revealing:

> Chomsky's type of explanatory adequacy leads away from speech, and from languages, to relationships possibly universal to all languages, and possibly inherent in human nature . . . . The complementary type of explanatory adequacy leads from what is common to all human beings and all languages toward what particular communities and persons have made of their means of speech. It is comparative and evolutionary in a sociocultural, rather than a biological, sense.
>
> (Hymes 1977:203)

The emphasis is upon the fact that man constitutes a subdivided species with culture, and language, as something which contains culture, being the basis of that subdivision. Yet it would seem that the preceding argument suggests that some languages are better suited than others for adaptation and, subsequently, survival. Evolution as a manifestation of group contact becomes a matter of culture rather than politics.

The second point that must be developed refers to Hymes' claim concerning the potential equality of all human groups:

> Many linguists, like many anthropologists, believe that no group of human beings is innately incapable of the highest achievements

of civilisation. . . . What they can speak to is the potential equality of all human groups.

(Hymes 1977:204)

It might be noted that the potential equality refers to groups rather than individuals and, as a consequence, obliges us to discuss inequality in terms of the groups and the features which characterise the groups – in Hymes' case, language and culture. Again what is referred to by Hymes is the claim that 'means of speech are what their users make of them', implying that difference is not a feature of race but of culture. That inequality exists is not challenged; that is, we are not referring to a matter of groups merely being different, but they are unequal and it would appear that, since language is a feature of culture, culture is the factor which accounts for this inequality. That is, evolutionism is a cultural phenomenon which accounts for inequality. Again it would appear to be an argument in favour of a single, universal culture.

Evidently the argument concerning evolutionism within the ethnography of communication is not new. It is one which we have encountered in previous chapters even though minor variations might be discerned. What is increasingly evident is how this evolutionary view mirrors the predominant American political philosophy with its emphasis upon individual freedom, social and cultural diversity and an unwavering dedication to democracy.

LANGUAGE AND SOCIAL NETWORKS

One piece of work which claims an affinity with the ethnography of communication is that of Lesley Milroy (Hymes 1987:223; Milroy 1980). It is a piece of work which has received attention far in excess of its theoretical merits, largely, I suspect, for its attempt to introduce methodological novelty into sociolinguistic research. It is also a work which highlights the limitations of, not only the ethnography of communication, but also other areas of sociolinguistics. Thus the rest of this chapter will be devoted to a discussion of this work.

The study of social networks derives, not from the work of social anthropologists during the 1950s as Milroy (1980:46) suggests, but from the psychometric work of psychologists and it is there that we encounter the interpretation of social groups as the amalgam of social interaction, a major weakness of the perspective, and a conception far removed from Durkheim's idea of the social as involving a *conscience collective*. It is essentially a methodological procedure and even though social networks were referred to by

Radcliffe-Brown (1940) and Fortes (1949), it is in the more recent work of social anthropologists (see *inter alia* Boissevain 1974, Mitchel 1969, Kapferer 1969, Bott 1971 and Cubitt 1973) that the link between method and theory is evident to the extent that implicit theoretical assumptions are drawn into the use of the method. This interest emerged from a dissatisfaction with the functionalism in Radcliffe-Brown's work and involved a claim, somewhat similar to that of the ethnomethodologists, that such a perspective made human actors into dupes. In its place there was a need to study the interaction of individuals in actions which were capable of altering the institutions in which they participated. It was of some significance among social anthropologists and, to a lesser extent, some sociologists, during the 1960s but has received scant attention since that time.

The emphasis of network analysis is fundamentally interactionist, and involves a conception of interaction as involving the negotiated relations of individuals seeking to arrive at a consensus which involves agreement. It is easy to see how Milroy has linked network analysis to the ethnography of communication since both emphasise the importance of the transactional content of interaction and that social relations are negotiated. Yet another feature of network analysis that must be mentioned is its link to rational choice or exchange theory with the emphasis upon individuals operating on some principle of optimisation. There is also a link to the tendency, which we have already encountered, for sociolinguistics to emphasise the normative in that network analysts claim it is the frequency of close interaction which contributes to the development of behavioural norms, with members of clusters exerting pressure on each other for conformity. This linking of social order to normative consensus is highly evident in the work of Boissevain (1988:166), as also is the belief in the ability of the individual to adjust his/her behaviour to conform to different norms – both viewpoints also being fundamental premises of conventional sociolinguistics.

As a consequence of the sharing of assumptions about individual behaviour, and of the ramifications of such behaviour, it is easy to understand how both sociolinguistics and network analysis place emphasis upon the concept of community and tend to have a broadly similar understanding of that concept. Thus the community is seen as the focus of normatively established order and, as we have seen, may even be defined in terms of social or linguistic norms. Milroy seeks to remove the definition of community from the sociolinguistic tendency to conceive of it as deriving from a common agreement about speech norms. Whereas Labov's (1966:125) definition of community was normative, involving the idea that shared values lay behind agreed evaluation of speech, Milroy emphasises the spatial, interactional and psychological dimensions, involving a cohesive group to which its members feel a sense of attachment. It is a small-scale community involving face-to-face interaction within a defined territory. She claims that it encompasses Hymes' (1977) emphasis upon primary interaction. What is interesting about this conception of community is that it is not merely descriptive since it is placed in an economic context. It is a homogeneous entity in the sense that it is a single-class community – a working-class community. I shall have more to say about this conception of a single-class community, but for the moment I would like to emphasise Milroy's claim that the psychological feature of identity and its political corollary – loyalty – derive from the common demands of a population that is confronted by poverty. Solidarity is a feature, not of an allegiance to some norm whose source of origin is unspecified, but of a socioeconomic unity which must have political dimensions. This would imply that community is conceptualised in terms of a conflict orientation which focuses upon the contradictions of a class-based society. Alas this is not sustained since the argument focuses upon difference rather than opposition. We are never told what solidarity and loyalty are in opposition to, and it is only towards the end of the monograph that we have some strangely muted comments about the relationship between community and state. This silence is particularly strange since this relationship is a central feature of community discourse in the north of Ireland. This unwillingness to relate state and community is evident throughout the book. It is reflected in the claim that British society encompasses Irish society (Milroy 1980:180), in the reference to 'Northern Ireland', and in the equation of nation and state, despite the contrasting of local and national values (Milroy 1980:194).

This inability to develop a conflict orientation should not be surprising given that Milroy claims to be continuing the work of Labov and Gumperz while, simultaneously, representing Hymes' interest in communicative competence. The main thrust of the work involves the seemingly contradictory tendency for the stigmatised vernacular to be retained by the working class. In one sense this would appear to be a strange issue to address, for if, as Milroy maintains, this vernacular is a marker of the working class it is the evaluation of class position rather than its language marker that is problematic. That is, even if the stigmatised vernacular is not retained, some other form will be stigmatised in its place as a manifestation of class position – it is the class that is being stigmatised, and that as the consequence of a capitalist society constructed out of inequality and exploitation. Evidently for the question to be anything other than absurd it must be asked within the context of a conception of society as an open system of individuals who have unlimited access to social mobility out of the working class. Indeed it is this which does emerge in Milroy's work, with class being discussed either in consensus terms or being displaced by the focus upon interactional networks. For example, she claims that social class is an ethnocentric concept which does not allow for comparison across societies. Such an argument is only sustainable within the context of a conception of class in terms of status positions associated with culturally conditioned values. A conflictive evaluation of class as involving relationships to the means of production, for example, is perfectly capable of cross-societal evaluation.

Given her conception of class society it is not surprising that the communities which she discusses are variously described as 'working class', 'lower working class', 'industrial proletariat', and 'marginalised'. Despite claiming that community solidarity is a derivative of marginalisation (Milroy 1980:73), her allegiance to the consensus sociology of Labov, Gumperz and Hymes prevents her from pursuing the antagonisms which are a feature of marginalisation. Consequently marginalisation as an explanatory force is not analysed but tends to be taken for granted. The class polarisation is reduced to one involving status and solidarity, individual upward mobility and working-class cohesion, a perspective which, as I have indicated above, inevitably draws her into the consensus orientation of individual liberalism. She claims that each of these dichotomies represents different, rather than oppositional, values, involving local loyalty on the one hand and 'institutional provincial or national values' on the other. Despite drawing upon concepts such as the split working class, which posits the separation of what she refers to as the 'local community' from the 'upwardly mobile urban society', she fails to pursue the issue of class fractioning in a systematic way, with the consequence that community becomes synonymous with the residual of individuals within a fluid society consisting of individuals striving for upward mobility. As a consequence it becomes an argument similar to Durkheim's thesis concerning the functionalism of deviance through emphasising the norm, a view which prevailed among structural functional accounts of deviance of North American sociologists of the 1950s.

Given what has already been said it is not surprising that, once she has established that the communities which are the focus of her study are some kind of working-class community, the class analysis is abandoned in favour of an emphasis upon the social networks of indi-viduals. The assumption is, of course, that the social group is an amal-gam of individuals, a rejection of the fundamental basis of sociological analysis. Milroy claims that sociology treats individuals as 'blobs of clay moulded by social and situational constraints' (Milroy 1980:19), hence her preference for network analysis. However, social networks constitute more than a methodology in Milroy's work, becoming a concept which involves a set of role relationships (54). Social structure now becomes a network of relationships. This is far removed from a sociological analysis, no matter what its orientation.

The reference to role theory allows us to begin to comprehend how this work fits into the normative orientation of consensus theory. An empirical correlation is obtained between retention of the vernacular and the nature of social networks, leaving this correlation to be explained. The claim is made that norms are enforced, or are not enforced, in accordance with the nature of the individual's social network. Thus norms are enforced when networks are dense, with extreme density producing a homogeneity of norms and values. A tautological argument emerges in which loyalty to the vernacular speech norms is accounted for by a density of networks which is a consequence of that loyalty. Furthermore, the corollary of this claim is that loose networks fail to enforce norms and, consequently, the role of norm enforcement is assumed by institutions which enforce publicly legitimised norms. That is, we have an either/or situation with the emphasis upon the normative without any discussion of the ideological nature of these norms and values.

It is tempting to suggest that the use of network analysis derives not so much from the demands of a theoretical perspective as from the need to collect extensive data from a small number of individuals. Milroy admits that she employs the method in order to treat speakers as individuals so that *individual* behaviour can be explained, albeit in terms of what she refers to as corporate *group* membership. As I have stressed, the nature of this individual/group relationship is never clear except in aggregate terms. However, in implying that network relationships are, in effect, role relationships, we begin to see how individuals are conceived of as group members. Role relationships involve rights and obligations which are sustained by reference to the values implicit in the normative structure which brings her right back to her objection to conventional sociological principles. These values are subject to variation, not only from culture to culture, but also from community to community. References to culture are few and far between and when the concept does emerge the discussion is confused. We find reference to 'vernacular culture', to 'British culture', 'ethnic culture' and 'urban culture'. The idea of a superordinate, dominant, controlling culture which is divisible into subcultures is missing, as is the idea of any oppositional culture or subculture. What is clear is that culture, again in a manner consistent with the overriding consensus orientation, is treated as that which determines norms and, thereby, values. Thus, whereas there is an attempt to explain the production of a normative order, further regression leaves us with a free-floating culture as the ultimate consensual influence and the argument is reduced to a culturist, conservative stance. The radicalism of the initial reference to a marginalised, working-class community is entirely lost in an argument which is locked into a view of society as culturally conditioned.

It is evident why the concept of culture is invoked even though it is not made explicit. The exchange theory nature of the framework would insist that individuals operate on the basis of a rationally conditioned optimising behaviour. However, since the subjects of investigation reject the optimisation of upward social mobility, in order to avoid treating this rejection as irrational, the claim must be made that it is a consequence of a different rationality, one which derives from an alternative cultural source. Culture, in a manner consistent with the approach of cultural anthropology, is dealt with as that which conditions values and reason. Thus the communities in question are treated as residual categories somehow outside of the rational, normative consensus of normal society. This is a view which, as we have seen, one encounters time and again in the culturally based accounts of language contact.

Within this cultural framework, norms are treated as social meanings *à la* Hymes, with these meanings, presumably, being a manifestation of values. Since they are a product of culture, and since culture is variable, it is only the bearers of a specific culture which have access to these meanings. It is here that we encounter communicative competence. Thus, once again, it is culture that creates meaning and allows individuals to operate as social beings. The influence of North American cultural anthropology on sociolinguistics has carried way beyond the continent! What we have is an explanation for the social closure of the various communities couched in terms of a normative culture rather than in terms of any explanation that involves an analysis of material and political forces. Rather than conceiving of the diacritica of community as generated through confronting an external power, they are treated as a culturally determined set of strategies for survival adopted by those who have not achieved upward social mobility out of the community. It is yet another example of blaming the victim for not achieving the desirable upward social mobility that is magnanimously offered by a benevolent social and political order.

This leads us to consider the manner in which the individual is conceived of. The individual is viewed as a free entity who is free to express him/herself by employing linguistic resources, even though this freedom is fettered by social norms about how to use language that are imposed by the primary group. Thus individual choice is governed by the values of vernacular culture that are involved in the conveying of social meaning. It is also constrained by an insistence upon conformity with the basis of the social order of the community. Within this conception of a relatively free individual it is claimed that there is a freedom to employ speech in order to symbolise social identity, something which, in turn, is dependent upon social and psychological factors. Thus the individual employs the resources of linguistic variability in expressing social values. Evidently the expression of identity is a feature of the expression of values. In this respect Milroy follows closely the work of Le Page (1968) who claims that the individual creates his/her system of verbal behaviour so that it resembles those common to the group(s) she/he wishes to identify with. However, the individual must be free to change his/her group affiliation from time to time, and thereby must have access to the various linguistic markers of group identity. The associated integration into the group involves an acceptance of that group's norms and values. This implies an openness of the social system, with individuals occupying social places or positions by choice – the constraints of socioeconomic forces are ignored and the argument is close to that of the American Dream within which anyone can succeed if they try hard enough. Thus integration is rationally induced rather than being a consequence of structural position or power based opposition. All that is required is an allegiance to the normative consensus of community based social order. Speech, as a symbol of community loyalty, is no longer viewed in terms of loyalty against some external force, but rather as a feature of integration through conformity with a specific set of norms. Presumably the state becomes a feature of a social order that is a constitution of the sum of its parts – the multiplicity of communities that lie within its territory. Such an argument screams for comment given the nationalist discourses in the north of Ireland.

The relevance of the tendency for exchange theory to emphasise the manner in which individuals rationally achieve agreement and cooperation should be evident. The free individual is striving for such cooperation which is linked to the manner in which the close-knit network exercises control over its members (Milroy 1980:194). We have a situation in which every individual, regardless of his/her position in an unequal social structure, yearns for integration into a social order. Such a perspective is sustainable only if society is seen as a system of opportunities for the enterprising individual, rather than as an oppressive, exploitative system, sustained by power in the name of social order. The normative order is a matter of reciprocal agreement over the nature of social order even though it is claimed that peers supervise the normative order and that the peer group controls that order, thereby conveying the impression that the group, in this case a fraction of the working class, is the guardian of a social order which, presumably, can be in opposition to any other source of social order.

Thus the individual is viewed as a free, rational being whose striving for cooperation with her/his fellow being leads to a desire for social conformity and social order. Language, on the other hand, is the means by which this is achieved. It is a symbolic system which, as such, is a means of conveying social meaning. Thus the use of language becomes a matter of free choice among rational individuals seeking to convey their desire for various social identities to their fellows, these social identities being a manifestation of belonging and integration. Language is functional and is a reflection of social order.

One further issue must be addressed – that of evolution. Hidden in the analysis is a very clear account of the evolutionary role of language in society. It is an account which reiterates the Durkheimian account of the shift from mechanic to organic solidarity. It posits one form of society which is expressed in terms of rural, traditional and tribal with an opposite form which is modern, urban and industrial. The former is seen as homogeneous and solidaristic, involving an organic form of primordiality while the urban, industrial society is individualistic in nature. The relationship between them is expressed in temporal, causal and unidirectional terms, with urban, industrial society being responsible for the 'break up of close knit, territorially based networks' (Milroy 1980:185). Superimposed on this argument is an account of language which results in linguistic traits being described as 'archaic' and as a manifestation of conservative behaviour. It seems that the working-class communities which Milroy discusses are located at the rural end of this continuum, being treated as an extension of rural society. Thus, implicitly, the allegiance to a stigmatised vernacular becomes an archaic feature of tradition which is opposed to the modern, progressive behaviour and language of upwardly mobile individuals. It would seem that the very perspective employed by Milroy merely serves to accentuate the stigmatic nature of the vernacular!

In conclusion, apart from the application of network analysis to linguistic behaviour there is nothing that is new in Milroy's approach. In several respects it is reminiscent of Durkheim's discussion of the functional nature of deviance as developed by Merton (1968) and Albert Cohen (1955) albeit in a different context. Whereas Cloward and Ohlin (1961) interpreted youth subculture in the USA in terms of the frustration of non-achievers with the promised upward mobility of the American Dream, Albert Cohen (1955) assumed a functionalist position which read this subculture as resistance. This theme was further developed by British sociologists working within a Marxist perspective who clearly saw that the American Dream was not directly relevant to youth subculture in Britain, even if they did ignore the more universal philosophy of individual liberalism (see Willis 1977, Corrigan 1980). They pursued the theme of subculture as a feature of resistance. It is these studies which Milroy has been flirting with, but her failure to divorce herself from the consensus perspectives of North American sociolinguistics, and her adoption of the individualistic, rationalistic, interactionism of exchange theory and network analysis, inhibits her ability to project a radical analysis, especially since the predominant ingredient of exchange theory – power – was systematically ignored in her work. Given the problems which it confronts, and the issues it fails to resolve, it is little wonder that exchange theory has been rejected as a useful tool for theorising about social structure (Blau 1979–80).

CONCLUSION

Despite the occasional reference to Marx in the work of Hymes and to the implication of a Marxist conception of ideology in Gumperz's work, there is little to suggest such an orientation in the overall framework of the ethnography of communication. On the contrary, the orientation is far more Kantian in nature than it is Hegelian. This should not be surprising since, as I have emphasised above (pp.172–3), it derives from the concerns of Herder through the North American emphasis of cultural anthropology in the work of Boas, Sapir and Whorf. As such we find the Kantian emphasis upon the constitution of experiences gaining a place of prominence within the ethnography of communication.

From time to time a conflict orientation is claimed for the concept of communicative competence by reference to Habermas' use of the concept. Despite Habermas' grounding in the Marxism of the Frankfurt School his more recent work appears to have abandoned the fundamental premises of Marxism. Habermas, along with the ethnographers of communication emphasises that the speech act is the fundamental source of what he calls the 'intersubjective mutuality of reciprocal understanding, shared knowledge, mutual trust and accord with one another' (1979:24–5). For Habermas, in contrast to the ethnographers of communication, this is premised upon the relations of production which involve a form of social integration unified through values and norms (1979:146). Furthermore, in a stance not unlike the discussion of evolution which we have encountered above, Habermas claims that it is this 'principle of organisation' that determines a society's level of development, expressed in its learning capacity. Not only does Habermas assimilate the evolution of society to that of individual agents but he 'assumes that society is constituted by communication', that 'other forms of social action – for example, conflict, competence, strategic action in general – are derivatives of action oriented to reaching understanding' (Callinicos 1983:143). As a consequence, as Callinicos emphasises, opposition to human emancipation is irrational, and the exploitation, antagonism, conflict and struggle of Marxism are denied by the consensus perspective Habermas adopts.

That there is little ground for claiming that the ethnography of communication involves some semblance of Marxist conflict theory is evident in, among other things, the manner in which fundamental societal concepts are discussed. Thus, for example, social class is conceived of in terms of status and wealth rather than relationship to the means of production. More importantly perhaps Hymes would appear to be as guilty as Habermas in seeking to distinguish and separate communicative action involving language and culture from instrumental action. Such anti-naturalism appears to involve Fichte's notion of reason as inseparable from the quest for human emancipation. The role of rational action in relation to social evolution which I have outlined above makes this clear (pp.187–91).

What then is the theoretical status of the ethnography of communication? We have already qualified its relationship both to Marxism and ethnomethodology. In many respects there is an appeal to Parsonian structural functionalism. In this respect the phenomenological orientation is misleading. The theory of communicative competence is seen very much as part of the scientific endeavour involving the discovery of a theory of language. This involves the discovery of the patterned complexity which is claimed to be involved in communication. The theoretical status involves the ability 'to predict and judge as appropriate or inappropriate what is, in principle, an infinite amount of cultural behaviour' (Hymes 1977:11). The order which exists in communication and which, as we have seen, is the basis of any cooperative endeavour, can be discovered and theorised within the conventional terms of social science. Thus Saville-Troike (1982:108) states that the initial goal is to 'formulate possible hypotheses concerning the diverse ways . . . socio-cultural phenomenon might relate to patterns of communication'. There appears to be a reluctance to suspend judgement as Schutz would advocate. None the less Hymes appears to distinguish between predictive and descriptive theory, arguing that it is only the latter which is currently possible for those involved in the ethnography of communication. The background assumptions which structure such a descriptive theory are treated as heuristic in nature:

> A descriptive theory requires some schema of the components of speech acts. At present such a schema can be only an etic, heuristic input to descriptions. Later it may assume the status of a theory of universal features and dimensions.
>
> (Hymes 1977:53)

However, even such a theory which involves creating taxonomies of speaking and descriptions which will, in turn, result in an adequate classification of languages based upon function, defined as the interaction between social role and features of languages (1977:35), have a limited scope:

> Yet a general theory will always be open. It may define the parameters and grounding of human communicative competence, and guide specific studies and applications. It will not be able to specify absolutely and in advance the character of communicative competence for a particular case, for that will be relative to the persons, activities and needs involved . . . it may be able to anticipate, but not predict configurations of communicative ability yet to emerge . . . .
>
> (Hymes 1987:225–6)

Evidently the aversion to empirical positivism (Hymes 1977) seems to imply a rejection of the predictive nature of such theory, but it does not encompass a suspension of the theoretical endeavour; rather it assumes the necessity of a theoretical framework which serves as a guide for the evaluation of the relevant behaviour. The subscription of objective scientific principles are still very much in evidence.

The associated methodological approach is revealing. There is an emphasis upon the ethnographic nature of research, involving extended periods of participant observation within different societies and cultures; that is, the work is simultaneously ethnographic and comparative. Within this context the emphasis is upon features of communication involving an approach which synthesises a linguistic and an anthropological input. Such an approach claims to 'extend the etic frameworks and to ascertain emic relevance' (Hymes 1977:27) for the data collected by ethnographic means. Since observed behaviour is held to be a manifestation of a deeper set of rules and codes, it is claimed that ethnography can and should focus upon discovering the rules necessary for communicative behaviour. However, the reflection thesis, which states that linguistic variability is socially conditioned, evidently makes the nature of the conception of the social on the part of the investigator an essential aspect of the collection and interpretation of data. Thus, viewing the concepts which constitute the social as the product of a particular theoretical perspective, that is, as a discourse on society, it is clear that they condition the nature of the linguistic data which is gathered. That is, by retaining the importance of theory, even if only within a heuristic context, there is an element of inevitability in the data that is gathered. The ethnographers answer to this tends to be to fall back upon the emic nature of the perspective, claiming that interpretation of the data derives from the actors themselves. Thus it is claimed that the informant can be trained to give either etic or emic information, a claim not unlike that of the ethnomethodologists who state that everyone is a sociologist. Yet this position is not carried to the extreme of the ethnomethodological perspective since the methodological approach appears to be more reminiscent of Weber's ideal types (1964a:106), where a heuristic model is tested by the collection of data and that model subsequently refined through comparison with the data elicited.

The explanatory discourses which are interspersed through the various writings are essentially culturist and, as a consequence, conservative in nature. Culture is the independent variable which accounts for variation in the nature of communicative competence. Furthermore, culture is a normative system of symbolic order which conditions social organisation, including role relationships, values and so on. In this respect culture is the basis of social order. The relationship between language and culture involves language being viewed as an expression of culture, an expression which informs the world view of the individual. It might also be noted that the approach is normative in a different sense as well, in that the tendency is continuously to view the ethnographer's culture as normative and to view other cultures in terms of variations from this norm while also asserting that each cultural system has its own integral autonomy.

Despite claiming that the speech community is socially differentiated, and is established on the basis of speech patterns which reflect this social differentiation, the integrating role of culture lends an element of homogeneity to the unit. This unity is represented by the language which the community is built out of, and, it would seem, reminiscent of Labov (1966). Surface (social) differences in language are not evident at the deeper (cultural) level. At this deeper level the various linguistic/social groups share a common linguistic/conceptual world. This is akin to the mentalist/rationalist position of Chomsky in which the essential equality of humankind – or at least of the members of the speech community – is stressed, and variations at the social level are unfortunate but inevitable. The retention of the scientific perspective, with its emphasis upon the natural nature of language, involving laws or patterns to be developed, tends to lead to language being treated as a 'natural' rather than as a 'social' phenomenon. The 'laws' to be discovered exist at two levels, the social, of which language is a reflection (and this reflection is an essential ingredient of such a perspective), and the cultural level, which subsumes the social.

The nature of the social actor within this wider context is constructed out of the philosophy of individual liberalism which involves a strain of both mentalism and rationalism. Despite the constraints of the normative order, the individual is essentially a free and creative agent capable of expressing social identity in a rational manner, even if that rationality is culturally conditioned. The range of social identities which the individual possesses are expressed through language since language is a reflection of the social. That is, features of language are social markers. The social order pre-exists speech, but it should be noted that Gumperz seeks to avoid the mechanical nature of this argument by focusing attention upon interpretation rather than expression. Interaction involves the negotiation of identity through speech and this is achieved in a rational manner. Thus speech situations are goal orientated and the use of language is grounded in a knowledge of rules and relationships. What we have is a version of linguistic pragmatics of speech acts within the context of the interactive process in which culture is a crucial ingredient.

There are several reasons why a view of language as involving communication-intention should be rejected. One objection is that it is not possible to attribute intention without interpreting speech since intentions, beliefs and speech are part of a single project. Presumably the ethnographers of communication seek to overcome this problem by insisting upon the emic explanation of the speaker after the act. A second objection is stated by Rosen (1985) in what he calls the conventionalist account of meaning – the meanings of expressions are determined by the implicit inter-subjective agreement that is expressed in the rules governing speakers' linguistic practice. He argues that communication presupposes rather than facilitates the existence of beliefs shared by all of the interlocutors. Such communication-intention theory is, in the view of Callinicos (1983:146) 'a softened, socialised Kantianism, which substitutes for the transcendental subject an intersubjectivity whose tacit agreement on the rules of language renders communication possible'.

The conception of speech acts as goal orientated inevitably leads to a functionalist argument. However, function tends to be equated with meaning since the function of language is to convey social meaning. Hymes (1977:146) systematically avoids this issue except to state that his brand of functionalism bears no relationship to behaviourism. However, it is impossible to avoid functionalism, given that language is conceived of in terms of rational, goal orientated, identity expressing actors. Furthermore, language also functions in a pan-individual sense since it is the basis for the separate identity of the speech community. It is here, once again, that the absurdity of the concept of speech community, defined in terms of language, albeit a language that is claimed to reflect social structure, raises its head. Initial scrutiny conveys the impression that functionalism is avoided by drawing upon the argument in terms of purposive action or goal orientated activity, but the functional need that is addressed involves the establishment of effective communication, the basic essence of the social order. This assumption of a teleological quality of the social system in which communication exists because it contributes to the functional need of social order or the persistence of cultural diversity is, evidently, unsatisfactory.

Given the fundamentally consensus nature of this perspective on language and society, it is not surprising that issues of conflict in society are either ignored or are subsumed within a consensus orientation. Saville-Troike (1982:51) makes reference to the concept of domain but does so without any reference to the issue of power and domination in the structuring of language group relations. She also implies that social control derives from culture, this being a normative argument involving rules being seen as norms rather than involving control and power. Since the normative order is an expression of the society, social control is a matter of consent on the part of the people. Hymes (1977:104–5) does make reference to the link between language and social structure seen as an 'unequal and unfair' system, claiming that, as a consequence, code switching is a feature of power and domination. Not only are such references rare within the overall consensus perspective, but they also result in the conception of power and domination as features of interpersonal relationships rather than as features of society.

8   Ethnolinguistic vitality

An area of work which pursues some of the issues discussed in preceding chapters, albeit within a more specifically psychological context, is that of Giles and his associates. They build upon the work of social psychologists such as Wallace Lambert and Henri Tajfel who have pioneered the link between language and psychology. Their main concern is with the variety of attitudes expressed towards speakers with different speech styles (Giles 1987:585). Recent years have seen a proliferation of this field of study, both in terms of the number of active participants and in the volume of work it has produced. At first glance it might appear that such work rightly belongs in psycholinguistics rather than sociolinguistics but, as we shall see, there is a concerted effort to emphasise the social context to the extent that it does overlap with the interests discussed in preceding chapters.

VITALITY

The social parameters are most evident in the concept of vitality. It is claimed that a language group is an ethnic group since language is a symbol of identity and, if people feel themselves to be members of a group, that group must exist regardless of the nature of its basis. The collective nature of this group may well be a subjective phenomenon, but an attempt is made to relate it to objective criteria through the concept of vitality by arguing that the strength of the identity varies in accordance with objective social factors. If, as it appears, ethnic identity is a feature of culturally conditioned subjectivity, this would imply that social factors condition culture. Yet the social tends to be dealt with in terms of behaviour, which would suggest the converse – that the social is culturally determined. This contradiction is evident throughout the discussion of ethnicity

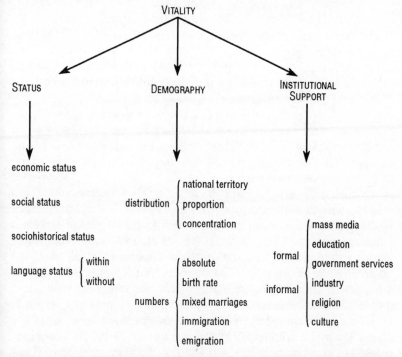

Figure 8.1 Taxonomy of the structural variables affecting ethnolinguistic vitality.
Source: Giles, Bourhis and Taylor (1977) p. 309, fig. 1.

as we shall see below (pp.215–21). For the moment I would like to elaborate upon the multi-dimensional nature of the vitality concept.

An attempt is made to develop a typology of vitality which can encompass the variation in the strength of ethnic identity as a continuum. This is encapsulated in fig. 8.1.

The vitality of an ethnolinguistic group, or the propensity of individual members of such a group to turn to other members of the group rather than to 'act as isolated individuals' (Giles, Bourhis and Taylor 1977:308) is the ingredient that makes a group behave collectively. That is, a group is viewed as a feature of behaviour and involves the sum of the actions of the individual members. Behaviour therefore involves two possibilities – to behave with reference to a particular group, or to operate as an individual, the two presumably being mutually exclusive. It is a position which we have encountered before in the context of the tendency to contrast the individual achievement of a modern society involving organic solidarity with the solidaristic orientation of traditional society with its mechanical solidarity.

The direct referent of status is not individuals but rather the various ethnolinguistic groups, with individuals presumably acquiring the status of their particular group within an overall system of ranking of such groups. Furthermore status is divisible into different dimensions. This treatment of social differentiation in terms of status is the inevitable consequence of an approach which focuses upon subjective evaluation, with status referring to the normative evaluation of social or occupational groups which are subsequently ranked relative to one another. It is not surprising then that one of the major endeavours of this group of researchers is to establish a series of stereotypes of ethnolinguistic groups by using the Matched Guise methodology, and relating these stereotypes to a status ranking. However, with reference to the vitality index, social status: 'refers to the degree of esteem a linguistic group affords itself.' (Giles *et al.* 1977:310). This refers merely to the in-group evaluation. If, as appears to be the case, the ethnolinguistic group is a cultural group, and if status evaluation is a feature of culturally conditioned values, the out-group evaluation derives from a different set of values and it is futile for Giles *et al.* to suggest that 'often, this amount of group self-esteem closely resembles that attributed it by the out-group' (310). Furthermore, unless the concept of group is treated as the sum of its constituent members, the whole idea of an ethnolinguistic group's self-evaluation is meaningless, and we have already emphasised how such a conception of a social group is remote from the conventional sociological meaning.

Economic status, on the other hand, refers to 'the degree of control a language group has gained over the economic life of its nation, region or community' (Giles *et al.* 1977:310). At first glance this would appear to be a more acceptable criterion in that it is an objective dimension. The problem arises with the concept of 'control'. The implication is that the control of resources, whether they be human or material resources, is equated with group closure. If there is an attempt to maintain that this closure is the basis for control *à la* Weber, it should be made clear that this is merely one way in which resources can be controlled. If, on the other hand, and this seems to me to be the gist of the argument, it is claimed that control over resources leads to group coherence or closure, then, if it is accepted that control over resources is the main feature of power relationships, it is essential to discuss how ethnicity relates to other dimensions of inequality such as gender and social class. I shall have more to say on this issue (see p.220). Suffice it to say, for the moment, that if we are addressing the relationship between language and control over economic life, then it is essential to discuss the issue of language prestige, or the value of a language for social mobility, in a far more systematic manner than occurs in this thesis. As it stands it would appear that what is referred to as the ethnolinguistic group's 'control over its own economic destiny' is akin to language or ethnic groups 'maintaining themselves as distinct collective entities'. That is, rather than a group being created out of the social conditions of oppression and denial of control, it would appear that groups exist only as a feature of power and control. This means that it is difficult to conceive of a minority group in terms other than those of an assimilation typology associated with the possession/non-possession of power and control.

It would appear from the above statement that a language group is not synonymous with either nation, region or community. This means that we are discussing plurilingual situations involving more than one language group. It also means that control over economic life must involve a struggle between members of different language groups over the economic order. Thus the groups that are referred to are merely a feature of their markers – the various language markers that pertain to the situation. Therefore, the groups will disappear when their markers disappear as a result of failure in the struggle that is an essential feature of language group relations. It is highly reminiscent of the assimilation thesis which argues that ethnic change derives from the erosion of cultural traits and their replacement by the cultural features of the host society. The perspective is inevitably static and involves a continuum from the retention of traits to assimilation. Little reference is made to struggle and there is a tendency for the discussion to lead to suggestions of tautological ethnic conservatism and primordial allegiances (G. Williams 1978).

The third status factor of ethnolinguistic vitality is termed language status and involves the manner in which 'history, prestige value and the degree of standardisation may be a source of pride or shame' (Giles *et al*. 1977:312). What is puzzling here is that, if a language group is a social group, then how does language status differ from the social status referred to above? Since nowhere are we told of anything about the relationship between the variables which determine ethnolinguistic vitality, it is impossible to determine whether the two variables are distinct and, if they are, how this is achieved.

The measure of language status is a 'sense of pride or shame' in the language or variety, a subjective quality. Pursuing the issue of the relationship between variables it seems that we have both subjective and objective variables seemingly holding the same analytical position *vis-à-vis* the determination of vitality. Yet one would expect that the objective dimension would assume the status of independent variable with the subjective dimensions being dependent variables, which merely raises the question of the relationship, if any, between the intervening variables. However, without clarification this assumption is of little value.

The final status factor which contributes to ethnolinguistic vitality is labelled 'sociohistorical status' and involves the symbolic value of history for the ethnolinguistic group. Since historical interpretation is a matter of conjecture in the sense that it is a feature of ideological production it is yet another subjective variable. We do find reference to groups locked in struggle 'to defend, maintain or assert their existence as collective entities'. Yet if the existence as a collectivity is largely a subjective criterion which is necessary in order for the group to assert itself then we have a blatantly circular argument. Furthermore, there is no elaboration of the nature of the struggle apart from repetitive, descriptive, anecdotal case studies which are employed to justify the statement.

In addition to these status factors we have demographic factors involving territoriality, population density, endogamy/exogamy, fundamental factors of demography and geographic mobility. Without denying the relevance of these factors for the attempt to create a vitality typology, there is one glaring omission. Nowhere is there reference to the fact that a numerical minority can be a majority in power terms with the consequence that its vitality is high. That is, there is a danger of confusing the demographic concept of minority with the conceptualisation of minority in terms of power and dominance, something that has little to do with demography. Of course it can be argued that this issue is addressed in the final set of vitality variables – those implicated in institutional support. However, these variables entirely ignore the relationship between language and ideology which we addressed in chapter 5. Consequently, the institutional settings controlled by the state may appear to contribute to a positive vitality whereas they merely serve to integrate the ethnolinguistic group ideologically. That is, institutions are treated merely as a backdrop for language rather than as analytical categories in a sociologically meaningful sense.

It is this ethnolinguistic vitality that conditions the individual's evaluation of the ethnolinguistic reference group. In order for choice to be relevant to this argument it must be assumed that there are alternatives to this reference group, but, apart from the individualism referred to above and the reference to particular case studies where the tendency is to oppose the ethnolinguistic group with the dominant group, we learn little about the nature of such alternatives. That is, there is a general tendency to conceive of the ethnolinguistic group in terms of an ethnic minority even if the nature of the minority position, and thereby its relationship to power, is not specified. But there is also a silence with reference to alternative social bases of identity. What we are told is that the rejection of the identity associated with the ethnolinguistic group is accompanied by a social mobility from that group to a superior group, this being a manifestation of the individual will of the actor. It would appear, therefore, that social groups are subjective creations in the minds of the actors despite the attempt to make vitality an objective concept or to see collective action as an objective quality. It seems therefore that a variety of linguistic forms, be they languages or varieties of a language, are associated with different populations of variable size which are unevenly related to economic resources and power, and have contrasting relevance in the institutional structure. These variables condition vitality such that the various groups are capable of being ranked on a vitality continuum which involves the potential for survival of the respective groups. One must assume that the condition of highest vitality is reserved for the dominant group, unless that group is not conceived of in terms of ethnicity, with all other groups occupying lower positions. If this is the case then the dominant/subordinate relationship is not so much one of power but rather it is a measure of demographic, institutional and status factors as they relate to individual evaluation, unless these can, somehow, be equated with power. As such it appears that the omission of any discussion of power as a feature of evaluation obliges us to conclude that the relationship of dominance and subordination involves a normative process based upon rationality.

It would seem that this is an ill-constructed attempt to develop a Weberian analysis of language groups as status groups. Language groups would be ranked economically and the status that accrues to the members of the language group derives from this ranking. Furthermore, the power of the group is analysed in institutional terms following the Weberian belief that there is a high degree of correlation between power, wealth and status. Such an analysis is obliged to demonstrate how the status group which, after all, is constructed out of cultural attributes, relates to the objective class structure as an inherent feature of the economic order. It should also demonstrate how conflict derives from the denial of the rewards of power, wealth and status to specific incumbents and it will be evident from what is to follow that the work of those associated with ethnolinguistic vitality systematically fails to address this issue. A failure to achieve these objectives merely creates confusion and obscures the essential ingredients of Weberianism.

INTERGROUP RELATIONS

The second facet of the work of Giles and his associates involves the manner in which the vitality factor is implemented in terms of intergroup relationships. These relationships are discussed in terms of Tajfel's (1974) thesis on social change. It is essentially a psychological perspective. Individuals are claimed to be active agents in defining themselves and the social world through the active categorisation of people into groups. Here social identity involves the individual's knowledge and evaluation of his/her membership of social groups. Part of this evaluation involves comparison with other groups, with the individual operating on a principle of optimisation in striving for affective satisfaction and pride. As a consequence, and inevitably so, there is a tendency, not merely to create social boundaries through evaluation, but also to evaluate the in-group more favourably than the out-group along dimensions that are significant and meaningful to the individual. Giles *et al.* (1977:319) claim that this process of aggrandisement and denigration involves 'material possessions, social power, abilities, personal attributes and so forth'. That is, it involves both esteem and status features. It is this evaluation that accounts for a positive identity.

What is difficult to fathom in this argument is precisely how a negative identity, based upon the same attributes, can exist, since, in a manner similar to the consensus argument involving a view of society as involving a never-ending process of upward mobility for the enterprising individual, the logical conclusion of Tajfel's argument involves the universal quest for positive identity through comparison, this leading to a denial of negative identity. Once again it is the motivated individual, constantly seeking upward mobility, that is the driving force of social change. As we have seen in our discussion of the work of Labov and Milroy this problem is common to much of orthodox sociolinguistics and derives from the emphasis upon the free, rational, individual operating in an open society where mobility, and, as a consequence of the particular philosophy of language, an associated change in identity, is not only possible but desirable. Sociolinguistics then becomes reduced to a discussion of the different identities within this type of society and how such identities are expressed through language within the context of the reflection thesis. The rational ingredient of such behaviour involves a desire for the shift from mechanical and organic solidarity and, where this shift is related to a vision of society as progressing through such rational change, it invariably leads to an explicit or implicit evolutionary statement. It seems that, in this particular argument, we encounter another example of how the consensus nature of the perspective creates the problem of how to explain the persistence of a negative identity and affiliation. It would seem that groups with a negative identity will be abandoned by their incumbents who will, if we follow the preceding argument, opt for individualistic behaviour in their quest for positive identity. Giles argues (1987:588) that if a negative identity is the product of a negative evaluation of subordinate groups, the persistence of that identity must involve the difference between what he calls practical and idealistic or personal motivation, a contrast similar to the individualistic/solidaristic opposition in Milroy's work. There is no need to repeat the objections to this argument except to re-emphasise that it fails to conceive of the dichotomous opposition in terms of power and opposition.

The resolution of the problem of the persistence of the negative identity involves the qualification of the argument by the fact that not everyone will be 'aware that cognitive alternatives to the existing status relationship between it and the superior group are possible' (Giles *et al.* 1977:319–20). Two conclusions are evident. First, that this is a clear case of blaming the victim, with a negative identity being the consequence of an inability to conceive of alternatives. Second, intergroup differences derive from an individual propensity for recognising cognitive alternatives, and acting according to the principle of optimisation rather than from the relationships of the respective groups to the material order.

However, the quest for a positive identity does not appear to rest entirely with the individual for, in some unspecified way, there is also a claim that group members will work in tandem for collective upward social mobility. This is achieved in a number of ways: through cultural and psychological assimilation into the dominant group, through re-evaluating the symbolic basis of the negative identity, by creating new dimensions of distinctiveness, or by direct competition with the dominant group. Some aspects of this part of the argument are reminiscent of Milroy's work where solidarity is contrasted with individual upward social mobility, but with the difference that the basis for cohesiveness and solidarity is claimed to derive, as we have seen in the discussion of vitality, from psychological orientations rather than from the structural order.

SPEECH ACCOMMODATION

This social and psychological backdrop must, of course, be related to features of speech and this is achieved through what Giles, Bourhis and Taylor (1977:321) refer to as 'Giles' theory of speech accommodation'. It rests on the awareness that individuals are capable of producing a variety of speech styles and that this ability is rationally employed in order to express social position *vis-à-vis* significant others in interaction. Thus 'people are motivated to adjust their speech style, or accommodate, as a means of expressing values, attitudes and intentions towards others' (322). That is, it is a perspective that involves the claim that language reflects society and that society largely consists of a series of social roles. Convergence refers to the tendency where the accommodation of speech style in interaction reflects a shift towards the style of the other, this being a manifestation of a desire for approval. However, whereas, as we have seen, many sociolinguists assume that there is a universal striving for approval and reciprocity in interaction, Giles, Bourhis and Taylor also refer to divergence which involves a shift away from the other's speech style, this reflecting a desire to remain distinct from the social group of that other. Since it is the degree of ethnolinguistic vitality that determines the tendency for in-grouping, and if divergence is an expression of that in-grouping then, evidently, it is vitality that is responsible for the propensity towards either convergence or divergence. We are told that 'non-converging speech is an important medium often used by ethnic groups as a symbolic tactic for maintaining their identity and cultural distinctiveness' (323). It seems therefore that maintaining identity and cultural distinctiveness is a feature of speech which is employed rationally and consciously. It is employed not so much by individuals as by groups, the implication being that individual speech is conditioned by group membership while simultaneously being a feature of that group. That is, the group is created through speech while also conditioning that speech. This is a fascinating suggestion, partly reminiscent of the ethnomethodological position. However, it does not appear to have any relevance for Giles, Bourhis and Taylor since it is not elaborated upon and the discussion of group focuses upon that which we encountered in the discussion of intergroup relations above. What is not discussed in detail is how the tendency for divergence is to be accounted for. We do have various suggestions such as 'cultural pride', 'outgroup membership', 'undesirable attitudes, habits or appearance', none of which is very satisfactory since they do not involve any conception of the relationship of the respective groups to the material order. This tendency to revert to descriptive discussions of psychological propensity associated with various case studies is characteristic of the discussion of speech accommodation.

ETHNICITY

As the title of the chapter implies, much of the work of this group of sociolinguists involves the concept of ethnicity, and it is essential to consider the implications of the manner in which the concept is discussed and employed. The claim is made that since language involves thought, symbolisation and emotion, it functions to help comprehend inter-ethnic relations. Language is held to be inherently linked to ethnicity because it is symbolic of dominance and oppression, with ethnic group relations being conceived of in such terms. It is the dominance and oppression that obliges people to accept a social identity which they don't necessarily want. That is, if language is one of the diacritica of ethnicity, and if identities are created out of the stereotypification of people on the basis of language and speech, it follows that ethnicity involves the evaluation of people on the basis of language. Language is the embodiment of ethnicity and is implicit in the concept of an ethnolinguistic group. It is maintained that people subjectively categorise others into social groups and, in so doing, evaluate themselves and others in positive and negative terms. Part of this categorisation involves the use of language in developing the subjective category of ethnicity. Ethnicity invariably is treated as culturally determined, with the defining force involving some feature, be it language, behaviour, norm or belief, which varies by culture. In this respect it is the converse of a materialist conception which defines a group in terms of its location in the economic system. It is this distinction between the two orientations which lies behind the tendency for many Marxists to treat ethnicity as the basis of false consciousness deriving from a non-material base. Thus we have a struggle of ideological discourses which involves different arguments about what is the basis of the mobilisation of interests. Of course, if we do accept that society is organised in terms of the ability of groups to mobilise their interests, there is no reason why more than one basis for such mobilisation cannot be put into operation, sometimes simultaneously. Thus, for example, the concept of the cultural division of labour (Hechter 1975) implies that the economy is organised in such a way that there is an overlap of ethnic and class divisions such that the lower and upper classes consist of distinct cultural or ethnic groups. None the less, the ethnic group is still defined in cultural terms even if it is subsequently related to the economic system.

Clearly, in the work of Giles and his associates ethnicity is treated as a sort of identity, in the sense that people conceive of themselves as something and act accordingly, this being encompassed in the manner in which people speak. The implication is that since this identity is culturally determined, with culture being conceived of in terms of way of life, there is an identity with some form of shared way of life with which there is an affective attachment. Both self and other categorisations are involved in stereotypes which create the boundary between ethnic groups. However, this boundary only exists as a feature of that which is responsible for the stereotypification – culture. As a consequence the argument is circular.

One of the most evident features of work on ethnic groups is the exclusion of the dominant group from the concept of ethnicity. Thus, for example, in the work of some students in Wales (see Carter 1988) the Welsh will be conceived of as ethnic whereas English in-migrants are excluded from such a categorisation. It is also evident among the work of those whose work is the subject of this chapter. This tendency derives directly from the cultural nature of ethnicity and its relationship to ethnicity. A feature of the psychological nature of the argument is that people organise their motivations on rational grounds. However, reason is culturally conditioned, not only in consensus arguments but also in the false conscious theme of some Marxists. This means that the dominant group and the ethnic group operate on different, culturally conditioned, principles of reason. This difference is then subject to a normative evaluation which involves giving precedence to the dominant group. Thus the rationality of the ethnic group is, from the standpoint of the dominant group, not rational nor other-rational, it is deviant. Thus the concept of ethnicity is denigratory in the sense that it treats ethnicity as deviation from the dominant norm and it is little wonder, therefore, that the dominant group tends not to be conceived of in terms of ethnicity. Regardless of any claim for cultural relativity, this much is evident in the various studies of acculturation and assimilation. I have tried, throughout the preceding chapters, to emphasise this tendency to denigrate minority groups, whether they involve language groups or groups which speak varieties of a language, by asserting that it derives from the tendency for the consensus theory that prevails in sociolinguistics to be normative in nature. If indeed this is the case then it is time to abandon the concept of ethnicity and to analyse language group relationships in social rather than cultural terms.

The evolutionism of the nineteenth century has some relevance for this argument. As I argued in chapter 1, evolutionism was associated with the idea of social and cultural change as progress. Different cultural groups were aligned at different points on the evolutionary continuum. Since progress was destined to lead, ultimately, to perfection, those groups highest on the evolutionary ladder were closest to perfection. The consequence of such an argument is that 'modern' societies are treated as temporarily most recent and are thereby are closest to 'perfection'. The converse, 'traditional' society, is consequently denigrated through comparison and 'modern' society is the normative order against which all other societies are compared. In the Durkheimian schema the markers of this distinction tend to relate to the mechanical/organic solidarity dichotomy, whereas cultural features can provide the same function in this and other problematics. Once the limitations of this line of argument, together with the relationship between the theoretical orientations and the conceptualisation of ethnicity, are recognised it becomes evident that ethnicity cannot be anything other than a concept which denigrates those to whom it refers.

Another disturbing feature of the work on ethnolinguistic vitality is the failure to distinguish between ethnicity and ethnic group thereby failing to recognise a central problem in the sociological and anthropological work on ethnicity. One fundamental problem of the concept of ethnic group has already been addressed – it is a static concept in the sense that the group exists because it is different. If ethnicity is a subjective dimension of the process of the recognition and maintenance of cultural difference, involving the development and maintenance of ethnic awareness or identity through rationality, then any social boundaries which exist are merely subjective boundaries. Social boundaries rely on the perception of group differences. That is, not only does the argument lack any concept of reason associated with objective criteria but, as I have emphasised above (p.214), it also implies that the rational is irrational. The focus remains very much on the phenomenal level of relationships. It becomes a general theory and analysis of the development and maintenance of social boundaries based on the assumption that cultural difference is synonymous with ethnic difference, and that this ethnic difference constitutes the boundaries of ethnic groups. The boundaries appear to derive from a culturally conditioned rationality rather than from the material structure – the fundamental basis of struggle. In fairness to Giles, Bourhis and Taylor, they do not disregard the social and political structure. However, their discussion of ethnolinguistic vitality seems to bear little relationship to ethnic group relations and the main thrust of the argument remains at the phenomenological level of relations, involving a general theory and analysis of the development and maintenance of social boundaries. It continues to rest on the assumption that cultural difference, as manifested in language, is synonymous with ethnic difference and that it is this ethnic difference that constitutes the boundaries of ethnic groups.

The context in which the work of Giles and his associates departs from the static nature of the discussion of ethnic groups involves their discussion of ethnic relations. The emphasis is placed upon members of ethnic groups as active subjects who act in accordance with rational intentions. The member of the ethnic group is no longer a passive subject who is discriminated against, even though some of their work on stereotypification does tend to imply this, but rather she/he is an active participant in the process of ethnic relations. This much is evident in the key concept of speech accommodation which appears in the literature as a novel contribution to sociolinguistics. Yet, as we have seen, it does share much in common with other interactionist theories of language in society, particularly in the emphasis given to the idea of rational actors, consciously seeking approval in interaction. It is here that, once again, we encounter not merely the idea of the rational actor, but also that of the rational actor who is locked in a process of optimisation as in the rationality that is built into exchange theory: 'An elaboration of the theory (of speech convergence) *vis-à-vis* congruence has been formulated with regard to a number of sociopsychological processes, including similarity-attraction, social exchange, causal attribution and gain-loss' (Giles *et al.* 1977:322). It is not surprising that divergence receives far less attention than convergence since, if they are processes which express values, attitudes and intentions towards others, the focus on interaction must assume that accommodation is the norm otherwise interaction breaks down in that the pursuit of common goals cannot be sustained.

It is also clear that by developing primary categories by reference to social consciousness, historical and structural processes are either ignored or are marginalised. It is these processes which set the parameters of social boundaries, parameters which are not necessarily evident in social consciousness. Structurally determined interests are not necessarily recognised in terms of everyday consciousness which means that we must seek to explain why these essential relationships are not reproduced within phenomenal relationships. A failure to confront this issue results in work which merely documents ethnicity as an awareness of the significant distinction between in-group and out-group. That is, it becomes impossible to move beyond analysing the perception of difference. In his recent work, Giles (1987:597) appears to acknowledge this weakness but appears to imply that the solution lies in a different consideration of the relationship between attitude and behaviour. This, of course, should not be surprising given that social psychology, at least as employed by Giles and his associates, rests on the assumption that observable behaviour is merely a manifestation of inner psychological conditions and that the study of the former will result in the discovery of the latter.

Perhaps the most difficult aspect of the sociopsychological endeavour is the need to integrate the micro with the macro, the individual with the social structure. I have already identified this as a crucial weakness in this body of work, with the concept of group being equated with the sum of its constituent members. Furthermore, since the focus is upon goal orientated behaviour, there is a tendency to assume that there is an overlap between individual and group goals. Group goals become an elaboration of individual goals. Thus the approach appears to have more in common with the social network approach than the more conventional sociolinguistic orientations as is clear in the following statement: 'the more vitality a linguistic group has, the more likely it [is] . . . that ingroup members would turn more to one another in intergroup situations rather than functioning as isolated individuals' (Giles *et al.* 1977:308–9). This becomes particularly problematic with reference to the concept of speech accommodation. It is assumed that if individuals strive for accommodation in interaction then this is a feature of different groups striving for accommodation. It becomes impossible to envisage a scenario where individuals avoid personal antagonism through convergence while being aware of any inherent antagonism between the relevant social groups, the classic feature of deference.

As a consequence of this conception of individuals in interaction we are left with an impression of individuals who are capable of manipulating language and thereby manipulating the reaction of others to them. I have already suggested that it is misleading to think of such a position as being reminiscent of the manner in which roles and identities are negotiated in the ethnomethodological perspective since the situation does not involve free individuals who actively create society. Rather we have a situation in which constraints derive from the normative nature of stereotypification, a social convention (Edwards 1982). That is, the constraints derive from a social consensus in contrast to a stereotypification which might derive from ideological practices. Such social conventions do not merely generate stereotypification of speech variation but also produce evaluations of status and prestige. This should not be surprising since, if language reflects society, an evaluation of speech is, simultaneously, a social evaluation. What is more interesting is the implication that status and prestige are normative in nature. That is, social class, gender, ethnic and any other social differences derive only indirectly from the material order, the normative evaluation of these differences having priority. This means that social differentiation becomes a subjective, phenomenological dimension, only vaguely related to the material structure.

This normative emphasis allows us to clarify the relationship between the micro and the macro. I have already indicated that the vitality concept is largely subjective and is claimed to generate further subjective evaluations in the form of individual behaviour. A particularly interesting consequence of this orientation involves the manner in which regional dialects are subject to variation in status, a phenomenon which has received considerable attention from this group of researchers. The comments made in chapter 7 are worth repeating here. There is no reference to the relationship between regional dialects and social class and subsequently, of course, to the relationships between social classes. Neither is there reference to the relationship between the variation in status and class fragmentation. Indeed we are left with the impression that it is language that carries status thereby falling into the trap of reification by ignoring the claim that language is a social entity. More importantly, perhaps, the conception of social class as involving polarised social groups related to the material order is lost, not merely because of a preoccupation with the status and prestige dimensions of social division, but also because of a lack of sufficient awareness of the relationship between language and social structure.

What I have argued above is that the conception of an ethnic group as a self-defined group with beliefs and behaviour seen as distinctive through the association with culture means that culture is viewed as a universal, collectivist phenomenon that explains the totality of belief and behaviour of the individual as member of the ethnic group. The associated tendency to separate both cultural differentiation and the idea of group identity from a material structure leads to a tendency to disregard other bases of social differentiation such as social class. I am not arguing in terms of an either/or perspective reminiscent of the false consciousness argument, but, rather, I am suggesting that members of ethnic groups must, simultaneously, also be members of other groups, be they class, gender or age based. It is imperative to consider this inter-relationship between different dimensions of inequality across the entire population in a manner which the work of Giles and his associates does not even approach. If the concept of ethnic boundaries, their creation and maintenance, is to have any significance, an attempt must be made to establish the significance of social as well as cultural dimensions.

Furthermore, it is essential to recognise that interests are structurally determined and that they are not necessarily recognised in terms of everyday consciousness. This means that it is necessary to explain why the essential relationships are not reproduced within phenomenological relationships. It is necessary to identify the economic, political and ideological conditions which allow the attribution of meaning to occur. That is, meaning must be attributed to the bases of difference in order for those differences to be effective in terms of social relationships. Thus, it is essential to proceed beyond simply cataloguing the individual's perception of difference by a consideration of the material bases of the reproduction of social life. It is here that it is most evident that the analysis and identification of stereotypes must involve an understanding of the crucial importance of ideological production as it relates to the production of meaning.

IDENTITY

Giles, Bourhis and Taylor maintain that the individual acquires identity through socialisation from birth in that there emerges a capability to define oneself and others. Social identity involves people's knowledge of membership of social categories and the values that are attached to that membership. Furthermore, social identity is part of the self-concept and only acquires meaning through comparison. The conception of value is normative and in that sense we have the usual consensus view in which social identity is the basis of social order, with individuals finding their place within a universal consensus. The claim that social comparison makes the individual's own group appear favourable and psychologically distinct, thereby assuring that individuals have a desire to belong to groups that give them satisfaction and pride has already been discussed (p.214). It implies that while all of this is a psychological process associated with the individual in some unspecified way it leads to the existence of social groups. We have also seen that this overarching desire for a positive identity leads to the abandonment of affiliation with a particular group when intergroup relations result in the generation of a negative identity for members of that group. That is, the entire process of identity formation is conceived of in terms of an optimisation framework associated with the freedom of the individual to manipulate identities in order to achieve maximum psychological benefit.

The problem of identity lies in its involvement with the conception of rational actors with a view of the self. The manner in which Giles and his associates, and indeed most sociolinguists, approach the issue is via the traditional philosophy of language which claims that the meaning of a word is held to be the entity outside of language to which it refers. This is linked to theories of knowledge which suggest that conscious ideas mediate between human beings and the external world so that ideas are the signs of things and words the signs of ideas. Language becomes a collection of signs whose nature is dependent upon the relationship to extra-linguistic phenomena. It is the conscious, thinking subject who gives meaning to words and ensures that they are correctly employed. As a consequence language contains consciousness and it is implied that there is such a thing as a society outside of language.

These issues are evident in the manner in which identity is discussed by reference to the conscious, rational actor manipulating language in order to negotiate identity. Even when the generalised approach of sociology, with its tendency to refer to societal concepts such as social class or gender, is evident, the explanation of the relationship between language and identity invariably relates to an inherent rationality associated with the centred actor. As we have already seen, identity is treated as a manifestation of the individual actor as a rational being possessing his/her perception of the self *vis-à-vis* society. The attributes of such a social identity tend to carry reference to the body – sex, race, age etc. – but, as in the case of the centrality of culture for the concept of ethnicity, also involves non-physical attributes which are claimed to contribute to the creation of identity. Such an identity is invariably premised upon the coordinates of the similarity that derives from difference. It involves concepts of person, thought and conscience, either in terms of Cartesian substantialism with identity seen as an indivisible feature of the individual; or as a Durkheimian spiritualism where different elements involved in the constitution of identity are a manifestation of consciousness. What is clear about Giles' work is that while he strives for the latter he ends up with the former.

The awareness of the multiplicity of identities involving the relationship between attributions, consciousness and the structured context to which these are related is missing in the work of the group in question. Thus the idea of a collective identity, which should be the central feature of the attempt to integrate the individual as a social entity involving not only the various identities of the individual but also the collective identity, is also missing. This manifestation of the Durkheimian *conscience collective* is usually arrived at by emphasising the commonality of the ingredients of identity, thereby giving the concept of identity a sense of unity in diversity. We do find the tendency to emphasise or to exaggerate difference, as for example in the difference between the internal and external world, us and them, in the sense of unity which, paradoxically, derives from a diversity of experiences, and in the idea of timelessness as the essence of an ahistorical and essentialist conception. This, in turn, generates a reification in which a transitory, historical condition is presented as permanent, natural, and somehow outside of time. It is this which leads the sociological tradition to persistently relate the issue of collective identity to that of social order, with the breakdown of order being seen as the failure of collective identity as in the discussion of alienation and false consciousness. It is also implicit in the work of Giles when, as we have already discussed, culture is claimed to involve alternative forms of rationality, only one of which is treated as the normative basis of social order.

On the other hand, any attempt to treat identity as dynamic raises the question of causality as well as the problem of the maintenance of the collectivity within such a dynamic. I have already indicated that this is a central problem in the work under scrutiny here, with the assumption that a positive identity is a universal goal contradicting the persistence of negative collective identities. This problem, and its resolution, involves the tendency to confuse identity with the attributes which it is held to embody. The symbolic elements of identity are taken as given without much consideration as to how they achieve meaning while also incorporating a mechanical behaviourism with its allied empiricist conception of the subject.

To labour a point, it is clear that within the conception of identity as involving a symbolic manifestation of difference, the cultural is prominent to the extent that it becomes the predominant feature of causal analysis. Again the confusion of identity with its attributes is evident, these attributes being seen as the *sine qua non* of identity and, consequently, as the driving force of behaviour. Unlike sex, race and age, ethnicity does not relate to the body but is socially constructed.

As such its conception varies in accordance with the nature of the associated problematic. What I have sought to emphasise is that the problematic assumed by those associated with ethnolinguistic vitality carries with it associated meanings which point the analysis in a specific direction.

CONCLUSION

This penultimate chapter has sought to develop a critique of an area of work which is more explicitly psychological than that which we encounter in most of sociolinguistics. As such it inevitably involves a focus on the individual, albeit within a social context. At times, as in the reference to dominance and oppression, it would appear that there is an attempt to deviate from the more general consensus orientation of sociolinguistics. It is here that another difference from the preceding chapters becomes evident in that we do have echoes of a Weberian analysis in the reference to status and ethnicity. However, this orientation is not entirely consistent. Thus, for example, the Weberian tendency to deal with the ethnic group as a status group which cuts across class lines is ignored and the argument lapses into consensus conceptualisations and a subjective orientation devoid of any meaningful development of the earlier promise.

More specifically, ethnolinguistic vitality is more of a typological construct than a refined concept. It suffers from a lack of integration of its constituent parts, as a consequence of which it is difficult to understand how the subjective and objective dimensions relate, if at all. As a consequence the associated concepts are evidently not clearly thought out, at least in operational terms. This means that it becomes difficult to establish the precise nature of the formation of ethnolinguistic vitality which, after all, is claimed to be the independent variable. If that is indeed its status, and if this does represent a Weberian framework, then it is to be expected that it should assume a degree of objectivity that is far from evident in the schema. It is little wonder, therefore, that this part of the exercise generates little more than a descriptive typology with little analytical significance.

When we turn to consider the issue of inter-ethnic group allegiance we discover that any semblance of an allegiance to an objective analysis within a conflict perspective is abandoned. In its place we have an argument couched in terms of individuals, rationally conditioned to behave in terms of optimisation, with the quest for status and the associated positive identity being the motivating force of behaviour. That is, we are locked into the same kind of analytical framework as that which we have encountered in preceding chapters. This orientation is linked to the culturist account of ethnicity. Thus cultural difference is held to be synonymous with ethnic difference, and it is this ethnic difference that constitutes the boundaries between ethnic groups. Other social dimensions are ignored and the subsequent analysis becomes fundamentally descriptive in its attempt continuously to refine the basic assumptions of the perspective. An attempt is made to integrate the perspective with the psychological commitment to the scientific endeavour by undertaking a series of empirical studies which seek to sharpen the conclusions. That is, the assumptions of the perspective are accepted and any forward movement lies not at the epistemological level but rather in terms of the cumulative knowledge associated with scientific experimentation.

The perspective has a strong functionalist ring to it. Language is functional in locating a language group in its heritage, in transmitting group feelings, and in defining a social boundary by signalling in-group membership while simultaneously defining social closure. This functionalism is often accompanied by the reification of language and its separation from the social context. The appearance of functionalism in any work which has affinity with that of Weber should not be surprising since the taxonomic approach for studying structures and processes derives fundamentally from the nineteenth-century concern with biological sciences that is reflected in his work. The tendency which Giles and his associates share with Weber of developing category systems first, followed by propositions among categorised phenomena, is at the centre of contemporary functionalism.

I have already implied that there is a degree of continuity between this sphere of sociolinguistics and what has been discussed in preceding chapters. Perhaps this is most evident with reference to evolutionism which derives from the same premise as we have already discussed. The distinction between individualistic action and collectivist solidaristic action is reminiscent of the Durkheimian distinction between mechanical and organic solidarity. Associated with the claim that linguistic diversity has a positive attribution within the context of social change (Giles 1987:585) we encounter the romanticism which relates mechanical solidarity to linguistic diversity while implying that the inevitable evolutionary thrust is in the direction of uniformity and individualism. The commitment to minority ethnicity conforms with this position and it is unfortunate that the denigration of the minority as a consequence of the association of that minority with a rationality which does not conform with the normative rationality of the established order exists alongside it. Once more it is an example of what we encounter time and again within sociolinguistics – evidence of an overriding desire to support the underdog, accompanied by a sociological perspective which reflects the power of the dominant.

9   Conclusion

A NOTE OF CAUTION

The preceding chapters have sought to demonstrate the consensus nature of most contemporary sociolinguistic theory. It has been argued that there is a remarkable continuity between what claim to be distinctive theoretical perspectives. This continuity derives from the grounding of the various subareas in a particular social philosophy whose roots lie in the eighteenth century. As a consensus philosophy on society it limits the adoption of alternative perspectives, and conditions the nature of the questions that can be asked and the answers which may be offered. In this concluding chapter I would like to develop the critique of consensus sociology in order to highlight the problems associated with contemporary sociolinguistics. In so doing I will return to much of the material that was discussed in the first two chapters. However, it will be evident that it is an oversimplification to divide sociological theory into opposed camps involving consensus and conflict perspectives, even though such distinctions may well apply at a general level. Such an exercise merely obscures what the two perspectives have in common while also ignoring perspectives which may not fit into one or the other of the two camps.

In sociology 'structural' refers to relatively stable points of reference of any system under consideration. Once such structures have been identified we need to consider what processes are necessary in order for such structures to be maintained. Within Parsonian structural functionalism the social system is conceived as a system of action whose structural aspects involve the relatively stable interactions of individuals. Action, it is claimed, is structured by social norms in the sense that interactions are not random but are mediated by common standards of evaluation, with individuals sharing definitions of the situation. In a sense such norms control the behaviour of social actors. What Parsons had to do was to consider the dynamic processes whereby social structures are maintained by considering how and why individuals are motivated to act in conformity with the normative consensus. He claimed that through socialisation individuals assimilated the normative into their personalities. Thus the normative components of interaction which involve the rights and obligations which are expected of interactional participants are internalised by the members of society. The structure of expectations is embedded in the playing of social roles which are associated with particular social positions. The particular expectations which serve to define specific roles are underpinned and influenced by the value system of the society in question. Roles are thereby seen as normatively conditioned and involve expected ways of behaviour. Thus social structure for Parsons ultimately derives from social values, a position which he inherits from Durkheim. Inevitably there arises the criticism that such a perspective views human behaviour as machine-like in that there is no room for a theory of action in which human beings are treated as knowledgeable beings. Social conduct is programmed by the influence of a social order that is normatively conditioned. Such a critique appears to make conversation analysis stand out from other aspects of the predominant sociolinguistic concerns. Yet, in other respects, it has much in common with those concerns.

This social system, despite its internal diversity, was conceived of as an integrated whole. Integration was associated with the idea of social equilibrium. A society in a state of equilibrium was one devoid of conflict, with every member knowing what was expected of him/her in any role, and where such expectations were constantly met. In a sense Parsons viewed this as an ideal type but also linked it to the idea of society as an evolutionary entity which was constantly striving for perfection in line with the idea of evolution as the striving for perfection. The attainment of such a situation of perfection was through socialisation, and social control with perfect equilibrium involved a corresponding relationship between the personality of an individual and the social structure. Clearly, conformity, consensus and cohesion are integral aspects of the perfect society and there is no room for conflict and disruption. Once a system that is in equilibrium is assumed, even if only for analytical purposes, the consequence is a focus on the elaboration of concepts promoting integration and equilibrium. Such equilibrium also relies upon the functional integration of the various parts of a society's social structure. However, where change occurs in one part, the other parts are obliged to respond through adaptation in order to sustain equilibrium. Thus society always seeks to achieve equilibrium and perfection.

Giddens (1982) has argued that it is a mistake to establish an opposition between consensus and conflict theories in sociology as has been the tendency, especially among North American sociologists. He claims that while the main influence on Parsons was Durkheim it is a mistake to think of Durkheim's work simply in terms of the problem of order which Parsons emphasised, a point recently developed by Pearce (1989). Rather, Durkheim's main concern was with the Kantian problem of the moral imperative rather than with the inevitable conservatism which the Parsonian emphasis would imply. The evolutionary influence in Durkheim's work led him to a consideration of the contrasts and continuities of what he regarded as traditional and modern societies and this was embodied in his concepts of mechanical and organic solidarity. He showed that the ideals of individualism, premised as they were on the idea of the freedom and dignity of the individual, were products of social evolution, being, in his view, differentiated in accordance with different societies founded on the division of labour. Thus freedom was no longer conceived of as the escape from moral authority but as the transformation of that authority through the new values of moral individualism. Furthermore, Durkheim did show an interest in socialism. Giddens is particularly severe in his castigation of Nisbet for claiming that Durkheim's work was fundamentally conservative, asserting that Nisbet confuses methodological and moral individualism. Durkheim's concern was on the latter which he claimed was a product of social evolution from traditional to modern society involving a transformation through the new values of moral individualism. This parallels Giddens' own claim that the main concern of sociology is a theory of industrial society which involves a particular set of ideas concerning the evolution of 'advanced societies', industrialisation being regarded as the main force transforming the contemporary world. This is an inherent feature of orthodox consensus which involves three elements: positivism as a logical framework, functionalism, and industrialisation of the driving force towards perfection. Lukes (1973:320) makes the same point about Durkheim, emphasising that this view of social change is associated with liberal rather than conservative political ideas. It would appear therefore that the emphasis upon social order is something that was resurrected by Parsons rather than being a preoccupation of nineteenth-century social philosophy.

Giddens (1982) also takes to task Dahrendorf's (1958) tendency to contrast the work of Durkheim with that of Marx with reference to the problem of order, the former, in Dahrendorf's view, claiming that order derives from consensus and the latter insisting that it derived from coercion. Giddens claims that both authors were in agreement with reference to rejecting the eighteenth-century claim that primordial society was a free society and that both sought to emphasise that social development involved freeing humanity from self-ignorance and bondage to nature.

Certainly there is every reason to take these ideas seriously and also to recognise that the work of Marx and Durkheim has much in common. Thus both are functionalist arguments which involve a heavily evolutionist orientation. However, they also differ in several respects and especially so with reference to the importance of social class. Whereas Marx saw class conflict as the driving force of social change, Durkheim emphasised that class conflict was not fundamental to socialist thought, claiming, in an argument derived from Saint-Simon, that tension in industrial society does not emanate from the relations of production, but, rather, from the immaturity of the newly emerging organic solidarity.

However, what I have sought to argue in the preceding chapters is that the structural functionalism which most sociolinguists have inherited from Parsons and his followers, and which remains at the heart of the sociolinguistic endeavour, involves a distinctive orientation whether it be referred to as conservative or liberal. It is a perspective which involves employing the natural sciences as a model for a social science, it emphasises functionalism and has a model of social change in which an evolutionary development towards perfection relates to the forces associated with industrialisation. Beyond this it emphasises a social order which derives from normative consensus, with the individual operating in line with specific social constraints which derive from this social agreement. The specific nature of the perspectives are outlined in the following section.

PREDOMINANT THEMES

I have already stated that the majority of work in sociolinguistics, no matter what subdisciplinary banner it goes under, shares a common orientation to language and society. It is time to spell out the precise nature of this discourse and to establish which practitioners preach which aspect of the general discourse.

The general discourse is what I have referred to as the normative consensus view of society. The central feature of the discourse is that language reflects society, that is, language is social in the sense that it is merely a mirror of society. Thus the essence of society and social behaviour can be encountered by studying language. Therefore all that is required is to translate what is discovered in the patterning of language as behaviour into what is claimed to be known about the nature of society. Such a society is claimed to exist, not simply as a subjective point of reference, but as truth or reality itself. It seems that there is a direct correspondence between language and social practice. In this respect language is not so much social, as a representation of the social, a social which pre-exists the speech act – ethnomethodology is an exception in this respect. As Achard (1986:8) has stated, ethnomethodology and, to an extent, the ethnography of communication treat language as underlying the spontaneous consciousness of acting subjects. Social structure will therefore disappear and reflection, seemingly, becomes impossible. Certainly the issue of the relationship between micro and macro perspectives disappears. However, the transparency of language does not disappear but is merely displaced into a different model of reflection, one of communication.

The speaking subject is presented as a free, rational individual capable of employing language not only to express meaning, but to convey a social identity. Again language is a manifestation of the thinking subject who consciously employs it in interaction in order to establish understanding. The individual subject clearly has a privileged access to the contents of its consciousness. It therefore seems that human thought, and the world that is reflected in that thought, cannot be understood separately from its expression in language, a distinctively Kantian position in which thought is akin to discourse.

Most features of social enquiry tend to treat the actor as behaviourally and attitudinally rational. This may involve a behavioural rationalism in which the agent's action is an intelligible outcome of patterned beliefs and desires, or it may involve an attitudinal rationality in which the agent is responsive to inconsistencies in, and counter-examples to, this pattern (Macdonald and Pettit 1981:65). Thus action is seen as intentional, with other sorts of explanation presupposing it. Macdonald and Pettit (1981:94–100) argue that this orientation cannot involve the positivistic development of hypotheses which are superior to existing ones, but that rather it involves applying the 'indutible explanatory principles' within this 'orthodox conception of human agents' to specific cases. Since social action is held to involve regularities which transcend and constrain the intentions of agents, something other than rationality is involved. The 'orthodox conception of human agents' tends to treat these supra-rational features as marginal to their endeavour. This was the case in the work discussed in chapter 8 and also in the work of Milroy where groups tended to be seen as the aggregate of individual rational behaviour. In a sense this should not be surprising since the importance of functionalism in this line of enquiry means that any phenomenon is accounted for in terms of its effects, with human behaviour tending to be explained in terms of its contribution to the reproduction of society. I shall return to the issue of functionalism momentarily. The important point is that accounting for human conduct has a limited range of possibilities within a functionalist argument.

To a certain extent it is this limitation which lies behind the tendency for ethnomethodologists to reject structural functionalism in favour of methodological individualism. The problem with this development is that it treats social regularities as the unintended consequences of individual actions, with little reference to the manner in which such regularities precede and structure individual choices. Conversation analysis, no matter what else it rejects, retains the goal orientated nature of communication, that goal involving the intention of being understood in order to establish inter-subjective mutuality of reciprocal understanding in order to promote mutual trust and accord. The main objection to this stance is that contradictions and conflicts are concealed in the sense that they are subsumed in the overriding claim that action is directed towards reaching understanding. It would seem that if cooperation is the basis of reason then any opposition to human emancipation is seen as irrational (Callinicos 1983:143), and there is the danger that it tends to be reduced to the application of such a principle.

In seeking to avoid reducing social behaviour to the rational behaviour of the agents, sociolinguistics invokes a particular view of society as a system which constrains. The society within which the free, rational subject exists is a very specific form of society. It is an open society full of opportunity of which the rational and enterprising individual actor, operating on the basis of an inherent desire for social status, will be able to take full advantage. This is the normative nature of society, and, conversely, failure to take advantage of the opportunities afforded by society is treated as an aberration, as deviance. That is, the social norm is seen as the product of the rational actor who conforms and cooperates in social action. Those who do take advantage of the opportunities will invariably be socially mobile and will, as a consequence, assume a variety of identities which will be expressed and conveyed through language. The emphasis on individual creativity involving freedom and diversity remains. The social norm is viewed as a homogeneous will of society at large, a will which promotes conformity through cooperation and an overriding desire for social approval, thereby engendering social order. It is also an expression of value, and, in social terms, of shared values. Thus society precedes language, and despite its propensity for change it assumes a structure which can be identified and which determines human behaviour. It is only in the work of ethnomethodologists and in Milroy's work on social networks that the tendency for such a perspective to treat the social actor as predetermined and constrained, that is as a 'dope', is rejected. I have already discussed what the ethnomethodologists do with this (p.156). Milroy resorts to methodological individualism as the alternative and treats interactional regularities as social. In so doing she retains another feature of the general sociolinguistic discourse, the emphasis upon social roles as a form of social agreement between individuals, in the sense that roles involve rights and obligations. Unlike the ethnomethodological tendency to treat social roles as created in social interaction, Milroy tends to treat roles as fixed and given, in common with the other uses of the concept in sociolinguistics, as the consequence of behaviour learnt through socialisation.

I have already referred to the manner in which social order deriving from the consequence of striving, achieving, rational individuals tends to be treated as normative, with the order involving a faith in the form of rational action and mentalism. This means that alternative behaviour is treated as deviant behaviour. This has numerous consequences. When the concept of social change as involving progress is invoked we have the same tendency to create dichotomies which involve norm/deviance within the context of social evolution. Invariably the norm involves the powerful element and the deviant involves the adversary which is placed in time through dichotomies such as modern/traditional which derive from typological constructions which are assumed to reflect new and old forms, despite the fact that they both sit together at the same moment in time. This can only be substantiated by assuming that the new or modern is in the process of displacing the old or traditional, and that this displacement takes place within a natural process of social evolution devoid of power and interest. Language is superimposed upon this vision of society by relating different language forms, whether they be languages or varieties, to the dichotomous relationships of society. Thus, as traditional and old are denigrated through a conception of them as obsolescent survivals, so also are the language features which relate to them denigrated. Thus language death, as it is referred to, is perhaps an unfortunate term, but it is also an inevitable consequence of progress seen as natural and inevitable. Survival is the antithesis of progress. The issue of language death is particularly relevant here in that it highlights the biological analogy which underlies this form of functional argument. Languages fail to survive, not because of aspects of power involving social groups in conflict, but because of the failure of language, in its reified form, to adapt to modern conditions. Languages do not disappear because people cease to speak them but because of some inherent weakness in language. It is not surprising therefore that evolution as progress involves a drive towards linguistic, if not social, homogeneity, even if only because progress and development are a consequence of communication, as we saw in chapter 4. Power relationships between language groups or between the groups represented by language varieties need not enter into the discussion since the process of change is clearly defined in terms of direction and is, in any case, inevitable.

The main feature of this evolutionism in social terms involves a change from mechanical to organic solidarity, commensurate with the shift from traditional to modern society that was referred to above. Both the direction of change, its inevitability and its desirability are taken for granted, leaving an air of social fatalism. Language merely reflects this shift from one basis of social contract to another. The shift from mechanical to organic solidarity involves a shift from corporate to individualistic bases of social contract. Since the main evaluation of the social involves a claim for the preference of a social order deriving from, and involving, rational individuals who act in accordance with freedom from the constraints of tradition, it is not surprising that the same form is encapsulated in the progressive end of the evolutionary schema. Furthermore, the temporal coexistence of a new or 'modern' form with a pre-existing or 'traditional' form leads to the spatial preoccupations of geolinguistics in which the same societal prejudices are given a spatial justification.

I have suggested throughout the preceding chapters that this model of society is very close to the North American world view, and to the individual liberalism which it encapsulates. What is implied is that what passes for objective sociology is, simultaneously, a subjective expression of the North American common-sense understanding of the nature of society. Yet this individualism does not fragment society, not merely because of the constraints upon individualism that exist in the form of social parameters, but also, it would seem, because the underlying driving force of action is a desire for cooperation and cohesion. Thus the need for freedom and diversity as the *sine qua non* of individual creativity is justified insofar as it does not negate a social responsibility which involves an awareness of communal responsibility. It is hardly surprising, given this emphasis upon social responsibility and the need for cooperation and cohesion, that concepts of community derive from integration rather than opposition. Thus evolution can not involve a polarisation between individualism and corporatism.

This issue invariably obliges us to consider the manner in which the concept of culture is invoked. While the social tends to be employed in terms of constraints on social action, culture is invoked as that which conditions social behaviour. It is most explicit in the work on communicative competence where it emerges as the very basis of social order, and in the work on ethnolinguistic vitality where culture is the basis for the definition of ethnic groups. Yet it is not absent from the other orientations. Ethnomethodology treats culture as the basis of social cohesion with meaning being conditioned by the shared features of culture. Perhaps the most common understanding of culture is as some totality or structure which defines the society in that it is the source of the values which determine behaviour. Rather than being some *ex cathedra* force external to actors, it is part of an overarching stock of knowledge employed to facilitate interaction. It is reproduced in such a way that it allows actors to understand their respective subjective points of view while also coordinating their actions. Thus while culture subdivides, it also integrates those allocated to the various subdivisions. If the objective of society is to facilitate integration and cohesion then certainly culture is a facilitating force in that it is the very basis of effective communication which is presented as the *sine qua non* of integration. However, in a cross-cultural context it is an inhibiting force that generates 'conversational interference', to invoke a concept employed by Gumperz (1982:153). It would seem therefore that cultural assimilation is a desirable process.

CRITIQUE

Having identified a general discourse on language and society, it is time to offer a general critique of that discourse. Incorporated in this discourse were the following features: evolutionism, functionalism, social order and individualism. These must be the starting point of our critique.

Functionalism seeks to demonstrate how both order and change derive from the same conditions. It is claimed to replace the evolutionary analysis of the nineteenth century which emphasised the universal nature of social change. However, it should be clear that the two are not necessarily alternatives since time and again in the preceding chapters we have encountered arguments that simultaneously draw upon both functionalist and evolutionary arguments. Before considering the implications of this unity I would like to consider them separately.

The most obvious feature of functionalist explanations is that they tend to substitute a rationality which appears to involve society at large for that of the individual, as if societies have needs or even reasons. Their importance in social science relates to establishing the difference between the intentions of the actor and the consequences of that action. Thus both Durkheim and Weber underlined the importance of moral values in generating unintended consequences, and in so doing they both expressed the importance of the non-rational in humankind. Durkheim saw these moral values as a source of solidarity and as the basis for pattern-maintaining, as the basis of social order. In this respect functionalism can be regarded as a unified theory of order and change since it demonstrates how both derive from the same conditions. Consequently functionalism tends to ignore the actor's rationality in order to develop an account in terms of what is regarded as the 'real' cause. This focus involves a biological analogy that is so evident in the work of Comte, in which society is likened to the anatomical whose structure operates to create a system, this operation being akin to function. Thus control does not lie in the hands of the individual agent and his/her reason, but relates to the wider system which functions in accordance with a social reasoning. Systems have functional needs which are allocated explanatory value. Evidently functionalism emphasises unintended consequences of action, claiming that when these consequences are patterned or reoccur regularly, this accounts for institutionalised aspects of social systems. However, as Giddens (1984:xxxi) has rightly shown, one can only refer to unintentional consequences if the intentional aspects of action are known, which must involve a highly sophisticated interpretation of agency. Similarly, Callinicos (1985:107) states that we

> must reject functionalism in the absence of a specification of the mechanism which permits the explanandum to have the effect attributed to it and in particular in light of treating the social structures as self-sustaining.

Generally the tendency is to resort to some functional need of the system with the consequences somehow filling that need. What tends to be missing is some mechanism whereby the functional need and the consequences are causally linked.

As I have claimed, the distinction between functionalism and evolutionism is by no means clear cut and the link between the two, as in the work of Comte, involves some form of organic metaphor. The organism has an internal potential for growth and most theories of social evolution adopt this premise claiming that it represents an orderly series of changes representing the different stages in evolution. There follows a tendency to develop a taxonomy or typology of these various stages, assuming that they can then be placed in sequence, and an explanatory framework is superimposed in order to justify the evolutionary nature of the change, each type or form growing out of, and tending to displace, the preceding type or form. The only additional element that is necessary is the assumption that the most recent type is the most superior because it is closest in time to the end result of evolution as progress – perfection. A denial of this claim for the potential achievement of perfection severely limits the entire argument. The driving force of the entire schema tends to be adaptation. Fishman's discussion of language domains which we encountered in chapter 3 fits neatly into this framework even though he does not claim that it is an evolutionary schema. In a sense it is possible to conceive of evolution in terms of a justification of the rule of the dominant with the overlap between the more recent form or type in the evolutionary schema corresponding with the features of the dominant society. Thus it is in the natural order of things that the prevailing system of societal differentiation should exist. Similarly, it is natural that the preceding forms have outlived their usefulness and will be replaced by the modern form. There is no reason to lament the disappearance or death of 'traditional' languages since they are simply being displaced by languages which are closer to perfection.

The feature which links functionalism and evolutionism in sociolinguistics tends to involve the implication that the shift from mechanical to organic solidarity, with its relationship to distinctive role structures, is an evolutionary phenomenon in which society establishes and re-establishes social order. This was perhaps most evident in the discussion of Milroy's work. The progression from mechanical to organic solidarity is taken for granted, not simply in terms of their being different social forms, but also in terms of their respective preference. The contrasting social forms are then empirically related to different speech patterns, and the interactional orientations claimed to relate to the respective forms are then claimed also to relate to the speech patterns.

Some of the objections to evolutionism should already be clear. It tends to impose time upon difference in such a way that one aspect of the difference must give way to the other, and, as a consequence, the two aspects are presented in terms of superiority/inferiority. This also involves viewing change as an inevitable process of nature driven by some inner social mechanism that remains unspecified, thereby ignoring aspects of social power that are involved. Change, be it social, linguistic or both is viewed as inevitable, natural and desirable.

It is common to associate the idea of adaptation with evolutionary theories, the biological analogy once again being the feature which leads to a discussion of response to the change that is implicit in evolution. Usually the concept is employed in such a way that it tends to be a vague notion totally incapable of explaining anything. With reference to social change there is a tendency to assume that societies, or any societal feature which has survived over time has done so because it has adapted, whereas those that disappear do so because of an inability to adapt. As a consequence, evolutionary theory lacks the necessary explanatory force which can account for the succession of social forms associated with time.

Perhaps the best known problem associated with adaptation is its limitation with reference to social change. There is a tendency, only too obvious in Parsonian structural functionalism, to treat social change in terms of stages. Thus the biological analogy informs us that a society which is subject to change is out of equilibrium and must adapt in order to re-establish such an equilibrium. Thus we have a series of stages of equilibrium interrupted by an associated series of adaptations. Process tends to be explained away by the concept of adaptation and all that we encounter are the various features of the stages in equilibrium.

One of the tendencies in evolutionary theory which is very common in the sociology of language is to generalise from a few cases so that general laws are established. Thus stages are established and the claim for a universal process is made. It is this that forms the expression of inevitability in evolutionary thought since the stages are held to run in sequence. With reference to language, as Fishman's discussion of domains makes clear, the tendency is to emphasise the claim that language reflects society and that the different features of language reflect different types and scales of society thereby establishing stages which tend to relate to one another in historical sequence. Alternatively, as suggested above, the tendency is to relate the mechanical/organic solidarity difference to time, suggesting that organic solidarity is the necessary outcome of the disappearance of mechanical solidarity.

This is echoed in the tendency to view the world in terms of a modern/traditional dichotomy, the former being regarded as superior because it is the more recent and the latter, consequently, being an inferior survival which must in time give way to the modern. However, there is also a discontinuity involved in that a causal relationship between them is never posited. Thus it becomes impossible to suggest that the traditional exists as a consequence of the existence of the modern, and in particular the power relationship between them. Even though both exist at the same moment in time the claim that one derives from the other means that they will be seen respectively as 'of the present' and as a 'survival from the past', this leading to a denigration of tradition through not being modern. Durkheim's emphasis upon persistence being seen not as survival but as the consequence of on-going function and the basis of social order is lost. It is hardly surprising that the modern is equated with a Eurocentric discourse which in the nineteenth century identified Europe as the pinnacle of civilisation.

What is evident here is that evolutionary theory links not only with functionalism but also with the comparative method in such a way that the denigration of languages and cultures is the end result. This is nowhere more evident than in the study of language contact or bilingualism. The linking of evolution with a diachronic study results in culture being viewed as static rather than as dynamic and creative. It involves viewing the past as the source of a culture which is diluted with time and through contact with 'superior' cultures. Consequently, not only is it impossible to conceive of culture as dynamic and contemporary but also it means that there is no way in which culture can be viewed as the creation of meaning as resistance.

Various commentators on language contact in France (Calvet 1974; Achard 1980; Balibar 1985) have commented on reason as part of the ideological discourse which asserts language dominance. The language of the state as the language of legal and other discourses of status is claimed to be the language of reason, thereby relegating all other languages within the state territory to the realm of non-reason. The claim is made that progress depends upon reason, that reason depends upon thought and thought depends upon language, so that language is a feature of progress. Given this ideological discourse it is not surprising that language is linked to aspects of personality in the form of thought. Thus even though no sociolinguist would suggest that there is any relationship between the complexity of linguistic structures of a language and stages in the evolutionary schema, there remains a tendency to treat some languages as modern and others as non-modern. It is hardly surprising that minority languages have such a struggle to enter into the domains of state administration. Indeed, in many cases it is claimed that the economy and commerce rely upon the same claim for reason, and it is held that minority languages are not 'commercial languages'. This should not be surprising given the tendency to treat language as a reflection of society, for if the assumption is made that the level of complexity of societal organisation is mirrored by that of personality development, then it follows that evolution involves not merely personality development but also language development. Carried a step further it becomes a manifestation of the preoccupation of Bacon and Locke who claimed that complex ideas cannot be translated, and that it is this which creates barriers between communities. That is, language divides and prevents progress towards uniformity, the absence of conflict, and progress.

The issues of biological analogy and social change are not missing from a discussion of power, for if we consider what has been said about change and adaptation, it should be evident that the outcome of change is equilibrium or social order, each condition of equilibrium being interrupted by change, seen as disequilibrium associated with adaptation. Thus society will always be built around social order, and permanent conflict is denied. Furthermore, the emphasis upon normative consensus as the basis of social integration which we have encountered time and again in preceding chapters merely involves the issue of contestation of norms, and the source of their existence as it relates to interests. Not of course that power has to be linked with conflict, for even though it does constrain, it also involves the ability to achieve outcomes. What is clear is that social order, within this perspective, derives from consent rather than coercion, this being the main division between what is held to be consensus and conflict orientations. If social order does derive from consent then there can be no reason for anyone to consider a revolutionary change which, by definition, seeks to establish a different form of social order.

It should be clear that my objection to the normative consensus of orthodox sociolinguistics rests on the unquestioned adoption of a specific conception of society by what are either naive or politically motivated practitioners. The arguments against this particular perspective, it should be evident, are numerous. It is not that I would wish to argue that such a perspective somehow fails to correspond to some form of truth or reality, but that there should be an awareness of the limitations of the perspective assumed. Such an awareness would, presumably, lead to a consideration of alternative perspectives and it is two such alternatives that I now wish to address.

MARXISM AND LANGUAGE

Having subjected mainstream sociolinguistics to a sustained critique associated with the overriding involvement in orthodox consensus, it is hardly appropriate to conclude without considering alternative approaches which might redress what has been claimed are deficiencies in the mainstream approach. Yet, as will be clear, these alternatives are not devoid of problems, many of which they share with the orthodox consensus view of society. The two perspectives which I would briefly like to consider are Marxism and what has become known as French Discourse Analysis (FDA), which focuses upon the theoretical work of Michel Foucault.

While maintaining that there is a general orientation that is shared by the majority of sociolinguists it was not my intention in the preceding chapters to suggest that some sociolinguists have not been associated with the alternative perspectives which I intend to discuss. Indeed there is a considerable interest in Marxism and language even though little of this recent work has developed on the early work of the Moscow Circle, Marx, Lenin and Gramsci among others. An exception is the work of Voloshinov which has received considerable scrutiny in recent years. In addition there are those sociologists and linguists who operate from Marxist principles in developing theories of language and society – those that come most easily to mind are Pecheux, Bourdieu, Hodge and Kress. I do not wish to focus attention on what has been achieved by such workers and their predecessors – that is the work of another volume, one that is much needed in the English language. Rather I would like to consider how Marxism can address some of the problems I have identified above and how it fails to address other problems.

In claiming that Marxism represents an alternative to the orthodox consensus perspective it is necessary to reiterate the warning expressed at the beginning of the chapter concerning the oversimplification of creating a consensus/conflict opposition as exemplified by the work of Marx and Durkheim. None the less it should be evident that there is a fundamental difference in the assumptions about society that underlie the two perspectives.

Marx assumed that change was an inherent feature of society, this change being orderly in the sense that it was patterned and that it was the relationship of people to the economic order which was the key to this patterning of change. Marx shared the belief that society should be treated as an interrelated system of parts with his contemporaries who laid the ground for structural functionalism. For Marx the economy was responsible for shaping the other parts and in this respect it was the determining force.

While Marx held that people were rational, intelligent and sensitive he also claimed that circumstances could influence people in such a way that they became irrational, unintelligent and insensitive. This occurred when the social arrangements of society were such that a few were able to pursue their own interests at the expense of others. This feature of exploitation was the central aspect of the conflict in Marx's conception of society. The manner in which he and Engels criticised the followers of Hegel – specifically Feuerbach and Stirner – gave rise to the view that social theory must be critical of oppressive arrangements and should present emancipatory alternatives. The Young Hegelians were criticised for their treatment of the world as reflective of ideas, with the dynamics of social life revolving around consciousness and other cognitive processes. For Marx this was nothing more than a conservative ideology that helped further the oppression of the many by the few. He claimed that humans were capable of a conscious awareness of themselves and their situation, and held that their assessment of their position in society derived from their daily existence, the most important feature of which was the process of production. However, productive activity generates a division of labour which, in the long run, deprives humans of their capacity to determine their productive activities. Furthermore, through their involvement in productive activities people generate private property and capital for those who control the modes and means of production, this being the very element that enslaved them. Thus, the productive process involves those who have only their labour power to sell and to survive with – the proletariat – and those who have the means with which to purchase this labour – the bourgeoisie. The exploitation of the labour power of one by the other in order to realise material profit is the very essence of a society riddled with inherent conflict. Thus any semblance of order is an order which reproduces this relationship of exploitation.

Thus capitalism is an economic order in which there is the naked exploitation of the many by the few, this being the inherent feature of social class relationships. It is a system that is also typified by contradictions, strains and tensions which are created by the system. As a consequence, Marx foresaw an inevitable situation of drastic change to the system. One element which delays this inevitability is the ideological process whereby the conflicting interests are instrumental in obscuring the collective interests of the proletariat. Another is the structural bond whereby both social classes depend upon one another for survival.

However, capitalism is merely the latest of a series of modes of production, and the one which preceded the communist mode of production. That is, there is a heavy evolutionist strain to the Marxist argument. Progress towards perfection, the central tenet of nineteenth-century evolutionism, is evident in the claim that a socialist society, devoid of exploitation, is the feature of the final mode of production. Thus, all preceding modes of production, be they the lineage, Asiatic or feudal mode, are merely stages in the inevitable drive towards perfection. It is claimed that neither Marx nor Engels implied that a process was inevitable and that this position was one adopted by Marxists such as Plekhanov. However, this would appear to be difficult to sustain given the nature of the driving force for change and the directionality of change within the overall perspective.

The forces of production and the relations of production constitute what Marx called the 'economic base' but which is often referred to as the infrastructure. The other feature of society is the superstructure and includes the religious, familial and political institutions. The economic determinism in his argument derived from the claim that the superstructure is shaped by the infrastructure. Yet, this relationship between base and superstructure has been highly problematic in recent Marxist debates, and the nature of the determinism is a highly contentious issue, far too involved to be debated here. This is also true of the concept of ideology which is of crucial importance in any discussion of Marxism and language.

The essential role of ideology is in preventing the transformation of latent class interests into manifest class interests which, under additional conditions, would lead to the polarisation of society into classes joined in conflict. That is, it inhibits the transformation of false consciousness into class consciousness. As such it permits the perseverance of domination. It is this that lends it a critical connotation in the sense that it encapsulates a belief that social theory must be critical of oppression and domination. It is this understanding of ideology, with meaning as the basis of sustaining domination, which has been at the centre of most studies of language among contemporary Marxists, leading to what is referred to as critical sociolinguistics.

Perhaps it is here that one should begin outlining some of the problems of Marxism. In the sense that it is a negative quality ideology becomes, as Thompson has emphasised (1984:1), the production of the other: 'the thought of someone other than oneself'. This is part of the problem; it is the result of conscious production. As such there is a tendency to treat ideology as conspiratorial, as the conscious production of an individual or group whose objective is the subversion of some other group. This was one of the problems with the early work of Hodge and Kress and their colleagues (Fowler *et al.* 1979) who explicitly saw newspapers as conscious ideological production. Perhaps it is more explicit in the work of the Glasgow Media Group (1980) and their discussion of television news. Raymond Williams (1973) has underlined the oversimplistic nature of such a conception in that it implies that all that is necessary for the implementation of change is the removal and replacement of the forces responsible for ideological production. Such an act would be far from sufficient to readjust the forces of capitalist domination. It is akin to the claim of some feminists that sexism can be 'cured' by adopting non-sexist language.

Being a conspiratorial entity, ideology is equated with rational and conscious actors who constitute ideology prior to action. The problems of the centred, rational actor have been emphasised in the preceding chapters and I will momentarily return to the opposing debate, one that has been incorporated into some Marxist arguments, which claims that ideology is not constituted before the act but is the act itself, when I discuss French Discourse Analysis. For the moment, suffice it to say that regarding language as part of the superstructure does not necessarily involve identifying language as the communication of a sense between persons, as is the case in most of linguistics, a position which obstructs theoretical advance and closes off important areas of ideological struggle. As a consequence language is indifferent to class struggle, but class struggle is not indifferent to language. This is the location of much of the recent work among Marxist linguists.

It should immediately be evident that ideology in its rationalist conception carries a functionalist connotation since ideology is claimed to function in order to sustain domination. However, this is not the only functionalist reference within the Marxist perspective. It has been most evident in the base/superstructure relationship where it is claimed that the superstructure exists in order to sustain the infrastructure. In this respect it also becomes a reductionist argument with the superstructure being reduced to an image of the infrastructure as in Lukacs' famous reflection and lags thesis.

G.A. Cohen (1978:250) has sought to avoid the problem of function-alism by distinguishing between 'attributing a function' and 'providing a functional explanation' where one avoids the claim that ideology exists because of the need to conceal contradictions by restricting the claim to 'attributing a function'. Cohen also distinguishes between functionalism and functionalist explanations, claiming that Marxism is an example of the latter.

Yet another problem which relates to the relationship between social class and ideology involves the problem of agency in social change. If the bourgeoisie is the benefactor of ideological produc-tion and its effect upon class relationships, and if the proletariat is influenced by ideology to the extent that it conforms with its own domination, then where lies the agency for change and resistance? The answer lies in what resembles a residual afterthought in the form of the intellectuals who, presumably, act in opposition to their class interests in supporting the proletarian cause.

The reductionism alluded to above boils down to the claim that all ideas have a class basis. This in turn underlines the problem of an over-emphasis on social class as the dimension of inequality above all others. This is partly why feminists have identified Marxism as a male discourse, with the consequence that Marxist feminism becomes impossible. Similarly there is a tendency to reduce all other forms of domination to a discussion of class, the prime example being that of ethnicity, the claim being not merely that class analysis is ignored but that ethnicity is itself ideological in the sense that it inhibits the development of class consciousness. Evidently such a view denies the relevance of alternative dimensions of inequality as the bases of struggle and inhibits seeing the various dimensions of inequality as coexisting (this issue was considered in chapter 8).

Since Marxism is premised upon the belief that social order derives from coercion – even if that coercion does involve a consensus, it is a consensus which does not reflect 'reality' – it would appear that many of the problems which we have associated with mainstream sociolinguistics can fruitfully be considered by reference to a Marxist orientation. However, it is also evident that the two perspectives share what we have recognised as problems in the analysis of language in society. It would seem that any argument that is premised upon the concealing effect of ideology must inevitably be functional. As I have implied this problem may be ignored if the problem of conspiracy can be overcome. This has been the focus of recent work on ideo-logy which involves a focus upon language leading to an argument which seeks to demonstrate that, even though ideology may not be conspiratorial, none the less it does serve to sustain the dominance of the bourgeoisie, doing so within a broad spectrum of what can be said without undermining the capitalist order. It is only at the borders of this spectrum that the problem of conspiracy will arise. The work of Althusser has been important with reference to this development but it must be emphasised that although his work has had considerable influence upon those working exclusively in the English language, his own work owes much to other French language sociologists, particularly Bachelard, as well as to Gramsci. The contribution of Bachelard in terms of what can and cannot be said within discourse becomes evident, as also does the work of Foucault. These two ideas are among the most important and influential contributions to French sociology and it is little wonder that they have had such a far-reaching influence on French Marxism.

Another French sociologist who has grappled with Marxism and language is Bourdieu. However, there is a sense in which much of his work reflects an underlying Durkheimian evolutionism, with society evolving from a simple to a more complex stage. The main thrust of his work involves language as a basis for communication, but he also seeks to establish the nature of structural constraints on this process. In so doing he seeks to integrate interactionist accounts of language. He claims that language standardisation is subject to legitimisation in such a way that it serves specific class interests. While structural functionalism tends to refer to the social conditions of communication, Bourdieu emphasises the social character of these conditions, an important distinction in the shift from a consensus to a conflict orientation. Yet there remains a sense in which he appears to draw upon an analysis very similar to the normative consensus of structural functionalism. This much is clear in the way in which linguistic features of speech are socially marked. No attempt is made to establish the way in which this marking is institutionalised and legitimised, apart from a general appeal to the class variations in socialisation. Bourdieu links power and domination through the concept of symbolic violence which, as Thompson (1984:42–73) states, is an unreified concept which is linked to questionable assumptions about social reproduction. Indeed, Thompson (1984:59) states explicitly that Bourdieu resorts to a 'consensus model of social reproduction'. While the central point which Bourdieu seeks to emphasise, that legitimation involves the misrecognition of domination, is important, it is by no means a novel development.

These various attempts to develop Marxist analyses of language in society find it difficult to avoid the problem of language as reflection since the argument relies upon a preconceived and preformed conception of society. The analysis of language is then brought together in order to justify the implications associated with that particular model of society. Language in the form of discourse becomes a reflection of social inequality in all of its ramifications; it becomes an entity separate from, but reflecting, society.

In the same vein, discourse is treated as resistance. The problem here is that both dominance and resistance are treated as non-conspiratorial with the consequence that if resistance is not conscious it can be of little value as a counter-effect of dominance, and so resistance is reduced to little more than an unconscious ritual. The discourse in question is frequently denoted as a discourse of resistance on the basis of the class position of the *enonciateur* rather than on a thoroughgoing analysis of the content.

It is on ideology that one must concentrate with reference to the Marxist potential for sociolinguistics and the sociology of language. The translation of Gramsci's seminal work into English in 1971 was a tremendous boost to British developments in the study of ideology. His suggestion that, to an extent, the superstructure can be regarded as distinct from the infrastructure, followed by Althusser's important contributions (1969, 1971) led to a re-evaluation of the role of language in ideology. French sociologists have been particularly prominent in this development and it is evident that these resolutions must be taken on board by those working with language in society, before even considering what Marxism has to contribute. There is some evidence that this is not happening but one must also point to the contributions of Hodge and Kress (1988 *inter alia*) and Thompson (1984) as exceptions, despite the fact that Thompson's work is more of a critique than an elaboration. The work of Hodge (1990) is particularly interesting in that he seems to be moving progressively in the direction of FDA while sharing with many Anglo-sociologists a reluctance to relinquish the Marxist concern for the rational centred subject (G. Williams, forthcoming), partly, one suspects, because of the strong Fabian influence on the history of English sociology and partly because of the personal political allegiances of the individual sociologists. As we shall see in the following section, numerous sociologists have concentrated, above all else, upon resolving the problem of the conspiratorial nature of ideology by drawing upon many of the ideas which derive from French Discourse Analysis and it is to a consideration of that alternative that I now wish to turn.

FRENCH DISCOURSE ANALYSIS

This area of study goes under a number of titles including post-structuralism, *pouvoir–savoir* perspective and Foucauldian discourse analysis. This is partly because of the confusion associated with the concept of 'discourse'. Like the concept of 'social class' its meaning varies in accordance with the theoretical problematic in which it is found. Yet 'discourse' tends to be used in such an indiscriminate way with reference to theory that inevitably it is the source of no little confusion. On the one hand, it is employed in the type of analysis which seeks to highlight the rules and dynamics of speech and conversation in relation to social situation as in the work of Gumperz (1982) which was discussed in chapters 6 and 7. Perhaps it is this use which is familiar to most sociolinguists. However, the term is also used in work which seeks to relate language to the possible positions of human subjects in language as in the work of Benveniste (1973 *inter alia*).

There are two further uses of the term 'discourse' which are more relevant to what I wish to discuss. There is a sense in which the two uses overlap. First, discourse is treated as ideological production. Here we find evidence of a Marxist perspective which I will return to at the end of this section, with discourse sometimes being treated as conspiratorial (Monteforte Toledo 1980), and sometimes retaining the Marxist functionalist orientation, with ideology functioning to preserve class interests even if that function is not the consequence of conspiratorial action (e.g. Pecheux 1982). Second, there is the line of enquiry which denies the existence of epistemology by claiming that the subject is not constituted outside of discourse. Discourse becomes the source of the constitution of the human subject. It is this line of argument which I propose to entertain but I will return to the manner in which some of the ideas from FDA have been adopted by Marxist analysts without pursuing the consequences of the adoption to their logical conclusion.

The inspiration for the theoretical work of Michel Foucault and consequently for FDA was the nineteenth-century German philosopher Nietzsche and the very Young Hegelians whose idealism Marx and Engels criticised. Following the discussion from Nietzsche through to Foucault and FDA it is tempting to believe that perhaps Stirner was correct in claiming to witness the Hegelian absolute in theoretical generalisation with the concept of humankind being a secularised version of that of God, the struggle for power being the substitute of one master for another, thereby making Marxism a fusion of ancient theology and modern totalitarianism as the *nouveaux philosophes* who spawned FDA have claimed. Clearly those who have sought to implicate FDA in Marxism are barking up the wrong tree. Foucault said of the ideas of Nietzsche:

> The only valid tribute to thought such as Nietzsche's is precisely to use it, to deform it, to make it groan and protest. And if commentators then say that I am being faithful to Nietzsche, that is of absolutely no interest.
>
> (Foucault 1980:53–4)

Nietzsche realised that what posed as objectivity merely masked subjective motivations. Thus history could not be conceived of as the development of Truth or as the embodiment of Freedom. The historian's tendency to depict the present as finite, limited and despicable, relied on locating differences in the past; things were not always the way they are, differences existed. This, as we have seen, is the cornerstone of the evolutionism and the idea of inevitable progress which we have so severely criticised. Nietzsche referred to genealogy as the means whereby the present is delegitimised by separating it from the past. Neither could the foundations of morality be found in ideal truth. Rather history was made up of accidents, dispersion, chance events, lies, and the history of truth was the history of error and arbitrariness:

> The faith on which our belief in science rests is still a metaphysical faith . . . . The Christian faith, which was also the faith of Plato, that God is Truth and truth divine . . . . But what if this equation becomes less and less credible, if the only things that may still be viewed as divine are error, blindness and lies; if God himself turns out to be our *longest* lie?
>
> (Nietzsche 1969:288)

This suspicion of Nietzsche's led him to ground morality and social institutions in the tactics of individual actors, a highly paranoid and conspiratorial standpoint which, as we shall see, FDA departs from. Rather than being found in ideal truth, morality was founded and rested in *pudenda origo* or lowly origins and was associated with a clash of wills. Knowledge was enmeshed in the petty malice of this clash of dominations. It is here we must recognise that, having denied the possibility of objective knowledge, Nietzsche also denies the possibility of social emancipation, since knowledge, rather than being the source of emancipation, merely increases the dangers we face. This is because potentially everything is implicated in the networks of power which are ever increasingly associated with the advance of knowledge. Knowledge cannot be separate from power.

This claim that power and knowledge are not external to one another is linked to the Foucauldian claim that there is no knowledge outside of discourse and no discourse outside of language. Thus language is power. Let us consider these ideas as a means of introduction to the ideas of Michel Foucault. His concept of discourse does not involve seeing discourses as groups of signs but rather as practices that systematically form the objects of which they speak. Furthermore the preformed subject is dispensed with:

> Discourse is not the majestically unfolding manifestation of a thinking, knowing, speaking, subject, but, on the contrary, a totality in which the dispersion of the subject and his discontinuity with himself may be determined. It is a space of exteriority in which a network of distinct sites is deployed.
>
> (Foucault 1972:49,55)

The implication of this decentring of the subject, as it has become known, is that the conventional practice of sociology in which an individual or social group is responsible for, or at least is drawn upon as an explanation for action is no longer possible. Causality must be rethought. It is the implications of this which have disturbed many sociologists as we shall see in the following pages. More importantly, perhaps, from the standpoint of sociolinguistics is the recognition that the 'author' of a text is neither autonomous nor creative, but occupies a subordinate place within a given discursive practice. It becomes clearer how knowledge is constituted only within discourse.

The conventional view which we have challenged claims that 'valid' knowledge is possible and that knowledge correlates with reality. Objectivity is justified through an approximation between the discourse in question and 'truth', with 'truth' implying a correspondence between reality and thought. Since epistemology evaluates a discourse from the standpoint of its relationship to truth, if objective knowledge is denied then the discipline of epistemology is undermined. Norris (1985:143) claims that modern philosophy lost its way when Descartes, and subsequently Kant, focused their main concern on answering the problem of knowledge and epistemological doubt, a claim not unlike that of Michel Pecheux (1982) concerning the need to return to pre-Cartesian philosophy for an understanding of language.

The central assumption of the orthodox view is one that has been shared by so many philosophers since Aristotle: that there is an immediate, direct, intuitive contact between subject and object and that this is the basis of our knowledge of the world. This means that our knowledge consists of objects which are discussed in discourse, that is, objects and discourse are two separate entities. As should be evident from the preceding chapters, in the quest for truth the issue boils down to which of alternative theories gives the most accurate reflection of reality. Evidently epistemology involves a consideration of the objectivity of knowledge. Epistemologies are also empirical in that discourses are judged in terms of whether or not they add to our knowledge of truth or reality. This does not mean that empiricists and idealists cannot still disagree about whether the mind merely absorbs a given, objective reality in a passive way or whether it plays a more active role in shaping such a reality. Yet epistemology remains concerned primarily with how the subject can have knowledge of the object, that is, the subject is taken for granted as the origin and justification of knowledge. This has its parallels in the philosophy of language.

In most philosophies of language the meaning of a word is held to be the entity outside of language to which it refers. Linking this to theories of knowledge which suggest that conscious ideas mediate between human beings and the external world, we find that ideas are the signs of things and words the signs of ideas. Language becomes a collection of signs whose nature is dependent upon relation to extra-linguistic phenomena. It is the conscious, thinking subject who gives meaning to words and ensures that they are correctly employed. As a consequence language contains consciousness.

FDA, drawing upon Saussurean linguistics, negates this idea, and this has profound consequences for those social sciences where the rational actor is central to its theories and perspectives. The already existing actor is no longer at the centre of any explanatory conceptualisation. Discourse becomes the source of the constitution of the human subject who does not, and cannot, lie outside of discourse. Knowledge is no longer treated in terms of 'ideas' in the sense of mental representations tied to the production of thought by a human subject. The individual author is denied. If the human subject only exists within discourse then that subject cannot be the source of any action prior to discourse as is implied for example in the conspiratorial view of ideology. Neither can the human subject be the source of ideas since it is ideas which constitute the individual as subject. Evidently discourse must be treated as a sequence of verbal signs, as the first representation of thought. It is different from speech which tends to be treated as the way any individual uses language to express him/herself. To decentre the subject as the source of meaning and action is to raise grave doubts about most of what has become axiomatic in the social sciences, and especially in sociolinguistics.

A central tenet of this analytic force is that structures have no objective existence, but only assume meaning within discursive contexts, and that there is no level of the social formation which stands outside of the discursive formations in which the material activities of concrete human subjects consist. Thus the human subject is not seen as occupying a given 'place' within a 'social structure', but as constituted in the intersection of a determinate set of discursive formations in which they are articulated. To conceive of social practices which are non-discursive reduces ultimately to a mechanical behaviourism with its allied empiricist conception of the subject. Similarly social groups must be conceptualised not as categories of human agents but as categories of subject which only exist in struggle. Thus, if classes, for example, are not determined economically as in the orthodox Marxist position, but are the consequences of discursive practice, their form and effectivity is dependent upon the specific civil society in question. More importantly perhaps, it cannot be assumed that the constitution of such classes depends upon opposition to another social class, with the consequence that struggle need not necessarily involve opposition to contradicting classes. Furthermore, non-class dimensions of inequality including gender, ethnicity, nation, language groups etc., are located within various discursive features of popular-democratic struggle within which nationality assumes a particular significance. A language group, and indeed any other type of group only exists in struggle, and there is no reason why any one form of struggle should dominate other forms of struggle. Furthermore, since struggles are located within discursive contexts, part of the struggle over and in language involves the struggle to establish the salience of language. What is implied here is that individuals are formed as subjects through social experience, through their position in particular discursive formations where the individual is determined as a conscious, self-reflexive, independent subject.

Let us now turn to the power dimension of *pouvoir–savoir*. It involves something quite different from the anthropomorphic conception of power that we encounter in most social science. It is the nature of the discursive formation that determines what can and must be said from a given position, in a given conjuncture, involving, not merely the words used, but also the constructions into which these words are combined insofar as they determine the signification of these words. This much should be familiar to most sociolinguists through their acquaintance with Saussurean linguistics. However, there are also silences in the sense that there are certain things that cannot be said within a given discursive formation. It is here that we locate the concept of power, in the manner in which one discourse determines what can and indeed, must be said, within any given place. This is because the places are responsible for organising the objects of the discourse:

> To describe a formulation *qua* statement does not consist in analysing the relationship between the author and what he [sic] says . . . but in determining what positions can and must be occupied by an individual if he [sic] is to be the subject of it.
>
> (Foucault 1972:95–6)

These statements never exist in isolation since the discursive formation exists as the totality of its statements; it has an internal consistency. Thus it would seem that there is an internal organising force in all discursive formations, a force which conditions the production of meaning. The production of meaning arises in the relationship between a concrete discourse and a discursive formation; words, expressions and propositions have no meaning other than in the usage within a determinate discursive formation. Evidently this is quite a different conception of semantics than those in which it is implied that a word has a fixed meaning that is capable of translation. The various signifiers represent an indefinite set of ideas with very different signification according to the discursive formation in which they exist. Thus, for example, the signifier 'Wales' can vary immensely in its signification, and it is always a matter of struggle, over which no group can claim a privileged view, to situate it within the symbolic where it can gain a 'proper designation'. Clearly the formation of the subject is interwoven with the creation of meaning. Whilst the subject may not be aware of its existence within any discursive formation it can, none the less, as subject, never lie outside of the discursive formation. In this respect the system of places from which the discourses emanate is crucial for reasoning in terms of discursive formation and leads to Foucault's formulation concerning the determination of the point which can and must be occupied in order to be the subject. The subject thus constituted is formed within a certain number of enunciative places in such a way that there is no externality between the subject and its discourse (Marandin 1979:41). Social places are constructed within discourse and involve a rapport with a variety of other notion-objects. It is here that the concept of episteme is relevant:

> By episteme . . . we mean . . . the total set of relations, at a given period, the discursive practices that give rise to epistemological figures, sciences and possibly formalised systems . . . it is the totality of relations that can be discovered for a given period, between the sciences when one analyses them at the level of discursive realities.
>
> (Foucault 1972:191)

Achard *et al.* (1987:4) refer to episteme as 'not only that which locates a systematic indivisibility of the interdiscursivity of contemporary representation between them, but as a trace of the ideal unity of a privileged observation – that of power'. Crucial in this conception of the subject as located in discourse is the concept of interpolation. Pecheux (1982:92–3) refers to this in terms of the relationship between the Freudian idea of the conscious and the Marxist conception of ideology, claiming that ideology interpolates individuals as subjects, and referring to the Althusserian claim that 'The individual is interpolated as a (free) subject in order that he shall submit freely to the commandments of the Subject, i.e. in order that he shall (freely) accept his subjection' (Althusser 1971:169). Presumably this does not imply that the individual as a subject can exist prior to discourse since it is only within discourse that the subject is created. In this respect there may well be a disagreement between the proponents of FDA and the materialism of Pecheux's thesis. I shall return to this issue momentarily. What is evident is the central concern of Pecheux's work – the linking of the constitution of meaning to the constitution of the subject and the manner in which this involves the claiming of the subject into existence within discourse.

Pecheux's work sought to redress the orthodox linguistic emphasis on language as communication by referring to discourse as the production of a sense which is independent of language, and which is articulated to the ideological instant. Like Foucault, he claimed that there was no meaning outside of discourse but, simultaneously, he claimed that words, expressions and propositions take their sense from the ideological formation of which they constitute the discursive element. Discursive formations are a region of ideological formations which are themselves distributed by the ideological level and, in the last instance, by the economic. However, we are not told why the economic discourse should be so privileged.

The preceding discussion may suggest that all discourses within any discursive formation are equal. This is far from being the case. As the official discourse, associated with institutional legitimisation, that of the state invariably assumes a position of dominance. The different status associated with different discourses means that any statement is influenced by the conditions of its enunciation. Such conditions include economic, institutional and ideological factors. This is what is referred to as the 'place' of a discourse. However, there is also the principle that wherever there is power there must be resistance. Thus the official discourse, partly through its guise of social policy, has such an effect. However, it also, in its dominance, to an extent constrains the nature of the alternative discourse in that any resistance must bear relevance to that which it resists. This obliges us to return to the conceptualisation of power in that it involves the manner in which one discourse determines what can, and indeed, must be said within any given place. This is because of the manner in which discourse is responsible for organising the objects of the discourse. What is inferred is that there is an internal organising force within discursive formations, a force which conditions the production of meaning. In a sense, even though a discursive formation retains its internal integrity, it also conditions the production of discourse since it limits what can and cannot be said: 'The analysis of statements and discursive formations . . . wishes to determine the principle according to which only the "signifying" groups that were enunciated could appear' (Foucault 1972:118). Both power and resistance reside in discourse. The relationship between power and knowledge is treated in terms of how the relations of power define the fields of knowledge and produce objects of knowledge. Furthermore, the production of meaning is rooted in struggle since truth is a contentious issue rather than an absolute, and as such it is the site of permanent struggle. Power needs resistance as one of its final conditions of operation and it is through the articulation of resistance that power spreads through the social field. Indeed the space within which the subject and the object occur is cleared and defined by struggle and its power/resistance constituents.

In pursuing its objective FDA has also redressed the tendency to see language as reflecting society as the following statement by Boutet (1985) indicates:

the words, the discourses, are not simply the representation of our acts and of our thoughts, they are not only there to transmit information or the ideas or the order. They are not the *reflection* of the social, they are a participating force and they are *active* on the social, and produce specific effects which the analyst can place reference points upon . . . the semiotic materiality that is language.

(emphasis in the original)

Language is not a representation, a simple commentary of social processes from which reality derives but an image in words and phrases of a symbolic language.

As I have implied above, many Marxists have accommodated several of the ideas of FDA, particularly those that relate to the link between language and ideology. This should not be surprising given that both FDA and the recent Marxist concern with ideology focus upon the same problem of the production of meaning. While this resolves some of the problems of Marxist analysis it merely raises further problems because of the retention of materialist causality, the *sine qua non* of Marxism. Thus the materialist thesis gives prominence to the economist discourse which stands outside of the general claim that there is no knowledge outside of discourse. Adopting some of the ideas of FDA leads to developing the work of Gramsci concerning the relationship between the superstructure and the infrastructure, resulting in the claim for a partial autonomy of the superstructure. However, to take that small step further would deny the fundamental ingredient of Marxism, that it is the infrastructure that is determinate. Allegiance to Marxist discourse, persisting alongside ideas deriving from FDA, in my opinion, merely produces contradictions which no amount of intellectual gymnastics can resolve.

FDA also redresses the tendency for Marxism to emphasise social class as the fundamental dimension of inequality in society. This development has appealed to both feminists and some members of minority language groups. However, among the latter the link between minority language movements and the desire for statehood by members of stateless nations means that the anarchist tendency in FDA loses its appeal, and the desire to stress the uniformity of the language group is another point of resistance to the development of such ideas.

While FDA may appear to resolve some of the issues and difficulties of sociolinguistics, it does not mean that it is divorced from other difficulties. One of the most obvious problems involves the link between theory and method. Achard (1986:11) has claimed that the analysis of discourse has not developed as an application of a theoretical programme but as a universe of methods. Recently J. A. Fishman (1990) said something similar about much of sociolinguistics, claiming that behind such work was intuition rather than carefully thought out theory. Evidently the link between theory and method is, in some respects, clearly thought out in FDA in that the objective of the methodological endeavour is to deconstruct discourse, not with reference to ascertaining some hidden truth as in the Marxist understanding of ideology, but rather to reveal the unintended in language and, through that, the nature of knowledge and power, without any pretensions concerning knowledge as truth. Yet there is a sense in which both objectives can overlap which is why there has been considerable interplay on the methodological plane between the respective theoretical perspectives. Both have drawn upon an analysis of discourse which rests heavily upon linguistics. The problem which this raises for FDA is that if linguistics is itself a discourse then, inevitably, a discourse is employed in order to analyse discourse!

FDA also leads to a rejection of the Marxist claim that history unfolds according to laws which dialectical reason can reveal. White (1978) sees 'the various "logics" of historical explanation as merely the legitimation cover adopted by different ideologies in search of narrative hegemony' (quoted in Norris 1985:22). This merely repeats what Nietzsche said about history with reference to its ability to suppress creative thought through the idea of 'tradition'. Thus the objective of history should not be to tell a story, as in a narrative, but rather to come to terms with explanations in terms of discursive formations. Ryan (1982) has argued that privileged concepts exert the kind of force which links them to forms of domination, that is, within the epistemological conception of theory the dominant discourse prevails. There is a necessary relationship, in Ryan's view, between the structures of thought and the structures of political power. What is required of both the historian and the sociologist is a critical reflection upon knowledge and interests. The critique developed in the preceding chapters, in a very unsystematic way, suggests that sociology itself is not an objective, privileged discourse but rather, as indicated in chapter 1, a historical discourse developed within an Eurocentric, imperialist and statist context by members of dominant groups within dominant states and, as a consequence, it systematically fails to address social and cultural issues from the place of the minority.

The distinction between Marxism and FDA referred to above is, to an extent, fused in the recent post-modernist debate. Post-modernism appears to contradict itself in, on the one hand, claiming to represent the denial of the truth claims of epistemology as in FDA and, on the other hand, paying lip service to the post-industrialism of those such as Bell and Richmond writing in the early 1970s whose work was based on precisely such claims. One of the assertions of post-modernism is that the grand theories, including Marxism, are no longer relevant in the post-modern world. Marxists, in turn, react to this red rag by seeking to engage the post-modernists by reference to the very truth claims which they deny. It is hardly surprising that the members of the two camps talk past each other, and that the debate would appear to be stagnant. However, this polemic has succeeded in highlighting the nature of modernism and the emphasis upon reason in the Enlightenment thought from which it derives. This has led to a reassessment of some of the central tenets of sociology. Without wishing to involve myself in the post-modernist debate I would subscribe to the need to deconstruct sociology. It is essential that sociolinguists should be part of that process since language must be seen as central to sociology as the study of society rather than the marginal topic it has thus far remained. In this respect this final chapter should not be seen as a summary of a critique followed by an easy answer in the form of a ready made alternative in the quest for 'truth'. Rather it seeks to present questions to be grappled with in the hope that it will lead to new directions for the sociolinguistic endeavour.

References

Abercrombie, D. (1967) *Elements of General Phonetics*, Edinburgh, Edinburgh University Press.

Achard, P. (1980) 'History and the Politics of Language in France', *History Workshop Journal*, vol. 10, pp. 175–83.

—— (1986) 'Discours et sociologie du langage', *Langage et Société*, no. 37, pp. 5–61.

Achard, P., M.P. Gruenais and D. Jaulin (1984) *Histoire et Linguistique*, Paris, Maison des Sciences de l'Homme.

Agar, M. (1973) *Ripping and Running: A Formal Ethnography of Urban Heroin Addicts*, New York, Academic Press.

Allardt, E. (1979) *Implications of the Ethnic Revival in Modern, Industrial Society: A Comparative Study of the Linguistic Minorities of Western Europe*, Helsinki, Commentationes Scientarium Socialum, 12.

Althusser, L. (1969) *For Marx*, London, Allen Lane.

—— (1970) *Reading Capital*, London, New Left Books.

—— (1971) 'Ideology and ideological state apparatus', in *Lenin, Philosophy and Other Essays*, London, New Left Books, pp. 177–202.

Appel, R. and P. Muysken (1987) *Language Contact and Bilingualism*, London, Arnold.

Aracil, Ll. V. (1977) *Bilingualism as a Myth*, Cahiers de L'Irsce IV, Centre Universitaire de Perpignan.

Arditi, G. (1987) 'Role as a Cultural Concept', *Theory and Society*, vol. 16, no. 4, pp. 565–93.

Atkinson, P. (1988) 'Ethnomethodology: A Critical Review', *Annual Review of Sociology*, vol. 14, pp. 441–65.

Attewell, P. (1974) 'Ethnomethodology since Garfinkel', *Theory and Society*, vol. 1, pp. 179–210.

Balibar, R. (1985) *L'Institution du français*, Paris, Presses Universitaires Françaises.

Becker, H. (1948) *Der Sprachbund*, Leipzig.

Benveniste, E. (1973) *Problems of General Linguistics*, Florida, University of Miami Press.

Bernstein, B. (1971–5) *Class, Codes and Control*, London, Routledge and Kegan Paul.

Blau, P. (1979–80) 'Elements of Sociological Theorizing', *Humboldt Journal of Social Relations*, no. 7.

Bloomfield, L. (1927) 'Literate and Illiterate Speech', *American Speech*, vol. 10, pp. 432–9.

Bloor, D. (1976) *Knowledge and Social Imagery*, London, Routledge and Kegan Paul.

Boissevain, J. (1974) *Friends of Friends: Networks, Manipulators and Coalitions*, Oxford, Blackwell.

—— (1988) 'Social Networks', in U. Ammon, N. Dittmar and K.J. Matthier (eds) *Sociolinguistics*, De Gruyter, Berlin, pp. 164–70.

Bott, E. (1971) *Family and Social Networks*, London, Tavistock.

Boutet, J. (1985) *Construction sociale du sens dans des entretiens d'ouvriers et d'ouvrières*, Paris, Université Paris VII.

Breitborde, L.B. (1983) 'Levels of Analysis in Sociolinguistic Explanation: Bilingual Code Switching, Social Relations and Domain Theory', *International Journal of the Sociology of Language*, no. 39, pp. 5–45.

Callinicos, A. (1983) *Marxism and Philosophy*, Oxford, Oxford University Press.

Calvet, L.J. (1974) *Linguistique et colonialisme*, Paris, Payot.

—— (1987) *La Guerre des langues*, Paris, Payot.

Cameron, D. (1985) *Feminism and Linguistic Theory*, London, Macmillan.

Carter, H. (1988) 'Yr Iaith Gymraeg yng Ngogledd Cymru 1951–81: Astudiaeth o'r Newid Lleoliadol', public lecture delivered at Oriel Llanberis, 18 March.

Cheshire, J. (1984) 'Indigenous non-standard English varieties and education', in P. Trudgill (ed.) *Languages in the British Isles*, Cambridge, Cambridge University Press, pp. 546–59.

Chomsky, N. (1966) *Cartesian Linguistics*, New York, Harper & Row.

Cicourel, A. (1973) *Cognitive Sociology*, Harmondsworth, Penguin.

—— (1981) 'Notes on the Integration of Micro and Macro Levels of Analysis', in A. Knorr-Cetina and A. Cicourel (eds) *Advances in Social Theory and Methodology*, Boston, Little Brown.

Cloward, R. and L. Ohlin (1961) *Delinquency and Opportunity*, London, Routledge and Kegan Paul.

Cobarrubias, M. (1983) 'Language Planning: The State of the Art', in J. Cobarrubias and J.A. Fishman (eds) *Progress in Language Planning*, The Hague, Mouton, pp. 3–27.

Cohen, A. (1955) *Delinquent Boys: The Culture of the Gang*, New York, Free Press.

Cohen. G.A. (1978) *Karl Marx's Theory of History*, Oxford, Oxford University Press.

Comte, A. (1896) *The Positive Philosophy*, London, Bell.

Condillac, E.B. de (1947) *Essai sur l'origine des connaissances humaines*, Paris.

Condorcet, Marquis de (1955) *Sketch for a Historical Picture of the Human Mind*, New York, Noonday.

Conklin, H. (1955) 'Hanunoo Color Categories', *Southwestern Journal of Anthropology*, vol. 11, pp. 339–44.

Cook-Gumperz, J. (1977) 'Situated Instructions: Language Socialization of School Age Children', in S.M. Ervin-Tripp and C. Mitchell-Kernan (eds) *Child Discourse*, New York, Academic Press, pp. 103–21.

Corrigan, P. (1980) *Schooling the Smash Street Kids*, London, Macmillan.

Corrigan, P. and V. Corrigan (1979) 'State Formation and Social Policy until 1871', in N. Parry, M. Austin and C. Satyamurti (eds) *Social Work, Welfare and the State*, London, Arnold.

Court de Gebelin, A. (1776) *Histoire naturelle de la parole*, Paris.

Cubitt, T. (1973) 'Network Density among Urban Families', in J. Boissevain and J.C. Mitchel (eds) *Network Analysis: Studies in Human Interaction*, The Hague, Mouton.

Cuff, E.C. and G.C.F. Payne (eds) (1979) *Perspectives in Sociology*, London, Allen and Unwin.

Dahrendorf, R. (1958) 'Out of Utopia: Towards a Reorientation of Sociological Analysis', *American Journal of Sociology*, vol. 64, pp. 115–27.

Davies, K. (1988) 'Story-telling and the Exercise of Power', in T. Hak, J. Hhafkens and G. Nijhof (eds) *Working Papers on Discourse and Conversation*, Amsterdam, Konteksten, pp. 107–21.

de Brosse, C. (1801) *Traité de la formation méchanique des langues et des principes physiques de l'étymologie*, Paris.

Deutsch, K. (1966) *Nationalism and Social Communication*, Cambridge, MIT Press.

Diderot, D. (1877) *Interpreter of Nature*, Amsterdam, Chez Marc-Michel Ray.

Dittmar, N. (1976) *Sociolinguistics: A Critical Survey of Theory and Application*, London, Arnold.

Dorian, N. (1982) 'Defining the Speech Community to Include its Working Margins', in S. Romaine (ed.) *Sociolinguistic Variation in Speech Communities*, London, Arnold, pp. 25–35.

Durkheim, E. (1915) *The Elementary Forms of Religious Life*, London, Allen and Unwin.

—— (1933) *Division of Labor in Society*, New York, Macmillan.

—— (1938) *The Rules of Sociological Method*, New York, Free Press.

Eastman, C. (1983)*Language Planning: An Introduction*, San Francisco, Chandler and Sharp.

Edwards, J. (1982) 'Language Attitudes and Their Implications among English Speakers', in E.B. Ryan and H. Giles (eds) *Attitudes Towards Language Variation: Social and Applied Contexts*, London, Arnold, pp. 20–33.

Ekeh, P. (1974) *Social Exchange Theory*, London, Heinemann.

Fasold, R. (1984) *The Socio-linguistics of Society*, Oxford, Blackwell.

Ferguson, C.A. (1968) 'Language Development', in J.A. Fishman, C.A. Ferguson and J. Das Gupta (eds) *Language Problems of Developing Nations*, New York, Wiley, pp. 27–36.

Ferguson C.A. and J.J. Gumperz (1960) *Linguistic Diversity in South-east Asia*, Bloomington, Indiana University Press.

Ferguson, C.F. (1959) 'Diglossia', *Word*, no. 15, pp. 325–40.

Fishman, J.A. (1968) 'Some Contrasts between Linguistically Homogeneous and Heterogeneous Polities', in J. A. Fishman, C.A. Ferguson and L. Das Gupta (eds) *Language Problems of Developing Nations*, New York, Wiley, pp. 53–68.

—— (1972)*The Sociology of Language*, Rowley, Newbury House.

—— (1974) 'The Sociology of Language', in T. Seebok (ed.) *Current Trends in Linguistics*, The Hague, Mouton.

—— (1980) 'The Whorfian Hypothesis: Varieties of Valuation, Confirmation and Disconfirmation', *International Journal of the Sociology of Language*, 26, pp. 25–41.

—— (1990) *Reflections on the Sociology of Language*, paper presented at Sociolinguistic Symposium 8, Roehampton.

Fishman, P.M. (1978) 'Interaction: The Work Women Do', *Social Problems*, vol. 25, no. 4, pp. 397–406.

Fortes, M. (1949) *The Web of Kinship among the Talensi*, Oxford, Oxford University Press.

Foster G., M. Diaz and J. Potter (1967) *Peasant Societies: A Reader*, Boston, Little Brown.

Foucault, M. (1969) 'La grammaire générale de Port-Royale', *Langages*, no. 7.

—— (1972) *The Archaeology of Knowledge*, London, Tavistock.

—— (1980) *Power-Knowledge*, Brighton, Harvester.

Fowler, R., R. Hodge and G. Kress (1979) *Language and Control*, London, Routledge and Kegan Paul.

Francis, W.N. (1983) *Dialectology*, London, Longman.

Gal, S. (1979) *Language Shift: Social Determinants of Linguistic Change in Bilingual Austria*, New York, Academic Press.

Gardner, H. (1973) *The Quest for Mind: Piaget, Lévi-Strauss and the Structuralist Movement*, New York, Knopf.

Garfinkel, H. (1963) 'A Conception of, and Experiments with, "Trust" as a Condition of Stable Concerted Actions', in O.J. Harvey (ed.) *Motivation and Social Interaction*, New York, Ronald Press, pp 187–238.

—— (1967) *Studies in Ethnomethodology*, Englewood Cliffs, Prentice Hall.

—— (1972) 'Remarks on Ethnomethodology', in J.J. Gumperz and D. Hymes (eds) *Directions in Sociolinguistics: The Ethnography of Communication*, New York, Holt Rinehart and Winston, pp. 301–45.

Giddens, A. (1976) *New Rules of Sociological Method*, London, Hutchinson.

—— (1982) *Profiles and Critiques in Social Theory*, London, Macmillan.

—— (1984) *The Constitution of Society*, Cambridge, Polity.

Giles, H. (1987) 'Research on Language Attitudes', in H. Steger, N. Dittmar and K.J Matthier (eds) *Sociolinguistics*, Berlin, De Gruyter, pp. 585–98.

Giles, H., R. Bourhis and D. Taylor (1977) 'Towards a Theory of Language in Ethnic Group Relations', in H. Giles (ed.) *Language, Ethnicity and Intergroup Relations*, London, Academic Press, pp. 307–48.

Gimson, A.C. (1984) 'The RP Accent', in P. Trudgill (ed.) *Languages in the British Isles*, Cambridge, Cambridge University Press, pp. 45–55.

Glasgow Media Group (1980) *Bad News*, London, Routledge and Kegan Paul.

Goffman, E. (1974) *Frame Analysis*, New York, Harper.

Goldthorpe, J. (1973) 'A Revolution in Sociology?', *Sociology*, vol. 7, pp. 449–62.

Goodenough, W. (1957) 'Cultural Anthropology and Linguistics', in P.L. Garvin (ed.) *Report of the 7th Annual Round Table on Linguistics and Language Study*, Washington DC, Georgetown University Press.

—— (1964) 'Cultural Anthropology and Linguistics', in D. Hymes (ed.)

Language in Culture and Soceiety, New York, Harper and Row, pp. 36–9.

Gouldner, A. (1971) *The Coming Crisis of Western Sociology*, New York, Avon.

Gramsci, A. (1971) *Selections from Prison Notebooks*, London, Lawrence & Weidenfeld.

Greenberg, J.H. (1968) *Anthropological Linguistics: An Introduction*, New York, Random House.

Gumperz, J.J. (1972a) 'Sociocultural Knowledge in Conversational Interference', in M. Saville-Troike (ed.) *Linguistics and Anthropology*, Washington DC, Georgetown University Press, pp. 191–212.

—— (1972b) 'Sociolinguistics and Communication in Small Groups', in J.B. Pride and J. Homes (eds) *Sociolinguistics*, Harmondsworth, Penguin, pp. 203–24.

—— (1982) *Language and Social Identity*, Cambridge, Cambridge University Press.

—— (ed.) (1984) *Discourse Strategies*, Cambridge, Cambridge University Press.

Gumperz, J.J. and D. Hymes (eds) (1972) *Directions in Sociolinguistics: The Ethnography of Communication*, New York, Holt Rinehart and Winston.

Habermas, J. (1979) *Communication and the Evolution of Society*, Boston, Beacon.

Hammersley, M. (1986) 'Putting Competence into Action', in M. Hammersley (ed.) *Controversies in Classroom Research*, Milton Keynes, Open University Press, pp. 93–103.

Harding, S. (1975) 'Women and Words in a Spanish Village', in R. Reiter (ed.) *Towards an Anthropology of Women*, New York, Monthly Review Press.

Harris, M. (1968) *The Rise of Anthropological Theory*, New York, Crowell.

Haugen, E. (1962) *Schitzoglossia and the Linguistic Norm*, Monograph Series on Languages and Linguistics, Washington DC, Georgetown University Press.

Hawkes, T. (1977) *Structuralism and Semiotics*, London, Methuen.

Heath, S.B. and F. Mandabach (1983) 'Language Status Decisions and the Law in the United States', in J. Cobarrubias and J.A. Fishman (eds) *Progress in Language Planning*, The Hague, Mouton, pp. 87–107.

Hechter, M. (1975) *Internal Colonialism*, London, Routledge and Kegan Paul.

Herder, J.G. Von (1803) *Outline of a Philosophy of the History of Man*, London, Hansard.

Heritage, J. (1984) *Garfinkel and Ethnomethodology*, Oxford, Polity.

Hindess, B. (1972) 'The "phenomenological" Sociology of Alfred Schutz', *Economy and Society*, vol. 1, no.1, pp. 1–27.

Hodge, R. (1990) *Literature as Discourse*, Oxford, Polity.

Hodge, R. and G. Kress (1988) *Social Semiotics*, Oxford, Polity.

Hymes, D. (1966) 'Two Types of Linguistic Relativity', in W. Bright (ed.) *Sociolinguistics*, The Hague, Mouton.

—— (1970) 'Linguistic Aspects of Political Research', in R. Holt and J. Turner (eds) *The Methodology of Comparative Research*, New York, Free Press, pp. 295–341.

—— (1977) *Foundations of Sociolinguistics: An Ethnographic Approach*, London, Tavistock.
—— (1988) 'Communicative Competence', in U. Ammon, N. Dittmar and K.J Matthier (eds) *Sociolinguistics*, Berlin, De Gruyter, pp. 219–29.
Jakobson, R. (1963) *Selected Writings*, The Hague, Mouton.
Kant, I. (1963) *Idea for a Universal History*, London, Longman.
Kapferer, B. (1969) 'Norms and the Manipulation of Relationships in a Work Context', in J.C. Mitchel (ed.) *Social Networks in Urban Situations*, Manchester, Manchester University Press, pp. 181–244.
Karam, F. (1974) 'Toward a Definition of Language Planning', in J.A. Fishman (ed.) *Advances in Language Planning*, The Hague, Mouton, pp. 103–24.
Kay, P. (1978) 'Variable Rules, Community Grammar and Linguistic Change', in. D. Sankoff (ed.) *Linguistic Variation: Models and Methods*, New York, Academic Press, pp. 71–85.
Kloss, H. (1969) *Research Possibilities on Group Bilingualism: A Report*, Quebec, International Centre for Research on Bilingualism.
Kremnitz, G. (1981) 'Du "Bilingualisme" au "Conflit Linguistique"', in J.P. Marcellesi (ed.) 'Bilingualisme et Diglossie', *Langage*, no. 61, pp. 63–74.
Labov. W. (1966) *The Social Stratification of English in New York City*, Washington DC, The Center for Applied Linguistics.
—— (1969) 'Contraction, Deletion and Inherent Variability of the English Copula', *Language*, vol. 45, pp. 715–62.
—— (1972) *Sociolinguistic Patterns*, Oxford, Blackwell.
Lakoff, R. (1975) *Language and Women's Place*, New York, Harper and Row.
Lambert, W. (1967) 'A Social Psychology of Bilingualism', *Journal of Social Issues*, vol. 23, no. 2, pp. 91–109.
Le Page, R. (1968) 'Problems of Description in Multilingual Communities', *Transactions of the Philological Society*, no. 195, pp. 189–212.
Leitner, G. (1980) 'BBC English and Deutsche Rundfunk Sprache: A Comparative and Historical Analysis of Language on the Radio', *International Journal of the Sociology of Language*, no. 26, pp. 75–101.
Levinson, S.C. (1979) 'Activity Types and Language', *Linguistics*, vol. 17, pp. 356–99.
Luke, A., O. McHoul and O. May (forthcoming) 'On the Limits of Language Planning', in R.B. Baldauf and A. Luke (eds) *Language Planning and Education in Australia and the South Pacific*, Clevedon, Multilingual Matters.
Lukes, S. (1973) *Emile Durkheim*, London, Allen Lane.
Lyons, J. (1972) 'Foreword', in W. Labov, *Sociolinguistic Patterns*, Oxford, Blackwell.
Macdonald, G. and R. Pettit (1981) *Semantics and Social Science*, London, Routledge and Kegan Paul.
Malinowski, B. (1944) *A Scientific Theory of Culture*, Chapel Hill, University of North Carolina Press.
—— (1961) *Argonauts of the Western Pacific*, New York, Dutton.
Malz, D.N. and R.A. Borker (1982) 'A Cultural Approach to Male–Female Miscommunication', in J.J. Gumperz (ed.) *Language and Social Identity*, Cambridge, Cambridge University Press, pp. 195–217.

Mandeville, B. (1962) *The Fable of the Bees*, New York, Capricorn.

Manicas, P.T. (1988) *A History and Philosophy of the Social Sciences*, Oxford, Blackwell.

Marandin, J.B. (1979) 'Analyse de discours et linguistique générale', *Langages*, no. 55.

Marcellesi, J.B. and B. Gardin (1987) *Introduction à la sociolinguistique*, Mont Saint-Aignan, IRED.

Maupertuis, P.L.M. de (1752) *Reflexions philosophiques sur l'origine des langues et la signification de mots*, Varia Linguistica, Bordeaux, Editores Ducros, in C. Porset (ed.) (1970).

Mayer, K.B. (1955) *Class and Society*, New York, Random House.

Mehan, H. and H. Wood (1975) *The Reality of Ethnomethodology*, New York, Wiley.

Merton, R. (1968) *Social Theory and Social Structure*, Glencoe, Free Press.

Milroy, L. (1980) *Language and Social Networks*, Oxford, Blackwell.

Milroy, L. and S. Margrain (1980) 'Vernacular Language Loyalty and Social Network', *Language and Society*, vol. 9, no.1, pp. 43–70.

Mitchel, J.C. (ed.) (1969) *Social Networks in Urban Situations*, Manchester, Manchester University Press.

Monteforte Toledo, M. (1980) *El discurso politico*, Mexico, Nueva Imagen.

Nadel, S.F. (1951) *Foundations of Social Anthropology*, Glencoe, Free Press.

Nagel, E. (1953) 'Teleological Explanation and Teleological Systems', in H. Feigl and M. Brodbeck (eds) *Readings in the Philosophy of Science*, New York, Harper and Row, pp. 537–58.

Nietzsche, F. (1969) *On the Genealogy of Morals and Ecce Homus*, New York, Random House.

Nisbet, S. (1969) *Social Change and History*, Oxford, Oxford University Press.

Norris, C. (1985) *The Contest of Faculties*, London, Methuen.

Page, C.H. (1969) *Class and American Society*, New York, Schocken.

Parkin, F. (1979) *Marxism and Class Theory: A Bourgeois Critique*, London, Tavistock.

Parsons, T. (1935) 'The Place of Ultimate Values in Sociological Theory', *International Journal of Ethics*, 45, pp. 282–316.

—— (1937) *The Structure of Social Action*, New York, McGraw Hill.

—— (1949) *Essays in Sociological Theory*, New York, Free Press.

—— (1951a) *Towards a General Theory of Action*, New York, Free Press.

—— (1951b) *The Social System*, New York, Free Press.

—— (1953) 'A Revised Analytical Approach to the Theory of Social Stratification', in R. Bendix and S. Lipset (eds) *Class, Status and Power: A Reader in Social Stratification*, New York, Free Press, pp. 92–129.

—— (1960) *Structure and Process in Modern Society*, New York, Free Press.

—— (1966) *Societies: Evolutionary and Comparative Perspectives*, Englewood Cliffs, Prentice Hall.

—— (1967) *Sociological Theory and Modern Society*, New York, Free Press.

—— (1969) *Politics and Social Structure*, New York, Free Press.

—— (1971) *The Systems of Modern Societies*, Englewood Cliffs, Prentice Hall.

Pearce, F. (1989) *The Radical Durkheim*, London, Unwin.

Pecheux, M. (1982) *Language, Semantics and Ideology*, London, Macmillan.

Peel, J.D.Y. (1971) *Herbert Spencer: The Evolution of a Sociologist*, New York, Basic Books.

Penalosa, F. (1981) *Introduction to the Sociology of Language*, New York, Rowley.

Piaget, J. (1935) *The Moral Judgement of the Child*, London, Routledge and Kegan Paul.

Pike, K. (1954) *Language in Relation to a Unified Theory of the Structure of Human Behaviour*, Glendale, Summer Institute of Linguistics.

Pitt-Rivers, A.L.F. (1906) *The Evolution of Culture and Other Essays* Oxford, Clarendon.

Poulantzas, N. (1975) *Classes in Contemporary Capitalism*, London, New Left Books.

Rabin, C. (1958) 'The Linguistics of Translation', in L. Forester (ed.) *Studies in Communication*, vol. 2, London, Secker and Warburg.

Radcliffe-Brown, A.R. (1940) 'On Social Structure', *Journal of the Royal Anthropological Society*, vol. 70, pp. 1–12.

—— (1935) 'On the Concept of Function in Social Science', *American Anthropologist*, vol. 37, pp. 394–402.

Robins, R.H. (1967) *A Short History of Linguistics*, London, Longman.

Romaine, S. (1982) *Sociolinguistic Variation in Speech Communities*, London, Arnold.

Rosen, M. (1985) 'Critical Theory: The Persistence of Philosophy', in S. Mitchel and M. Rosen (eds) *The Need for Interpretation*, London, Athlone.

Rousseau, J.J. (1950) *The Social Contract and Discourses*, New York, Dutton.

Rubin, J. (1968) *Nationalist Bilingualism in Paraguay*, The Hague, Mouton (earlier edition 1958).

Ryan, M. (1982) *Marxism and Deconstruction: A Critical Articulation*, Baltimore, Johns Hopkins University Press.

Sacks, H. (1963) 'Sociological Description', *Berkeley Journal of Sociology*, vol. 8, pp. 1–16.

Sacks, H. and E. Shegloff (1973) 'Opening up Closings', *Semiotica*, vol. 7, pp. 289–327.

Sapir, E. (1917) 'Do We Need a Superorganic?', *American Anthropologist*, vol. 19, pp. 441–7.

—— (1925) 'Sound Patterns in Language', *Language*, vol. 1, pp. 37–51.

—— (1932) 'Cultural Anthropology and Psychiatry', *Journal of Abnormal and Social Psychology*, vol. 27, pp. 229–42.

—— (1949) *Selected Writtings*, D. Mandelbaum (ed.), Berkeley, University of California Press.

Saussure, F. de (1915) *Cours de linguistique générale*, Paris, Payot.

Savage, S.P. (1981) *The Theories of Talcott Parsons: The Social Relations of Action*, London, Macmillan.

Saville-Troike, M. (1982) *The Ethnography of Communication: An Introduction*, Oxford, Blackwell.

Schutz, A. (1962) *Collected Papers*, The Hague, Nijhoff.
—— (1971) *Collected Papers II: Studies in Social Theory*, 3rd edn, The Hague, Nijhoff.
—— (1972) *The Phenomenology of the Social World*, London, Heisman.
Shuy, R., W.A. Wolfram and W.A. Riley (1968) *Field Techniques in an Urban Language Study*, Washington DC, Centre for Applied Linguistics.
Simpson, G.C. (1964) *This View of Life: The World of an Evolutionist*, New York, Harcourt Brace and World.
Smith, A. (1974) *British Broadcasting*, Newton Abbot, David and Charles.
Sturtevant, W. (1964) 'Studies in Ethnoscience', *American Anthropologist*, vol. 66, part 2, pp. 99–131.
Tajfel, H. (1974) 'Social Identity and Intergroup Behaviour', *Social Science Information*, vol. 13, pp. 65–93.
Thompson, J. (1984) *Studies in the Theory of Ideology*, Oxford, Polity.
Torode, B. (1984) *The Extra-ordinary in Ordinary Language*, Amsterdam, Kontexten.
Trudgill, P. (1971) *The Social Differentiation of English in Norwich*, Edinburgh, Edinburgh University Press.
—— (1984) (ed.) *Language in the British Isles*, Cambridge, Cambridge University Press.
Turgot, A.R.J. (1913) *Etymologies*, Paris, Schelle.
Turner, J. (1986) *The Structure of Sociological Theory*, New York, Dorsey.
Ure, J. (1982) 'Approaches to the Study of Register Change', *International Journal of the Sociology of Language*, no. 35, pp. 5–25.
Voltaire, F.M.A. (1953) *Correspondance de Voltaire*, Geneva.
Wakelin, M.F. (1972) *English Dialects: An Introduction*, London, Athlone Press.
Wardaugh, R. (1986) *An Introduction to Sociolinguistics*, Oxford, Blackwell.
Weber, M. (1964a) *From Max Weber*, H.H. Gerth and C.W. Mills (eds), Oxford, Oxford University Press.
—— (1964b) *The Theory of Social and Economic Organisation*, New York, Free Press.
Weinreich, U. (1963) *Languages in Contact*, The Hague, Mouton.
White, H. (1978) *Tropics of Discourse: Essays in Cultural Criticism*, Baltimore, Johns Hopkins University Press.
Whorf, B. (1956) *Language, Thought and Reality*, J.B. Carroll (ed.), New York, Wiley.
Williams, G. (1978) 'Industrialisation and Ethnic Change in the Lower Chubut Valley, Argentina', *American Ethnologist*, vol. 5, no. 3, pp. 618–31.
—— (1979) 'Language Group Allegiance and Ethnic Interaction', in H. Giles and B. Saint-Jaques (eds) *Language and Ethnic Relations*, Oxford, Pergamon, pp. 57–67.
—— (1987) 'Policy as Containment within Democracy: The Welsh Language Act', *International Journal of the Sociology of Language*, no. 66, pp. 49–61.
—— (1988a) 'Discourse on Language and Ethnicity', in N. Coupland (ed.) *Styles of Discourse*, London, Croom Helm, pp. 254–93.

—— (1988b) 'Bilingualism, Class Dialect and Social Reproduction', *International Journal of the Sociology of Language*, no. 66, pp. 85–99.

—— (forthcoming) 'Marxisme et l'analyse du Discours', *Langage et Société*.

Williams, R. (1973) 'Base and Superstructure in Marxist Cultural Theory', *New Left Review*, no. 82, pp. 3–17.

Willis, P. (1977) *Learning to Labour: How Working Class Kids get Working Class Jobs*, Farnborough, Saxon House.

Index